Wanda Banks
Kerr

SEVEN COTTON CROWNS

Wanda Banks
&
May Podbreger

VANTAGE PRESS
New York

FIRST EDITION

Published by Vantage Press, Inc.
516 West 34th Street, New York, New York 10001

Manufactured in the United States of America
ISBN: 0-533-12525-1

Library of Congress Catalog Card No.: 97-90983

0 9 8 7 6 5 4 3 2 1

To Jude, with love. He made the impossible dream come true.

Wanda

SEVEN COTTON CROWNS

ONE

Don't take sides. The affair is too complex for you to try to judge between right and wrong. Answer need on a person to person basis and stay away from politics, even in your thinking.

This is what nurse Hope Callaway had been told by the Mission Board in New York City when her application was accepted for the post of nursing superintendent at Beth Hanani Mission near Bethlehem, in that portion of Palestine that had been left to the Arabs when the country was partitioned in 1948 to make room for creation of the new state of Israel.

The year was 1953, the month was June, the morning was bright and hot, and Hope, just stepping out of a hospital side entrance, was able to see on the hillsides across from her, acres of brown tents packed so closely together that the tent pegs were nearly touching. These were the homes of Arab refugees for the past five years. Several such camps were dotted around the Hashemite Kingdom of Jordan. The Gaza Strip administered by Egypt was almost a solid mass of refugees, and there were even camps as far away as Lebanon.

In New York, Hope had wondered earnestly if she could avail herself of the advice she had been given. She knew herself to be a person of quick sympathies and prolonged loyalties—in short, she had the partisan disposition. Once on the scene and up to her ears in work, there had been no temptation at all either to uphold or to upbraid anyone. The extent of human suffering she encountered daily was so great, it became easy to view the cause as some natural disaster, some especially violent convulsion of nature that had laid waste to everything and everyone around it. Hope knew this viewpoint was unrealistic, but she cultivated it deliberately, less because it made life easier for herself than because, by keeping her mind clear of problems beyond her scope, she also kept herself at the peak of efficiency.

The rays of the rising sun silhouetting the tents sprawled on the hillsides across the highway told how early the hour was. Once Hope had fancied herself as a person who liked to lie abed in the mornings, but she knew about the sharp nips of despair that urged the people of the camps off their pallets long before daybreak. The usual daily lines of persons in need of medical attention would have started forming while the hospital grounds were still plunged in darkness. Every day, there were more patients and problems than could be crowded into the hours available; hence, this early morning stir, this miasma of anxiety that reached out to the staffers at the mission, pleading for attention.

Behind her, she heard footsteps, then Dr. Baxter's cheery British voice sang out a greeting and a casual, "Going my way?" As he came abreast of her, Hope began to trot. He noticed and shortened his stride, laughing. Dr. Baxter had a gift for laughing at people in a way to make them feel he was laughing with them instead. Hope saw through it but didn't mind; if her tininess amused him, so did his Saint Bernard massiveness amuse her; anyhow, his laughter was only an expression of his affection for her.

"I say there! Looks as if Yusef needs help," Dr. Baxter exclaimed, breaking into a run. Because of the uneven ground,

Hope was able to see the gateman on the other side of the wall that guarded the mission. Since the person he was trying to shield wore the blue uniform of a student nurse, she was one of Hope's charges, and the responsibility for protecting her was also Hope's. She sped after the doctor, hearing above the bee-hive hum of the refugees the angry shouts of Yusef. From the girl herself there was no sound. Hope noted this with approval even while skittering along at top speed; the habit of evaluating her charges during emergencies, which followed one another like birds in winter, was too strong to be suspended.

Since the refugees intended no harm to anyone, but were only acting out the need of each individual for immediate attention, the incident ended in no greater damage than a torn sleeve for the student nurse. Aida was still clutching in her left hand the numbered tickets she had been trying to distribute. With her right hand, she was holding together the edges of the tear.

"There are so many today, and they are fighting for the tickets!" she explained to Hope. Tears of fright stood in her large brown eyes and threatened to spill down her cheeks. "See what they did to my uniform!"

"That's just a straight tear and can be easily mended," Hope assured her. "Go and change into another uniform, and leave this one in my room. You know they didn't mean you any harm, Aida. They get excited and overanxious. I'm sure we would in their place."

Aida was Palestinian herself, but she had been born in that portion of the country that had been reserved for the Arabs. The experience of suddenly finding herself rootless would be as strange to her as it would be to those on the mission staff.

"I'll handle the tickets myself from now on," Dr. Baxter added, taking the packet from the girl's trembling hand. Spoken in a different tone, the words could have stood for a stinging rebuke; instead, Aida cleared up like a summer day after thunder.

Aida darted away, but Hope lingered to watch the distribution. She had long suspected that the doctors should see to it, rather than her student nurses, and what was happening now proved her guess had been right. The girls, half terrified by the press of so much urgent need, tended to thrust the tickets into the nearest hands outstretched. After spot checking the crowd with keen glances, Dr. Baxter went at it more selectively; quite frequently, his long arm reached out over the heads of those nearest to put a ticket in the hand of a pale and silent sufferer too sick to thrust himself forward.

Yusef began calling the numbers on the tickets and letting through those fortunate enough to have acquired one. Hope stood aside to permit them to pass her on their way to the clinic waiting room. Each one took time to greet her with a warm smile or a courteous inclination of the head. Occasionally a patient would pass with whom she had had previous dealing; without exception, these stopped to offer an effusive greeting in Arabic. She had cultivated a standard reply, *Shuk'ran* (thank you); accompanied with a smile, it seemed to suffice.

She thought how little change the past nineteen hundred years had wrought in either the costumes or the customs of these people of Palestine. Most of the men were garbed in the loose flowing robes, either plain or striped, that are believed to be the traditional type worn in biblical times. Their headgear was the white or red-checked shepherd's scarf, or *kafeeyah*, bound on with a double circlet of heavy black twisted cord. Coarsely woven brown cloaks were draped about their shoulders.

The women wore long black robes, many of them thickly encrusted with the beautiful bright cross-stitch embroidery for which the women of Palestine have been noted for centuries. One of the younger women who passed carried a small baby in her arms clad in a single garment of heavy muslin, crudely made. The toddler who clung to her skirts was similarly clad, but the garment she wore was so worn and scanty as to barely cover her thighs. From the painfully thin appearance of the young mother, Hope knew without a doubt that the last scrap of the long heavy muslin drawers customarily worn by male and female alike, had been sacrificed to provide the shifts with which to cover her babies. Evidently, not one stitch of under-clothing remained beneath that carefully patched black robe. It was obvious that her breasts were without milk. An allowance of seven cents a day per refugee for all needs—food, clothing, shelter medicine, education—was scarcely sufficient to encour-age lactation.

Most of the motley crowd were barefoot. A few boasted crude sandals, cut from old rubber tires and tied about the ankles with coarse rope. The only incongrouus elements in this otherwise ancient picture were the ragged, once elegant, men's suitcoats, recently discarded from Western wardrobes, and the cast-off, ill fitting foreign trousers, now worn by a few of the men and by most of the larger growing boys. The latter wore pieces of rope or twine to hold up the trousers around scrawny young waists. With rare exceptions, a pathetic lack of bathing and laundering facilities was glaringly evident throughout the entire group.

Hope noted that most of the patients were settling down on the bare, dusty ground to wait in the warm sunshine, rather than taking shelter in the small stone waiting room. During the cold, wet months of the previous winter, the waiting room had been crowded beyond capacity with shivering, desperately ill patients, for whom little could be done. Remembering that terrible winter, when they had seen tiny babies die of pneumonia even as they received the penicillin shot if administered in time could have saved their lives, she was thankful for this glorious warm day.

For hours she was frantically busy in the hot, crowded treat-ment room. During a lull, lasting only long enough for her to mop her face and neck with her handkerchief, she heard the piercing screams of a child accompanied by the sounds of hurrying footsteps. She started toward the commotion just as Yusef flung open the outer door to admit a frantic mother bearing a shrieking toddler in her arms.

The waiting patients pressed closer together to let her through. Hope hastened forward to take the child. With the mother close on her heels, she carried the baby into a smaller empty treatment room that was empty except for Warda, one of the students. Dr. Baxter followed her in, for only a deaf person could fail to hear those penetrating shrieks.

While he was examining the screaming child, the excited mother was shouting in Arabic, swiftly translated by Warda, how the baby had knocked a boiling teakettle off a lighted primus stove, scalding herself. The mother waved her burned hands to show how she had grabbed the primus before it fell, saving her own tent and perhaps the camp itself, from flames.

His examination finished, Dr. Baxter hastened back to the patient he had abandoned, leaving Hope and Warda to apply ointment, bandages, and administer penicillin. By the time they finished, Hope's clothes were alive with fleas acquired from mother and baby.

Back in the larger treatment room, Hope found Aida holding a syringe of vitamin B in her hand, oddly motionless. The explanation came quickly.

"Please give this one for me, Miss Callaway. There isn't a scrap of flesh to get the needle in," Aida said.

The shrunken buttocks of a frail baby draped over its mother's shoulder in readiness for the shot, was indeed a challenge to inexperience.

"You can do it, Aida," Hope said firmly. "You need to pinch up a long fold of skin and slant the needle in. Then you won't strike bone."

Aida shakily obeyed, finishing just as Yusef, who had entered unseen, pressed a note into Hope's hand. Mohammed Musa was at the hospital, waiting to confer with her.

She knew Mohammed's errand too well. In the four months since the opening of the training school he had already come three times to demand his daughter, Rehab.

The girl and her mother had been eager for her to enter the training class. In a weak moment her father had given reluctant consent. Almost immediately he regretted the decision. He had been causing trouble ever since. Each time he came, it took the combined pleas of Rehab and the nursing director, coupled with fervent silent prayer by the latter, to persuade Mohammed to allow his daughter to stay.

After making arrangements with Dr. Baxter to permit her to be off the floor for a time, Hope started toward the hospital, thinking about Rehab. Since a rare weekend visit with her family in Ramallah, Rehab's attitude had changed drastically. She seemed troubled. She avoided Hope and the other instructors, and her grades were dropping.

She found Mohammed Musa pacing the floor impatiently. He wore Western garb, which some of the well-to-do Arabs were now adopting. Hope courteously invited him to be seated. When they had exchanged the customary amenities regarding each other's health and the health of various relatives and associates, conversation lapsed. For once Mohammed seemed at a loss to begin. It was to loosen his tongue that she called Nadia, the maid, who was mopping the hall, and ordered Arabic coffee. Only lately she had learned that Arab etiquette decreed that a guest depart promptly after partaking, and she had no desire to prolong this interview.

A flicker of admiration was in Mohammed's eyes when he said, "You are busy, Miss Callaway. I am busy also. I will not waste words. I have come for Rehab."

"Rehab is on duty. She is enjoying her work here, as she has told you often. I will send for her and let her speak for herself."

She made a move toward the door. Mohammed checked her with an upraised hand. He looked amused.

"Did she not tell you? Rehab's betrothal was celebrated in our home a week ago. Her husband wishes to claim her tomorrow."

Hope was stunned. A Moslem betrothal was practically the equivalent of a wedding ceremony. A binding legal contract witnessed by all the guests was signed by the participants during the betrothal festivities. It lacked only the bridegroom's final claiming of his bride from her father's home for the marriage to be fully consummated. Anything further that Hope might say would be useless.

Mohammed's smile was now openly triumphant.

"Rehab didn't tell you?" he asked.

Hope mutely shook her head.

"Well, I am sorry," he said perfunctorily, "She should have done so. I must take her today. She is needed. Her husband is upset. His other wife is in a hospital. The neighbors are looking after the four children, but they can't be expected to do so much longer."

"He has another wife? And four children?" Hope whispered.

Evidently her stricken face aroused a sense of compunction in Mohammed's heart, because he began a blustering defense.

"It is a father's duty in this country to arrange a good marriage for his daughter. She must be protected. A father protects her. A husband protects her. Nursing does not protect her. It is degrading for the Arab woman. For *you*, no!" he added hastily. Hope already knew that European and American women in positions of authority were regarded by the Arabs as almost a third sex.

Mohammed went on, "I have made a good marriage for Rehab. Her husband is a good man, well-educated, highly respected in Jordan. He has a good position, a nice home. He can provide well for my daughter. He needs a wife. His children need a mother. Rehab loves children. She will be a good mother to them, a good wife for him. So, you see, Rehab must go. I must take her today."

Hope moved toward the door.

"Yes, I see. She must go," she repeated dully. "I will get her."

Nadia entered with the coffee. Etiquette demanded that a hostess serve her guest. Hope turned back to fulfill her obligation.

But Mohammed Musa was not to be outdone in gallantry. Seeing her falter he must have sensed the cruelty of the blow he had just dealt her. Having outwitted his opponent, he could afford to display the attributes of a true Arab gentleman. He bowed courteously, saying, "Miss Callaway, I fear I have detained you far too long from your duties. If you will permit me, I shall be happy to serve myself while you fetch my daughter."

Hope murmured an almost inaudible "Thanks." She turned hastily toward the door. Then realizing that her departure was altogether too abrupt, she turned back again and thrust her hand out impulsively in Western fashion. Mohammed grasped the hand eagerly and gave it a hearty Western handshake. He released her hand, stepped back, and executed a profound Eastern bow. By the time he raised his head, Hope was gone.

Two

THERE WAS WEARINESS IN Hope's step and heaviness in her heart as she climbed the stairs to the second floor and turned toward the women's ward at the south end of the hall. In the open doorway she lingered unnoticed, savoring afresh the cleanliness of the sunny room and the infinite possibilities for physical and spiritual ministries in the room.

Twelve beds were ranged down either side of the long room. In this needy land every one of those twenty-four beds was precious. Tuberculosis was rampant among the victims of the five-year-old partition of Palestine. This hospital specialized in the treatment of tuberculosis. The most vital factor known to date in the treatment of the disease was prolonged bedrest. With plenty of nourishing food and expensive new drugs such as PAS tablets and streptomycin injections, cures could be effected when lengthy treatment was given.

At present, lack of funds and acute shortage of medical and nursing personnel prevented full occupancy of the recently opened hospital facilities, and only six beds of the ward were occupied. The patients were grouped together at the right of the door. The nurses' station was in an entrance alcove just outside the door. It contained chart rack, washing facilities, a desk, chairs, and a rack for the nurses' isolation gowns.

Hope noted with approval the neatness of the bedside tables, the smoothly made beds, the immaculate appearance of the patients. A bouquet of bright flowers, freshly picked from the hospital garden, stood on a table by one of the large windows. Rehab and Aminah, the two student nurses, had completed their morning care of the women. Aminah was now distributing cups of yoghurt for the mid-morning nourishment. Rehab was propping pillows behind the latest arrival, a woman who appeared weak and listless, her eyes dull, face flushed with fever, seemingly indifferent either to food or the chatter going on about her.

The newcomer's hair was a soft golden blond and her eyes were deep blue. Her skin tones were remarkably fair for an Arab. Probably she was of Syrian ancestry, most likely from the Lebanon, where such coloring in the native population was sometimes seen. In good health, the woman would be strikingly beautiful. The students busy with their ministrations were also lovely to look at, Hope thought. Their thick dark braids wound around their heads in imitation of Hope's own hairstyle were a measure of the depth of affection existing between the nursing supervisor and her charges, for with the human young, it is natural to model yourself on what you admire and love.

With great patience, Rehab was attempting to feed the weary patient, and Hope tarried to watch, for it made a pretty picture.

"Hikmat," Rehab was saying with love and sternness, "You do want to get back to that baby soon, don't you?"

The stubborn mouth opened just wide enough to permit a swallow of yoghurt to be transferred from the spoon Rehab was wielding. For just a moment, Hope envisioned the nine snowy caps ordered from America, now reposing on the top shelf of her wardrobe. One of them was intended for Rehab, who was not to be permitted to claim it.

"Now Hikmat, once more, for the boy, yes?" Another spoonful was swallowed. What a nurse she would have made, Hope thought.

The five other bed patients, emptied their cups with gusto. Aminah began collecting them. Suddenly one patient spied Hope. She began shouting, "*Saïda, Sitt! Saïda, Sitt!*" (Greetings, Miss! Greetings, Miss!) Immediately, the four other patients took up the cry. Hope smiled, waved, and returned their "*Saïdas*" before motioning for the two students to join her in the hall. Aminah came eagerly, but Rehab hung back and approached her superintendent slowly with downcast eyes.

"The ward looks very nice today, girls," said Hope warmly. "You are doing a good job."

Aminah flushed with pleasure. Rehab looked miserable and frightened. Hope untied the strings at the back of the girl's isolation gown, whispering, "Your father is waiting, dear; you had better go get packed."

Without a word, Rehab slipped out of the gown, hung it on the rack, washed her hands in the basin of antiseptic, and hurried away. It occurred to Hope that Aminah seemed strangely incurious about the proceedings.

"Did you know about her engagement, Aminah?" she asked.

"Yes, Miss Callaway, she told me two days ago. I don't know why, except perhaps that we are both Moslem. I believe you know that the girls don't usually confide in me. I don't think any of the other girls know."

"They will all know soon enough," Hope said sadly. "I am afraid I must ask you to carry on here alone until I can find someone to help you. I will ask one of the maids, perhaps Taman, to help serve the lunch trays. She must wear an isolation gown, of course, and wash thoroughly afterward. Our new patient will need to be fed. She looks quite tired and feverish. For her sake, will you try to persuade the other patients to take a little rest this morning, as well as in the afternoon?"

Aminah smiled. "Don't concern yourself, Miss Callaway, I'll manage fine. I am sorry about Rehab. I was hoping that we might become friends."

Hope followed Rehab down the hall to the nurses' quarters. The door to the girl's room stood open. As Hope entered, Rehab lifted down a heavy suitcase from the wardrobe she shared with Regina. Hope noted that the shelves and hangers on Rehab's side, were entirely empty except for a single street dress and coat. Evidently the bag had been packed some time earlier.

The girl had her back turned at the moment. However, by the telltale flush that swept across the back of her neck, Hope sensed that her presence was known. Rehab unbuttoned and removed her blue uniform, hung it in the wardrobe, and donned the street dress. Then she stooped and pulled another suitcase, obviously filled, from under her bed.

Rehab must have been preparing secretly for flight all week. Had she expected to slip away without a word of explanation or apology?

Now Rehab stood aimlessly by her bed, head bent, hands twisting nervously together. Hope held out her arms and spoke her name gently. Rehab flew to her. For quite a while, the American woman and the Arab girl cried in each other's arms. Tears brought relief, and soon they were able to talk cheerfully about the marriage.

Rehab shyly admitted that her husband was very attractive. He seemed kind. No, she had never met him before, she replied in answer to Hope's direct question. But that was not unusual in Moslem marriages, she explained. He was not old, perhaps about forty. Some girls her age were married to men who were much older. Abu Ameer (father of Ameer—the oldest boy's name was Ameer) had experienced bad luck with his wives. The first one died giving birth to their second child. Now the second wife was too ill to care for them and for her own two little sons.

Even after she met Abu Ameer at her home during that special weekend Rehab asserted, she had held out against the marriage. But when he showed her a photograph of those four handsome little boys, she immediately took to about them, especially the youngest, only two years old.

"Just the age of Hikmat's little boy," Rehab concluded. "Hikmat feels so badly at having to leave her baby. She cried when she told me about him. It made me feel happier to know that I can love and care for some other woman's children while she is sick, so she will not have to worry as Hikmat does."

Although Hope could not help laughing at Rehab's extraordinary confession, the laughter was rather shaky. A lump rose in her throat at the prospect of the girl's future.

"Rehab," she probed gently, "how will you and his other wife get along when she recovers from her illness? Won't you both be unhappy and jealous of each other?"

"I don't know," the girl replied innocently, "but I expect that I shall find out."

"Yes, I expect you will," Hope agreed. She drew Rehab closer and whispered in her ear, "Will you promise to send your first daughter to Beth Hanani Hospital to train in your place, Rehab?"

Blushing furiously, the girl replied earnestly, "Indeed I will, Miss Callaway, and I promise to name her Hope!"

"In that case, I will certainly have to forgive you for leaving us," she said, rising and pulling Rehab to her feet. "Come, dear, we mustn't make your father wait any longer. I will ask Saleem to carry your bags down."

After Rehab and her father had gone, Hope sought the tearoom. It was late for mid-morning tea, but she hoped that Nadia had not yet removed the tea things, feeling need of physical fortification.

She found Dr. Baxter just pouring a steaming cup from a fresh pot wangled from the faithful Nadia. He promptly handed the first cup to her and poured himself another. Then he sat down opposite her and began offering condolences over the loss of Rehab. As Hope had expected, the news of the girl's betrothal and departure had already spread to the farthest corners of the mission compound. Hope answered him thoughtfully.

"I am very sorry that the man has another wife. Rehab has no idea of the problem she faces. But from our point of view, I am almost relieved. I knew we could not hope to keep her much longer against her father's violent objections. Rehab will be a much better mother and homemaker because of the training we have been able to give her."

Hope finished her tea, then continued, "I know it's only a drop in the bucket. Still the simplest rules of sanitation, not only in the refugee camps, but all over the Middle East, even that is better than nothing at all." After setting her cup down, she asked, "Isn't it time we got back to the clinic?"

"Relax," he said comfortably, "no rush. We got the treatment room cleared out fast after you left. While the girls were off to first tea. I saw a number of patients, so your girls have all the work they can handle right now. Plenty of time for another cup of tea."

He refilled their cups, saying, " You and Eileen Anderson have been doing a bang-up job of training the students. The Chief thinks so, too. I hope you don't think when I've finished that I'm just blarneying you to make matters easier for myself! Fact is, Hope, I've overstepped my bounds a bit in that direction, and I'm having a hard time confessing myself to you." Hope, who trusted Dr. Baxter implicitly, waited with a smile to hear what his confession could be.

"Y'know I've been wanting to do minor eye surgery outside of regular clinic hours at least an afternoon or two a week," he resumed. "There's this eye disease that leaves the upper lid curled inward, so that the lashes eventually scratch the eyeballs until sight becomes impaired. By slicing out a loose fold of flesh on the lid and stitching, the lashes can be pulled outward to normal position. It's practically painless and requires only a few minutes of time, but I would need an assistant to keep the patient still, and to hand me things, help clean up—all that sort of thing, y'know. But I know we're awfully short of staff."

"Surely planning a way for our team to be more helpful can hardly be called overstepping your bounds," Hope said warmly. "Whatever sacrifices are entailed, I'm sure we can manage. Do you want Yacoub for your assistant? He would seem the natural choice?" Unintentionally, she had ended the sentence on a note of inquiry.

"I have already asked Warda."

Hope stared at him. He looked back sheepishly, "I told you I had overstepped my bounds!"

"I agree that you have."

They sat quietly for a moment, sipping their tea, while Hope mentally reviewed Warda's history. She was the eldest child in a large Arab Christian family. Although barely sixteen, she had graduated the past spring from a secondary school in Bethlehem conducted by another Protestant mission, having led her class in high grades. But the parents were too poor to finance further studies for the brilliant girl.

Seventeen years had been set by Hope as the minimum age requirement for student nurses, but in the case of Warda Shaheen, she had consented to waive the requirement, bowing to the intense girl's desperate eagerness to acquire more education so she might help her struggling family. During two weeks of intensive training amounting to a crash course in the techniques of nursing tubercular patients, Warda had more than justified Hope's faith in her. But afterwards came exposure to the men on the mission staff, the patients, and even the mission employees, and Hope and her assistant, Eileen Anderson, were compelled to acknowledge that in the person of Warda Shaheen, they had a born flirt on their hands.

Ameer Shabeeb and Daoud Suileman, who were taking the six months' course for male attendants, were vying openly for this girl's favor. Even the old gardener, Issa, and the two gatemen, who had children as old as Warda, preened themselves when she walked by with a swish of skirts and provocative downcast lashes. Only Yacoub Kakeesh, who was taking the full course with his twin sister, Elizabeth, remained immune to Warda's charms, and Eileen had wondered aloud if the boy was nearsighted. That appeared to be the only logical explanation for his indifference, Eileen said.

Real trouble began when normal scheduling sent Warda to the men's ward for what was to have been three months' duty. In less than a week, Eileen, who was in charge of the practical training on the wards, reported to Hope that Warda's open flirtatiousness was causing disharmony; that already jealous quarrels had broken out over her among the patients. Considering the volatile Arab temperament, the matter was serious, and Warda was transferred to the clinic, where it was thought the rapid daily turnover of patients would keep her out of mischief. Also, it put her in the vicinity of Dr. Baxter and this was the result—a serious breach of ethics on the part of one staffer to another, which easily could lead to a serious breach in friendship between two people who were genuinely fond of one another. Hope bit her lip. The latter possibility could be averted only by herself.

Dr. Baxter had been watching the play of emotion across her face. Now he said gently, "Your suggestion about Yacoub did seem the natural choice, except I happen to know Dr. Dawson has his eye on the boy for training as his lab assistant. And that's what Yacoub wants, too."

Hope nodded, meaning these were legitimate reasons for not deflecting Yacoub's present course.

Dr. Baxter added in the same gentle tone, "I know I should have consulted you before speaking to Warda. I was swept off my feet, rather, by her vital interest in our work, her eagerness to learned — "

"When did all this happen?"

"This morning, while you were busy with Rehab and her father," he answered innocently.

Hope felt true anger. She had only to turn her back long enough to deal with an emergency, for the girl to be up to her tricks. That Dr. Baxter should have been her victim, that he should have succumbed so quickly to her wiles . . . the very strength of her emotion warned Hope to examine her own feelings with care.

She admired Dr. Baxter. She enjoyed his company. And she treasured the compliments he had given her from time to time, as a woman as well as a colleague and a nurse. The doctor was devoted to his family, red-haired Esther and their three children. Surely he was mature enough to keep a silly little girl, however beautiful, in her proper place. Hope saw that her flash of anger had cost her the game, because there would be no way now of reassuring herself that a refusal would not be based on subconscious jealousy of Warda's attractiveness. Even as she prepared herself to give in graciously, a flicker of unease persisted, as though intuition were trying to warn her that this would not end well for anyone.

"Perhaps the challenge of learning new things is just what Warda needs," Hope said.

"Bless you, m'dear. You could have been angry with me."

She walked back to the clinic in Dr. Baxter's company, their friendship safe — at least for now.

THREE

HOPE WAS IN HER office rescheduling the nursing shifts when she heard Eileen Anderson speaking impatiently to someone down the hall. As they drew nearer Hope could hear Eileen saying, ". . . And if you don't snap out of this foolishness, my girl, I can tell you right now that you will never be a nurse."

Hope looked up from her papers. Eileen was standing in the doorway, exasperation written all over her face. "I was hoping to find you here," she said. She stepped aside and motioned to a small figure behind her.

Regina meekly scurried past her and stood shrinking before Hope's desk. Her eyes were on her own hands, which were twisting nervously together.

"I don't know what we are going to do with this girl," Eileen began severely. "Ameer and Daoud can't be expected to bathe *all* the male patients who are on complete bedrest. Regina refuses to touch any of them. I always assign the weakest ones to the male attendants, of course. Those she is supposed to bathe can handle most of their baths themselves. But they can't bathe their backs, or do their own back rubs. All Regina does is make their beds. She won't touch the men. Says she can't. I certainly don't see why!"

Regina cast a look weighted with appeal and managed to whisper, "I can't, Miss Callaway. I want to. I really do try, but I I just can't." To this, Eileen responded with lifted hands and a despairing shrug.

"Suppose you leave her to me, Eileen," Hope suggested quietly.

"I'll be glad to," her colleague retorted. She marched off, leaving Regina standing forlornly before Hope's desk, head down, eyes contemplating the floor. Hope studied the miserable little face.

"This child needs your help. Love her," a familiar voice within prompted. She swept her papers into the drawer, rose, and put her arm about Regina's trembling shoulders.

"Let us go up to my room and talk for a while."

She led the girl upstairs to her own room and settled her in a low slipper chair, mindful of Regina's short stature. Being short herself, she well knew the discomfort of a chair that leaves one's feet dangling. Kicking off her own shoes, she curled up in the big armchair.

"Now, child, tell me what is troubling you."

Regina looked up from contemplation of her tightly clasped hands. Twice she opened her lips to speak. Twice she closed them and swallowed convulsively. Again her eyes dropped and her hands began their nervous twisting as if in complete despair over her inability to articulate her difficulties.

Hope waited patiently. Meanwhile she reviewed in her mind the facts she knew about the girl. Regina was nineteen, small but sturdily built. She seemed strong and healthy. She was the only daughter in a Christian household of moderate means. There were four older stepbrothers, now grown and married, and one full brother younger than herself. Her father's first wife had died in an accident when the boys were in their teens. Regina's mother was quite a bit younger than her father.

When Hope first visited Regina's home in Bethlehem on her quest for nursing recruits, she found both parents in a receptive attitude. They had carefully guarded their only daughter. They were happy to place her under the discipline and guidance of a good Christian mission. Regina herself seemed glad to come. At the time, Hope vaguely sensed in her a childish immaturity, but she attributed this to the girl's sheltered home life.

Regina displayed no signs of homesickness when she entered the training program. Her classroom work was not outstanding, but she was earnest and faithful in carrying out her duties on her first assignment in the women's ward. She had served happily until her transfer to the men's ward a couple of weeks ago.

The Nursing Director wondered now if strict home discipline could be the cause of the girl's difficulty in adjusting to men. But in view of the fact that she had grown up in a household with six men in it, that did not appear to be the logical explanation. Regina was a sensible, matter-of-fact individual in most situations. She displayed the fiery pride and the passionate loyalties of her race, but she also possessed the rarer qualties of transparent honesty and a willingness to own up to mistakes. Hope counted on the latter two traits to help her get to the bottom of Regina's difficulties. Finally she prodded the girl.

"You must believe that I want to help you, Regina," she began. "Cant you tell me what is troubling you?"

Silence.

"You are afraid of men?" Hope ventured. "Afraid to touch them, or to have them touch you?"

Regina nodded.

"Tell me about it," Hope said softly.

"You won't tell anyone else?" Regina asked.

"Not a living soul."

"I have never told anybody else, not even my mother. She would not understand."

The cry of daughters from time immemorial, Hope thought, they never give their mothers a chance to prove themselves.

Regina continued: "My father and brothers would think I am silly if they ever found out. They think all women are silly, and that only men have any brains. They think they never make mistakes, and that women ought to obey them like slaves. My mother doesn't do it, but she makes my father think she does. Men aren't one bit smarter than women. They just won't admit it."

Her tone was as scornful as that of a militant suffragette, and Hope suppressed a smile with difficulty. She remarked dryly, "I take it, then, that you are not afraid to match wits with men. But why are you so afraid to touch them?"

Fright flared again in Regina's eyes. She began to tremble and to twist her hands anew. Finally she whispered in a small voice, "Miss Hope, you are too far away. I can't tell you here. Maybe if I could get closer to you . . . ?"

Hope swung her feet to the floor and pulled forward a low footstool beside her chair. "Come, child," she invited.

Regina slipped over onto the footstool and laid her head in Hope's lap. Then, with Hope gently smoothing her hair, she haltingly began her story:

"I had a little girlfriend once. Her name was Suweylah. We grew up together and shared each other's secrets. She was Moslem. I was Christian, but it didn't matter. She was a year older than me. Her mother died when she was twelve. Her father took her out of school. He made her cook and keep house for him and her two older brothers. They treated her like a slave. She never had any pretty dresses, no earrings, no jewelry. She loved pretty things. She was very pretty herself.

"Once when my father gave me a new pair of earrings, I gave my old ones to Suweylah. She was so happy to have them. But my father missed them. I had to ask her to give them back.

"Soon afterward Suweylah showed me a prettier pair that a neighbor gave her. The man who gave them to her was married and had several children. She kept the earrings hidden from her father. Then she showed me a silver bracelet, and then a necklace. After a while he gave her a pretty dress, then some nylon stockings and pretty underwear. Everyone in the neighborhood looked up to the man with respect. He had a souvenir shop in Jerusalem. Suweylah went to visit him in the shop whenever she could. He always gave her a gift. She wore the pretty clothes under her old dress until she got out of sight of her home. Then she hid the dress under a bush and put on her jewelry.

"One day she took me with her to Jerusalem. The man took us into a little parlor behind the shop and gave us tea. He sat in the middle of the couch with us on either side. Suweylah let him put his arm around her and kiss her. He tried to put his arm around me, too. I didn't like it. I ran out past the curtain and waited for Suweylah in the front of the shop.

"A few days later my father told me that I was not to visit or talk to Suweylah anymore. She was a bad girl. Then I took sick with typhoid and was ill for a long time. I was so weak afterward that my mother kept me home for the rest of that school term.

"One day my mother went out to the market. I was alone in the house. Suweylah must have been watching. She came over right away and knocked on the door. I was afraid to let her in for fear she would catch the typhoid. But she started crying. She said I was the only friend she had left, and if I didn't let her in she wanted to die right there on the doorstep. So I let her in. But when I started to explain that I was afraid she would catch the typhoid from me and die, she gave a horrible laugh. Then she started laughing and crying at the same time. The sound was horrible. I can't forget it."

Regina was sobbing now at the painful memory. Hope stroked her hair and was silent. After a moment the girl wiped her eyes, blew her nose, and went on with her story:

"Now I know that Suweylah was what you call hysterical. When she calmed down she said she wished to get the typhoid and die. She said she was going to die soon anyway, and that she was going to have a baby. Her father and brothers would kill her when they found out. I asked her why she didn't run away. She said she had nowhere to go, that nobody loved her anymore. She made me cry, too. I said I loved her, but she said I couldn't do anything to help her, that nobody could. She wondered how they would do it. She thought her father would cut her throat with a sharp knife and she would bleed to death. Then her brothers would put her in a sack with heavy stones and drop the sack into a deep spot in the Jordan River. Then she kissed me and left."

Regina drew a long, quivering breath.

"I had a relapse of fever that night. I was sick again for a long time. I never told my mother about Suweylah's visit. I never asked my parents about her. When I went back to school the next term, the other children told me that Suweylah had disappeared one day. No one knew where she was. But I knew. I've known all these years. I can shut my eyes and see the blood running all down the front of her dress when her father cut her throat."

Regina shuddered and began to sob again. Again Hope held her close and comforted her until the sobs ceased and she was able to go on with her story:

"The man was never punished. Whenever I saw him strutting around town my flesh crawled to think that he had ever touched me. I hated him for what he had done to Suweylah. I was glad when he was killed in the war four years ago. Ever since Suweyleh died I have been horribly afraid to touch men's flesh, or to let them touch mine. Even my own father, and he loves me dearly. I know it hurts him when I won't let him kiss me or put his arm around me. He doesn't understand. I can't help it, or tell him why. I can't tell my mother, either."

Regina paused and looked wistfully into Hope's face. "I know it isn't normal to feel like this. I have tried to overcome it, but I can't. I thought being a nurse would help. I love to take care of babies and women. I don't mind touching their flesh. I don't really hate men, either. I don't hate my father and brothers. But I can't stand touching. I would sooner put out my hand to stroke a cobra. I keep praying for God to help me, but He doesn't."

Hope went on stroking the hair back from the distressed little face. She wished she had more knowledge of psychiatry or psychology. She realized that Regina's problem was a deeply rooted one that would not be easily resolved. At length she spoke, choosing her words carefully.

"My dear, this is not just a silly whim to be scoffed at, but an abnormal fear that has held you in cruel bondage for too many years. The trauma, or shock, that you went through with your little friend during your most impressionable years, would have been far less severe if you had not been in such a weakened condition from your illness. If you had confided in your mother at the time, I am sure she could have helped you. She is a far wiser person than you give her credit for, dear.

"I appreciate your confidence in telling me, Regina. I promised not to tell anyone, but I wish I knew better how to help you. I believe that psychiatry teaches that the first step toward a cure is for the patient to realize that she does have a problem. The second step is to discover the cause. You already have done both. The third step is to confide in someone else, which you did today. I admit I don't have much wisdom to offer. But we both know Jesus, who is the source of all wisdom and strength. You tell me that you have already been asking for God's help. Now we will both pray for the enabling amount of courage that you need. I have an idea that our combined prayers will bring a speedy answer. Meanwhile, you don't have to go back to the men's ward. You can take Hanni's place on night duty in the women's ward tonight. I will send Hanni over to take your place in the morning.

"Now, go wash your face. It is almost time for dinner. Try to get some sleep this afternoon so that you will be able to go on duty at nine o'clock tonight."

Regina bestowed a grateful hug and a rapturous "thank you" upon her benefactor as Hope accompanied her to the door. The customary Arabic response rose easily to Hope's lips. "For nothing!" she replied, with an encouraging smile.

She turned to her mirror, removed her cap, and began to repin her loosened braids. A gentle knock sounded on her door.

"Come in!" she called, busily pushing in the hairpins.

The door opened, and Aminah stood hesitantly on the threshold.

FOUR

REGINA SAID THAT I would find you here," Aminah began apologetically. "But it is almost dinnertime. If you are busy . . ."

"Never too busy to welcome one of my girls for a talk," Hope answered. "Come in and sit down, Aminah. I'll be with you in a minute."

Aminah obeyed, moving with the unaffected grace that was so much a part of her bearing. Hope studied the girl's reflection in the mirror while she pinned up her braids. Quite unconscious of the superintendent's scrutiny, Aminah dropped her mask of cheerfulness. A naked loneliness and hunger for friendship became evident in her expressive dark eyes and in the disconsolate droop of her mouth and shoulders.

Aminah was the one student recruited by Dr. Dawson himself. It had happened most unexpectedly. Her father was a wealthy Moslem friend of his. The two men happened to meet one day at noon in Jerusalem. Mohammed Abdullah invited the doctor to be his dinner guest at the Arab National Hotel.

During the meal, Dr. Dawson casually mentioned that his hospital nursing school was opening soon. He stated that his nursing superintendent was having difficulty in recruiting students, and jokingly suggested that Mohammed enter his daughter in the training program.

To the good doctor's utter amazement, Mohammed jumped at the suggestion. It so happened that he had just come from a most distressing scene with his daughter, in which Aminah had pleaded with many tears that he allow her to engage in some useful service, where she could have companionship with girls of her own age. It was four years since she had graduated from a private school in Jerusalem. Every one of her classmates had departed happily to colleges in Beirut, Cairo, or somewhere on the European continent, leaving Aminah bereft of her friends.

Although Mohammed could have well afforded to send her anywhere in the world to further her education, he could not bear the thought of parting with her for weeks at a time. Aminah was his only child. Following the death of her mother in the girl's early teens, the bond between father and daughter had become very close.

For a while Aminah felt flattered and content to stay at home and act as hostess for her father at the frequent dinners to which he invited distinguished friends of his own age. He was proud of his daughter. It never occurred to him that she was becoming unbearably lonely for companions of her own age. A few of the guests occasionally brought their wives to dine, but they were much older than their charming young hostess.

Margaret Dawson was one of the very few women to whom Aminah had confided her loneliness. Both the doctor and his wife felt very sorry for the girl. Because of the family's wealth, her duenna housekeeper guarded her from making "undesirable" friendships with young women in the immediate neighborhood who might have fortune-hunting brothers.

Periodically, Aminah made attempts to persuade her father to let her engage in some form of philanthropic work to relieve the monotony of her existence. He admitted to Dr. Dawson that she had disturbed him with such a request only that morning. He wondered if the training program might be the solution to their problem. He said he would discuss the matter with Aminah. If she were interested, he would bring her soon for an interview.

Hope had been frankly dubious regarding the ability of a pampered rich girl to cope with the discipline and distasteful chores required of nurses. However, she promised Margaret to give the girl a chance if she should apply. Within a few days, Hope received a summons to an interview with Mohammed Abdullah and his daughter in the Dawson home. The impropriety of holding such an interview anywhere but in Hope's own office had certainly never occurred to Mohammed, and perhaps not to Dr. Dawson, but on her way to the meeting, Hope was already regretting the promise she had made.

She was surprised to find a dignified girl, with lovely manners, but shy, eager to please, and with a hungry look in her eyes that went straight to Hope's heart. She agreed to give Aminah a trial after summoning the courage to let Mohammed know as tactfully as possible that his daughter would be allowed no special privileges. Her weekends at home would be limited to the number allowed all the other students. Furthermore, she would in no case be permitted the hospitality of the Dawson home in which to visit her father. He would be expected to visit her in the room provided at the hospital, or on the hospital grounds, and this only when Aminah was free from nursing duties.

Mohammed stared at Hope cooly while Dr. Dawson squirmed and looked uncomfortable. Aminah quietly stated that she neither expected nor desired any special privileges. Finally her father reluctantly agreed to abide by the rules, only requesting that his daughter be assigned a private room, since she was unaccustomed to sharing.

Hope was about to demur, when Dr. Dawson spoke up hastily, evidently wishing to mollify his ruffled friend. He assured Mohammed that it would be possible to make such an arrangement. Aminah's protests that she would be delighted to have a roommate were overruled. Hope let it go.

Thus, through no fault of her own, Aminah had gotten off to a bad start with her companions from the very first day. That she was a sweet, humble soul, eager to please everyone, asking no favors or exemptions from the most unpleasant tasks, made no impression. To the other girls she was a privileged snob with a room to herself and all the extra comforts that an affluent father could provide.

The other students took delight in shoving off the most distasteful chores upon Aminah's willing shoulders. She never tattled or complained. When Hope or Eileen caught the other girls shirking the dirty work and took them to task for it, Aminah suffered the results of their resentment.

Mohammed Abdullah visited his daughter frequently. He brought gifts of candy, English tea biscuits, fresh and dried fruits, and all kinds of sweetmeats for her to share. To her hurt dismay, the girls invariably refused everything she offered them. When they chummed together in each others' rooms they never invited Aminah to join them or accepted invitations to hers.

One door was wide open to her loving heart. That was the door of service to the patients. They responded warmly to her genuine concern for their comfort. She was unstinting in her ministrations to their needs. Soon she was the best-loved and most sought-after nurse in the entire hospital. While the affection of the patients for her only added fuel to her classmates' resentments, it kept her from being utterly miserable, enabling her to maintain a semblance of happiness before her father.

Aminah was not without her own brand of pride and loyalty. Her father never suspected the true situation. He firmly believed that his daughter was happy with her newfound "friends." Each week he arrived with more parcels of delicacies.

Up to this present moment Aminah had never confided her troubles to anyone. Hope felt this was about to happen and spoke encouragingly. Aminah blurted out, "I hate to trouble you, Miss Callaway, but it's about my room. It's so crowded! I don't know what to do anymore!"

Hope's sympathy vanished. She felt indignation and disappointment.

"Crowded?" she echoed sarcastically, "Crowded with what, may I ask?"

"The boxes," Aminah confessed meekly. "My father brings so many when he comes. Boxes and boxes of candy, you know, and dried fruits, and all sorts of tea biscuits, and things. I can't begin to eat them all. The girls won't take any. My father thinks they do. He keeps bringing more and more. I can't tell him not to bring them. It would only hurt his feelings. I don't know where to put them anymore. Can't you give them away for me, please, Miss Callaway?"

She paused, out of breath and slightly bewildered, for Hope was struggling vainly to choke back her laughter. Immensely relieved at the simplicity of Aminah's problem, Hope was thankful that the girl was completely unaware of her mean earlier thoughts.

Hope sobered, wiped her eyes, and said contritely, "Aminah, please forgive me for laughing. Truly, I wasn't laughing at you, only at myself. Of course I'll be glad to help you give away your goodies, if that is what you want. The Bethlehem homes for blind girls and boys will be happy to have some. Then there is Madame Wadea Malik's shelter for unfortunate women and children. It is just on the outskirts of Beit Jala. On your very next day off, I will arrange for someone to help you load up a car with your boxes and take you to the homes. You can have the fun of playing 'Lady Bountiful' yourself."

Aminah rose, shaking her head. "No, Miss Callaway, I want you to take them for me, please. I don't want anyone to know who sent them." Her lips quivered as she added bravely, "I have found that gifts can't buy love. I'd rather not try that way anymore."

Hope had to stand on tiptoe to get her arm around the proud shoulders of her tall young student.

"Right you are, Aminah," she said approvingly. "Gifts can't buy love, but love can win love. I have yet to discover anything but love in that kind heart of yours. I happen to know that you have won the love of every patient in this hospital. I hear them singing your praises whenever I enter the wards."

The dinner gong sounded.

"And I want you to know that I love you, too, Aminah," Hope added softly, swinging the door open wide, so they could pass through together.

"Thank you, Miss Hope," she whispered.

Shyly, but confidently, her arm found Hope's shoulders, and they walked down the hall together.

FIVE

ON THE FOLLOWING SUNDAY evening the blow fell that was to keep Hope away from the clinic for almost a fortnight.

At five o'clock in the afternoon she went to the kitchen to prepare the final meal for the day with the help of Tamam and Nadia. She had cooked supper the previous evening, as well as the breakfast and dinner today, for it was Rose Zaki's weekend to be off duty. Rose was their only cook; no assistant had been found to relieve her. So on alternate weekends Hope took over the kitchen.

Rose's husband had died two years earlier, leaving nothing except a small house on a steep Bethlehem hillside. Rose was supporting two teenaged children. Lydia, who was sixteen, kept house for her younger brother during their mother's absence. They attended a secondary school in Bethlehem. A neighbor kept a watchful eye on them and saw that they were safe inside their home at night. Palestinian homes were built of stone, with heavily barred windows and doors. No prowlers could enter once the doors were bolted from the inside. So Rose could manage her hospital duties without undue anxiety over the safety of her children. Her weekends off were needed to lay in supplies for the children and to help them solve their accumulated problems.

As Hope and the maids cleared away the remains of the simple evening meal, Hope sighed with relief that her stint was over for another two weeks. Rose was due back any minute on the bus. But when the bus arrived, Lydia appeared with the unwelcome news that her mother had fallen down the steep flight of stone steps leading up to their Bethlehem home. Her hip was badly fractured. She was now in a body cast at the Arab hospital in Bethlehem. Lydia would stay the night to help prepare breakfast, but must catch an early bus to school.

Neither one of the maids was capable of taking charge in the kitchen. So the daily burden of planning and cooking the meals for the entire hospital fell upon Hope, head chef now, as well as nursing director.

In the emergency, Eileen Anderson took over two of Hope's classes in addition to her own increased responsibilities at supervising. Hope shifted her ethics and anatomy classes to a later evening hour. The rest, perforce, were postponed. Everyone, even the patients, joined in trying to make things easier for Hope, who, thus supported, tackled her daily tasks cheerfully.

Her first flying visit to Rose, lying helpless and in pain on her hospital bed, banished all inclination to self pity. She returned to her duties with gratitude that she was spared such long weeks of suffering and enforced idleness as Rose must endure. Each morning she woke to claim God's promise of strength for the day. Each night her prayer of gratitude for His help concluded with a fervent petition, "Oh God, please send another cook in time for me to get the students prepared for the capping service next month."

On Friday, which was visitor's day, Hope and the maids were clearing away the noon meal when a series of piercing shrieks, emanating from the second floor, sounded down the stairwell. With pounding heart Hope dashed from the kitchen and raced up two flights of stairs to the women's ward. As she ran, the bloodcurdling shrieks changed to long drawn-out wails of grief. She arrived breathless at the door of the ward fully expecting to find nothing short of murder.

Her headlong rush carried her into the middle of the room. She stopped in bewilderment. Only one patient was wailing. At close range the sounds were so loud and penetrating that she clapped both hands over her ears. The two maids arrived, having followed at a slower pace. They were inured to the excitable ways of their countrywomen. Now they stood in the doorway grinning at Hope's perplexity. She stared about her in astonishment.

Five patients were sitting bolt upright, cross-legged in the middle of their beds, in typical Arab fashion. Apparently they were thoroughly enjoying the performance of the sixth patient, who was rocking to and fro emitting wails of anguish. Her headscarf was pulled down over her face. She was tearing at her hair in approved mourning fashion. By the golden hair Hope identified her as Hikmat, the newest patient. Whenever she paused for breath, her roommates egged her on to greater histrionic efforts by shouts of encouragement, and they joined in her rocking motions.

Aminah and Zacchis, the latter a nurse's aide, stood on either side of the bed to guard against the possibility of the mourner falling out. Neither made the slightest effort to restrain either her violent motions or emotions.

A woman in rusty black widow's garb leaned complacently against the nearby wall. Evidently she had been the bearer of bad news. She was now heartily enjoying the furor that she had created. Since it was half an hour till the official time for visiting, she must have managed to slip by the watchful eye of the gate-keeper, Saleem. Anger at the intruder's presence brought Hope into swift action. She swung round on the five patients with the sharp command, "Nammy!" (lie down). The women sank languidly down upon their beds with smothered giggles.

Then she stepped over to Hikmat's bed and snatched the headscarf from her face just as she was opening her mouth for another shriek. The woman's tightly shut lids flew open in startled amazement. Hope's hand came swiftly up under her chin and closed her mouth with a snap.

"That's enough, Hikmat!" she ordered sternly.

Whimpering, Hikmat subsided against Aminah's comforting shoulder.

Next, Hope turned to the visitor, who was edging past her. She seized the woman's arm and marched her over to the two maids, who were frankly eavesdropping.

"Nadia and Tamam," said Hope, "Please escort this woman to the gate. Tell Saleem to make sure she doesn't get in here again before visiting hours. Then kindly get back to your work."

The maids hustled the woman off down the hall. Hope turned back into the ward. The five women lay motionless, but their eyes sparkled with suppressed merriment.

Deprived of her audience, Hikmat was now submitting cheerfully to the ministrations of the two students brushing and braiding her long hair.

Hope was filled with curiosity.

"Tell me, Hikmat," she asked, "what was all that about?"

Genuine tears welled up in the patient's blue eyes. She answered simply, "My husband has taken another wife. He did not tell me." Her eyes closed wearily. The tears spilled out from under the lids and rolled quietly down her cheeks.

Hope surveyed her with deep pity, groping for words.

"I am sure it will be very hard for you to have another woman sharing your home and your husband's affections."

But Hikmat interrupted, hastily drying her tears as she spoke, "No, no, that is not why I cry. I wanted him—I begged him to take another wife. I am sick. I cannot care for our children. But . . ." she began crying again, "he did not let me choose her. He promised to let me choose. I do not mind another wife. But he has taken her before I could see her. That is why I cry."

She wiped her eyes again and lay back limply on her pillows, spent with emotion. Hope was speechless. She could only pat the woman's hand by way of further comfort.

There was a stir at the door.

A fine-looking Arab man in well-cut Western clothes entered hesitantly. He bore a huge bouquet of flowers and a large candy box wrapped in gold foil—a true picture of a guilty husband bringing his peace offerings to his offended wife.

Hope stepped forward to greet him. "You must be Hikmat's husband, Mr. . . .?"

"Yes," he said, bowing low over her hand, "I am Mustapha Hussein. You must be Miss Callaway. I have heard much about your many kindnesses. I am most happy to meet you."

He spoke in excellent English with a decidedly British accent. His glance slid apprehensively past Hope toward Hikmat. She was sitting upright, gazing at him reproachfully. Hope tried to escape, but Mustapha protested. "Please stay for a moment, Miss Callaway, I have a surprise for you both."

He placed the gifts on the bed beside Hikmat and went back to the door. Reaching out a hand to someone standing out of sight in the vestibule, he drew her into the room.

Hope gasped. So did Hikmat.

It was Rehab, blushing and smiling tremulously. She wore a smart blue street dress with a lovely matching scarf.

All the patients popped up in bed to shout, "Saida, Rehab, Saida!"

Mustapha led his blushing bride straight to Hikmat's bedside then went to stand on the other side of the bed.

After Hope's own first startled recognition of Rehab, she turned to watch Hikmat's reaction. The woman's eyes were searching every feature of the girl's face. Rehab stood with eyes timidly lowered. There was a strained silence. The other patients were holding their breath to listen.

"Look at me!" Hikmat commanded finally.

The girl meekly raised her eyes. They were brimming with frightened tears. Yet something else lay in their depths. Was it compassion? Tender understanding? Hope thought it could best be defined by the word "empathy," which combined the meanings of the other two words.

Hikmat continued her probing scrutiny until a couple of the tears overflowed and dried on Rehab's flushed face. Then the older woman held out her hand. Rehab took it. Hikmat's eyes continued to search the girl's face.

"Do You love my children?" she demanded abruptly. Rehab could only nod.

"Yes, I can see the truth in your eyes," Hikmat said. "You will take good care of them for me."

She leaned back wearily on her pillow, still gripping Rehab's hand. It had been an exhausting day.

"Allah is good," she murmured. "I am satisfied."

Her blue eyes turned wistfully toward her husband. His fingers closed tenderly around the hand she stretched out to him. She closed her eyes and drew his hand to her cheek. Then she pressed it to her lips.

"You are a good man, husband," she murmured. "You have made a wise choice for our children." Only a fleeting spasm of pain swept across Hikmat's face.

After a moment of silence she opened her eyes again and smiled gallantly up into the faces of the two whose hands she was holding.

"Kismet," she said clearly.

Then she drew the two hands together and joined them in a firm clasp.

Hope's own eyes were brimming as she made blindly for the door. Her soul felt humbled before the simple faith of this noble Moslem woman.

"Kismet," Hikmat had said. To many Christians and Moslems alike, the word merely meant a blind fatalistic acceptance of God's will. But Hope knew from the expression in Hikmat's eyes as she uttered the word, and by the gallant smile on her lips, that Hikmat well understood the full depths of its true meaning, which is, "acceptance of God's will *without bitterness*."

SIX

TEN DAYS PASSED. HOPE was still bound down to kitchen duties. The morning and evening meals were simple, requiring only the primus stoves for cooking. But the hearty dinner at noon, which was shared by the employees who came by the day and by some of the outside workmen, required more cooking space and far more time for preparation.

At eight o'clock, with breakfast out of the way, Hope knelt before the open door of the firebox in the side of the big black oil range, vainly trying to coax the smoldering oil into active flame. There was a daub of soot on her nose, considerably more on her hands, and a fresh burn along her left forearm. Her starched white nurse's cap sat tipsily askew on the loosened braids above her flushed forehead. She gripped a sooty poker in her hand. As she alternately poked and blew, she whispered childishly under her breath, "Please, oh, please, you big, black, beautiful brute, *do* get busy and start burning! Don't you know I need you to cook our dinner?"

"Miss Callaway!" the gateman's voice boomed down the stairway from the main hall.

"Down here, Saleem!" Hope called. She gave a last despairing poke at the smoldering oil and scrambled to her feet, shaking down the folds of the large blue pinafore that enveloped her from neck to heels.

Big Saleem lounged in the doorway. On his face was the ingratiating smile that Hope recognized as a prelude to wheedling a favor for himself or for one of his many friends. Her shoulders stiffened with instinctive resistance. Her chin rose in a gallant little fighting gesture which, quite unknown to her, had long since made Saleem her admirer. Washing her hands at the sink, she asked, "Well, Saleem, what favor do you want from me today?"

He looked aggrieved. "No, no favor from you. Today I bring you a favor. I bring you a cook!"

He stepped back and motioned dramatically to someone standing behind him in the hall. A huge figure billowed past him and stood smiling in the doorway, literally filling the opening from side to side.

Hope's mouth dropped open. Never had she seen so fat a woman. A tent-sized black robe of heavy material covered the massive body. Although shabby, the robe was spotlessly clean and carefully pressed. Its threadbare shiny expanse stretched snugly across bulging thighs and bosom, showing off to advantage every lavish detail of the beautiful cross stitch designs worked in brilliant colors from shoulders to waist and down the wide side panels extending clear to the floor. No doubt it was her wedding dress, Hope thought. It had seen many years of service since first it was made.

A black scarf such as worn by widows was draped over the woman's kinky gray hair. The dark-skinned moonlike face was a pleasant mixture of African and Arabic features. Above the three-tiered chin her white teeth flashed in a good natured grin. The twinkle in her black eyes brought Hope to the sudden realization that her own mouth was hanging open. She quickly closed it, trying hard to conceal her dismay.

Saleem's voice spoke from behind the woman's shoulder, "This is Fatmy, Miss Callaway."

Hope glanced up to see his head towering above the black headscarf. It gave her a queer sense of relief that Fatmy's height, at least, did not match her gigantic girth. She was scarcely taller than Hope herself. Still, she continued to eye the woman rather dubiously.

Fatmy's smile began to waver. She shifted her feet uneasily. Thus reminded of the courtesy expected in this country, Hope thrust out her hand, saying, "Good morning, Fatmy!"

The huge woman seized the proffered hand. She bowed gracefully from her waist to touch it to her lips, then to her forehead. As she did so, Hope became aware of an equally startling figure behind her. This was an extremely tall angular skeleton of a dark-skinned girl about seventeen or eighteen years of age. In sharp contrast to Fatmy, not an ounce of excess flesh was visible upon her bony frame. The same mixture of racial characteristics was apparent in both women, but there all resemblance ceased.

The girl's face was that of a comical clown. She had large, protruding ears, a large flat nose, high cheekbones, and a very wide mouth. Her kinky hair was tightly braided into two short thick braids tied with wide red ribbons. The latter stuck out like wings above her knife-edged shoulder blades. She wore a vivid red flowered cotton dress, ankle length, and a small red headscarf to match. Her height was equal to that of Saleem.

While Hope gaped at this second apparition, Fatmy sidled past her into the kitchen. Saleem drew the girl forward.

"This is Murshdeeyah, Miss Callaway," he announced. "Fatmy's daughter. She has to work with her mother. Fatmy doesn't understand much English."

Hope's hand rose in a quick gesture of protest, which Murshdeeyah misinterpreted. She seized the hand, as her mother had done, bent low over it, kissed it, and laid it against her forehead. As she straightened from her bow, her black eyes met Hope's. An expression of such childlike trust was in their depths that words of rejection died on Hope's lips. She stood helplessly while Murshdeeyah joined her mother in the kitchen.

In the hallway, she confronted Saleem, who was waiting to receive her approbation.

"You know we can't afford board and salary for two women just now. We have Rose's hospital expense, and Fatmy alone would eat enough to feed three women. I must have one cook who can speak good English. You will just have to go in there and tell those women that I can't possibly hire them."

Saleem was aghast.

"Miss Callaway, I told Fatmy you need a cook. She is a good cook. She loves to cook!"

"So I see. She loves to eat, too!"

"But I can't hurt her feelings," Saleem pleaded. "Maybe she does eat a little more than some people. But you can see that Murshdeeyah eats very little, and they need work. The family they worked for went back to America three months ago. They haven't found work since."

Hope shook her head.

Saleem persisted.

"They both work real hard, Miss Callaway. You said you could pay eight pounds. They will work together for only ten pounds. That is only two pounds more than you would pay for one cook. If you had two, you wouldn't have to do any cooking yourself. Murshdeeyah can do a lot of other things, too."

Hope began watching the women in the kitchen. Fatmy had gotten the oil burning steadily in the balky stove with utmost ease. The teakettles that Murshdeeyah had filled were already hissing on it. The two women began a delighted inspection of the kitchen equipment. Fatmy found some large knives in a drawer. She honed them lovingly on the edge of the stone sinkboard, testing their sharpness from time to time against her thumb. Murshdeeyah was sorting pots and pans.

"Miss Callaway," Saleem implored, "Please! You can't keep on doing all the cooking. And the teaching. And the nursing, and the mending, and shopping, and . . . and . . . everything. You will kill yourself! You need Fatmy! You need Murshdeeyah!"

Hope's eyes started twinkling. Fatmy now had the knives sharpened and was looking about for something on which to use them. Murshdeeyah discovered a basket of onions and some tomatoes. They pounced upon these with cries of delight and set eagerly to work washing and peeling them.

The two were evidently happily entrenched. Hope knew from past experience with Arab workers that it would be a well-nigh impossible task to dislodge them. Besides, anyone who could so easily master that brute of an oil range was certainly worth a try. Had she not prayed for a cook? If God chose to send two for good measure, who was she to question His judgment? She said to Saleem, "You can bring their luggage down to Rose's room. Then bring in another cot from the storeroom."

Saleem went off to fetch the luggage. Fatmy was already pulling the black robe off over her head, revealing a clean light cotton dress beneath. Hope stripped off the blue pinafore and held it out to Murshdeeyah. The girl donned it, wrapping the strings twice about her waist as Hope had done.

The director glanced at her watch and found it was time to prepare the mid-morning tea. She led the new employees to the room they would occupy and showed Fatmy where to hang her robe. The three then proceeded to the storeroom. Hope unlocked the door. She began measuring out the rice, oil, loaves of bread, and other supplies they would need for the day.

The two maids, Nadia and Tamam, appeared and were introduced to the newcomers. Hope selected two large pieces of lamb from the oil burning refrigerator, which she gave to Fatmy to carry. They all returned to the kitchen laden down with food.

Fatmy laid the meat on the wooden block. Hope explained to Murshdeeyah that it must be cut to serve thirty-eight persons.

Murshdeeyah relayed the message to her mother. Fatmy immediately set to work with a large knife, expertly cutting the meat into the required number of portions. These she put on to cook in a large stewing pot together with the onions and tomatoes already prepared. Hope watched approvingly while the maids, Murshdeeyah helping, prepared the tea.

Soon Jebra arrived on the bus from Bethlehem, bringing two large burlap sacks. He did the daily grocery shopping for the hospital. From the first sack he produced several stalks of small, sweet bananas, which he had carefully placed on top. Next were two kilos of firm green tomatoes, a half dozen large cauliflowers, some potatoes, and, in the very bottom of the sack, a quantity of green string beans.

As he shook the beans out into the two baskets that Tamam brought, Jebra explained that they were so fresh, and such a good buy, that he had bought double the quantity ordered, then glowed with pride at Hope's praise of his good judgment.

The second sack contained two large white flour sacks of double strength muslin. Divided between them were seventy-five loaves of round flat "aish," or Arabic bread, and four or five of the Western-style loaves, all freshly baked during the night at the Greek Orthodox bakery. An Arabic loaf hardly served more than one person, but was inexpensive and delicious.

I must order at least five more loaves of "aish" per day now, Hope thought, and added them to the list. Then she settled the day's accounts with Jebra and advanced him the estimated cash for the next day's needs.

The maids were carrying the new supplies to the storeroom, leaving one basket of the string beans for Murshdeeyah to fix for the noon meal. The girl surveyed the contents of both baskets. Then she scooped up a large double handful of the beans from her basket and dropped them into the one destined for the storeroom, remarking as she did so, "*Becafi* (enough) for today." Hope agreed.

The supplies were stored, then the maids carried off the tea trays to their various destinations. When they returned, Hope said, "Girls, I want you to stay here now and help Fatmy and Murshdeeyah with the dinner. Be sure to explain to them that everything used in the kitchen must be kept very clean. Any towels or dishtowels that happen to fall on the floor must be put in the wash immediately. I will be back before it is time to serve dinner."

She turned to find her way blocked by Murshdeeyah. The girl held out a handkerchief that she had found in the pocket of the blue pinafore. But as the director put out her hand to take it, Murshdeeyah's huge left hand shot out and grasped her chin. She tilted Hope's head back and wiped the soot off her nose as thoroughly as if she were a child. Exhibiting the soiled handkerchief, she restored it to the apron pocket with the explanation, "I wash."

Still blocking Hope's exit, she reached up both hands to carefully straighten the crooked nurse's cap, gently pushing several loose hairpins into place.

This done, she stood back and gravely surveyed Hope from head to foot. Inspection ended, she gave a final nod of approval and stepped aside from the doorway. Hope fled past her in utter confusion. Delighted cackles of laughter from the kitchen followed her all the way down the hall.

SEVEN

ON A SUNNY AFTERNOON in mid-July, Hope slipped out of a hospital side entrance and made her way down the hedge bordered path leading to the clinic. She was humming a silly little tune recalled from a game played in childhood,

"Where, oh where, is dear little Ruthie? Down in the paw-paw patch."

Where the hedge grew thickest she even indulged in a few little skips of pure joy. Her kitchen drudgery was over at last. Fatmy and Murshdeeyah had quickly grasped the strict rules of food sanitation. They were proving to be economical as well as efficient cooks. They could now be trusted to carry on their tasks with only a modicum of supervision. With no clouds visible on today's mental horizon, Hope skipped merrily along.

At mid-morning tea Dr. Baxter had invited her to observe an eye operation that he had scheduled for this afternoon. She welcomed the opportunity to observe his technique. Also, she had a desire to see how Warda was progressing. She had been away from the clinic for more than two weeks. Her only contact with

Warda during that time had been at the two evening classes that she had been able to carry on.

She was not surprised to find the compound deserted. No clinic patients were admitted at the south gate in the afternoons. Those with special appointments were admitted through the main hospital gate. Hope could see Yusef down there now chatting with Ahmed, the night watchman. Ahmed often slept in the gatehouse in the daytime. His home in the noisy refugee camp offered little opportunity for daytime sleeping. When he occupied the gatehouse, Saleem was free to perform extra chores around the hospital.

The outer door to the treatment room was ajar. Hope's crepe soled shoes made no sound as she entered and crossed to the smaller room beyond. A dark-robed figure, evidently the patient's companion, lay sprawled asleep on a bench in the main room, a white kafeeyah covering his face.

Hope passed him and stood unobserved in the doorway of the smaller room where the operation was already in progress.

The patient's chair was turned away from the door, facing the light of the west window. The backrest was lowered so that he lay in a semi-reclining position, head tilted well back. A Mayo table was adjusted to a convenient height above his chest. Hope noted with approval the neat arrangement of swabs, instruments, and sutures lying upon it.

Dr. Baxter's back was toward Hope. He was bent over the patient, absorbed in his work. Warda stood across from him, half turned toward the door. She was holding a small kidney-shaped basin against the patient's cheek with her left hand. A swab stick was poised in her right hand. But she was not watching the operation. Instead, her eyes were fixed upon the curly brown hair of the doctor. An unmistakable look of tender yearning made Hope draw back in shocked dismay.

Her first reaction was guilt, a feeling that she had unwittingly intruded behind a curtain into a private place that was not meant for her eyes to see. Then a wave of apprehension swept over her.

"Swab, Warda!" the doctor said sharply.

Startled, the girl returned to her task, hastily applying the swab stick as directed.

Hope slipped away unseen. The lightheartedness of a few minutes before was gone.

She spent a restless night, haunted by the look she had seen on Warda's face. Several times she woke from troubled dreams and knelt to pray for guidance.

By morning she had come to the decision to leave the problem in God's capable hands, and to say nothing to the good doctor. She knew that Dr. Baxter was a happily married man, and very devoted to his little family. Even if he were to discover Warda's infatuation, Hope knew that he would use his own good judgment in handling the girl, at least she hoped he would. On the other hand, he might be very flattered to know that such a beautiful young girl could think of him in such a way. That was the real problem, the unknown male ego. Here her thoughts remained. She could only wait and see.

Bringing her Materia Medica class to a close the next morning, Hope dismissed the students and hastened down the hall. Her mind was occupied with all the problems of the coming examinations, and she was quite concerned about some of her girls not passing. As she came neared Dr. Baxter's office, he came charging out of the doorway and they collided with a rather hard jolt. The doctor was very apologetic and quite flustered.

Hope laughed and assured him that no harm had been done, and then she started on down the hall.

"Hey, wait just a moment, please," he called out after her. "Something has come up that you might be able to help me with."

Hope stopped and turned back. The doctor came toward her and lowered his voice.

"Someone has been dipping into the clinic cashbox," he continued. "At first I thought a patient might be the culprit, but it happens too regularly for a day patient to be responsible. The nurses do most of the collecting when they dispense the medicines. I don't have much chance to keep an eye on the box when I have to be in my office. But I notice that some of the larger coins are disappearing. At the end of our busiest days we seem to have less in the box than on slack days. So far, there probably hasn't been more than fifteen or twenty plasters taken in one day. But we should put a stop to it before the thief gets bolder. I haven't said anything to Aida or Warda, since I don't suspect them, but I think you ought to know."

"Indeed, yes," Hope replied. "I am glad you told me. Even the small amounts in that cashbox are a great temptation to poor people, and it is too easily accessible. I shall try to guard it more carefully in the future."

Dr. Baxter smiled down warmly upon her. "It is certainly a relief to have you back."

Hope felt a warm glow inside as she turned to continue on her way. This feeling faded as she thought about what Dr. Baxter had told her.

"Dear God," she whispered, "please don't let me start suspecting anyone. And please don't let the thief be one of my precious girls."

EIGHT

A FEW MORNINGS LATER, Yacoub Kakeesh was waiting for Hope at the door of the classroom. He handed her a note from Dr. Dawson requesting her to come to his office as soon as possible. The summons was expected.

Some time before, at Hope's request, the chief had conducted a brief course in X-ray and laboratory procedures for the ten students who were taking the full two-year nursing course. Yacoub was the only male member of the group. His two friends, Ameer Shabeeb and Daoud Suleiman, had elected to take the six months' course for male attendants. But Yacoub was enrolled with his twin sister, Elizabeth, for the full course.

The boy was quiet and steady, conscientious, dependable. However, he showed no outstanding ability in either classroom or ward performance. Hope sensed no spark that distinguishes good from mediocre.

One glimpse into Dr. Dawson's microscope had lighted the latent spark in Yacoub, transporting him into the fascinating world of microbes. Noting the boy's keen interest, the chief immediately invited him to help with the laboratory and X-ray work during his free time, and gave him access to his own excellent library of technical books. Thereafter, Yacoub spent every spare moment studying and cataloging slides, developing and filing X-ray plates, and poring over the microscope and laboratory textbooks. As a consequence, his nursing studies suffered.

Hope was already resigned to the eventual loss of her one male student, so she was prepared for this summons. She thanked Yacoub, pocketed the note, opened her textbook, and rapped for the students' attention. Shortly before noon she dismissed the class and headed for Dr. Dawson's office.

The door was wide open. The chief was seated at his desk with the hospital account books spread open before him. The bookkeeper-accountant for the mission, Khaleed Khalil, stood beside him, a sheaf of requisition slips in his hands.

Dr. Dawson rose to his feet, and Khaleed sprang to pull forward a large upholstered leather chair. Dr. Dawson waved Hope into it, saying, "Please sit down, Miss Hope. Make yourself comfortable while we finish these accounts."

Hope relaxed contentedly, still basking in the sweetness of the chief's smile. She wondered how many people had been similarly blessed and influenced by the simple Christian love that shone out so brightly from the face of this saintly old servant of God. With a pang, she noted how feeble and frail he appeared today. Her glance shifted to Khaleed, envying for the doctor's sake, his youth and stalwart frame.

Khaleed was a muscular stockily built man with the typical dark eyes and handsome features of the Arab race. He was probably in his late thirties or early forties, unmarried.

Dr. Dawson first encountered him shortly after the 1948 partitioning of Palestine. At the time, the doctor was negotiating with Khaleed's cousin, Ahmed Khalil, for purchase of a plot of land south of Bethlehem. The chief wished to build his hospital and home in that locality. A devout Moslem, Ahmed professed reluctance to part with land that would be used for Christian purposes.

Khaleed was present at the interview, and he apparently had fewer religious scruples than his cousin. He joined Dr. Dawson in persuading Ahmed to sell, at a price higher than Dr. Dawson had expected to pay.

The deed was hardly signed before a refugee camp sprang up almost alongside the property. Soon nearly eight thousand refugees were quartered there in makeshift tents. A pressing need for medical attention quickly developed. Dr.Dawson was certain that God had chosen the location for his ministry. As Khaleed spoke excellent English, and the mission was in need of an interpreter to expedite dealings with government officials, contractors, builders, and the various workmen who were needed in the construction of the buildings, the position was offered to Khaleed, who accepted.

It developed that the young man was an expert accountant. He had been employed by a prosperous Arab businessman in Jerusalem ever since completing secondary school. But in the summer of 1947, in anticipation of the partitioning of his homeland, the employer liquidated his assets and departed for South America to start a new life in Brazil. This left Khaleed stranded along with many other young men whose employers sold, or lost, all their possessions. He was reduced to depending upon his cousin, Ahmed, for support. He lost no time in making himself indispensable to the mission.

By the time Dr. Dawson's residence was built and the clinic unit completed, the young Arab was handling all the business accounts and the payroll. Hope had to admit to herself that he did his job well. Now, watching the two, she speculated as to Khaleed's true feelings toward his benefactor and toward the Christian ministry as a whole. She knew that Dr. Dawson entertained high hopes for Khaleed's conversion, although he still attended Moslem services regularly in Jerusalem every Friday morning. His attitude toward Hope and the other staff members was always imperturbably courteous. She had no real reason to distrust him.

Just once she had caught him off guard, and she had never been able to erase the unpleasant memory of that experience. She came upon him unexpectedly one morning lounging in the doorway of his office. He was watching intently the movements of Nadia, the maid. She was unconscious of his gaze and of her well exposed limbs as she bent over from the waist to scrub the hall floor with a handcloth, in the manner of the Arab women. Avid lust glittered in Khaleed's eyes. Almost immediately, Khaleed caught sight of Hope. His face swiftly became expressionless. He turned quickly and strode back into his office. On her very next trip to Amman, Hope bought some longhandled mopsticks, and thereafter saw to it that the maids used them exclusively.

Now Dr. Dawson and Khaleed completed checking the accounts. Dr. Dawson wrote a check and handed it to Khaleed, who placed it carefully in his billfold, then bowed formally to Hope and left.

The chief swung his chair around to face her. Instinctively her spine stiffened. His eyes twinkled.

"At ease, Miss Hope," he commanded. She relaxed with a laugh. "Remember, we are not living in the 'good old days' of, shall we say, twenty-five years ago?"

"At least that," Hope agreed. "But they were good days, although at the time the discipline seemed terribly strict and hard to take. I can look back on them now with appreciation."

"My medical discipline began a good eighteen years earlier," he mused. "Isn't it amazing how time transforms the most tragic episodes of our student days into ludicrous, even happy memories?"

The clatter of the patients' lunch trays out in the hall brought them back. Dr. Dawson leaned forward in his chair and turned the full charm of his smile upon her.

"I suppose you know I have a favor to ask. As you know, I need a lab and X-ray technician. Yacoub is interested. I am hoping that you will release him from nurses' training. I would like to send him to the American University Hospital in Beirut for six months of intensive training. Special funds have just come in that can be used for the boy's board and tuition expenses."

"You don't need to wheedle, Doctor. I suspected your intentions some time ago. I am quite willing. In fact I'm very happy for Yacoub. I am sure he will justify your faith in his ability. The work is far more suited to his talents than nursing."

"Thank you," said the doctor gratefully. He settled back in his chair.

"As a matter of fact," he continued, "I am in correspondence with Dr. Lindquist, the roentgenologist at AUH. He and the lab technician are both willing to take the boy on for intensive training as soon as I can send him. The sooner he goes, the sooner I can get him back here to help me. I don't suppose that his parents will offer any objection to his going?"

"I hardly think so," Hope answered. "It is a wonderful opportunity for Yacoub. They should be grateful to you."

"No, my dear," he corrected, "their gratitude is due you, and so is mine. I know what a struggle you had to get your students. If you had objected to Yacoub's going, I would not have insisted."

He produced two overseas airmail letters from under his desk blotter and passed them across to her. "God willing" he said, "we shall soon have more helpers to ease your heavy burden. These both arrived yesterday. Read them at your leisure."

"For the present I shall brief you on their contents. The one from Germany is from a deaconess, Sister Marta Krueger. She is nearing seventy. She wants to spend some time in the Holy Land before retiring. She is willing to serve for board and room and pin money if we can find use for her. She is in good health. At present she is serving as night supervisor in a children's hospital, and prefers the night shift."

Hope's eyes sparkled. She exclaimed excitedly, "Of course we can use her. Molly Claiborne's young man in America is getting impatient. If she doesn't go home and marry him soon, he threatens to find another sweetheart. Please write and tell her to come right away."

The chief smiled at her eagerness.

"There are some strings," he said. "Sister Krueger has a nephew who wishes to come with her. He is a fully trained male nurse. He would need a regular mission salary as well as room and board. We would need to pay transportation expenses for both."

"But it is only from Germany. The fare for two of them would be less than it costs to bring one person from America. With Yacoub leaving we will need another male nurse in the men's ward. The beds there are filling rapidly. He could help Dr. Baxter part-time in the clinic, too."

"We can manage the funds somehow. But even if I write immediately, Sister Marta must give some notice before leaving her present position. It would be several weeks before they could get here."

"Of course," Hope murmured, feeling that each week of waiting would seem a year in length.

"Cheer up. I have saved the best for last. A Mrs. Ouida Prinstetter, a California registered nurse with whom I have been corresponding, is flying out at her own expense, but will need maintenance and salary. I haven't mentioned it before because I didn't want to disappoint you if she decided not to come. She is a widow in her mid-fifties, with three grown children, all married. She has been nursing mostly in doctor's offices for several years. I thought she might take care of the clinic work and pinch-hit in the ward when needed. She writes that she is interested in occupational therapy. I would like to see something of the sort started here, especially in the men's ward. The lady has already booked passage from New York on BOAC. She sent me the flight number."

He waited mischievously until Hope, no longer able to restrain her impatience, uttered the one word, "When?"

"Exactly two weeks from yesterday."

He leaned back in his chair chuckling as, forgetting all dignity, Hope clapped her hands in a transport of joy, and exclaimed rapturously, "Two weeks . . . I can scarcely believe it! Only two weeks!"

"Does this make up a little for the loss of Yacoub?"

"Oh, yes indeed, Doctor," Hope assured him.

Dr. Dawson cleared his throat. Then he lifted his right hand and solemnly intoned;

"I hereby promise, 'pon my honor, never to swipe one of your students again."

It set them both to laughing. Then he asked, "How are the rest doing with their lessons?"

Hope quickly sobered.

"I fear that one or two may fail in the qualifying examinations. If they do, they will not be eligible to receive their caps and continue further training. Without a good secondary education and a comprehensive grasp of basic English, they will be unable to complete the nursing subjects beyond the nurse's aide level of training. Most textbooks are still not available in Arabic, which is a big handicap for some. I dare not lower the academic standards that Miss Anderson and I have set up. As graduates of a Christian institution operating in a Moslem country where government officials frown upon our religion, our students will face discrimination enough when it comes to taking government examinations to obtain a license to nurse elsewhere than in our own hospital. Without a government certificate, their standing would be no higher than that of an aide."

"Well, nurse's aides can be very useful. They were all that I had to assist me in Ethiopia. I trained them myself." He chuckled at the memory. "Nothing wrong with having a good bunch of nurse's aides around here."

"Yes, I know," Hope agreed without enthusiasm. "But aides can never take over the responsibility of supervising and training others to take their places. We will not be here forever. Without the prestige of a government certificate, our graduates would be unable to command the respect of those they might attempt to train.

"Someday our work must be turned over to the nationals. You have said so yourself. Unless we leave behind some well trained leaders, the work we are trying to establish will soon collapse."

"You are absolutely right, my dear," he said. "Don't let this old man's outmoded notions lower your high standards. You are building wisely for the future. Have patience. God will choose your nurses for you and develop some leaders among them. Someday your students will rise up and call you blessed, then take over your job for themselves. Bless you!"

His parting smile was like an accolade.

NINE

It was long past midnight when Hope felt the quiet that had settled down over the whole of the mission compound. This was the first time that she had relaxed enough to realize how really late it was. The noisy generator had long since shut down. Now the faint glow from an oil lamp on the nurse's desk outside each of the two wards, and a third lamp on the floor at the top of the second stairway, were the only lights visible throughout the entire hospital. It was a comfort to know that two others, beside Eileen and herself, were still up. Daoud dozed beside the desk outside the men's ward, while Molly Claiborne was ruling some charts at her desk outside the women's ward. The heavy curtains were drawn across the windows to keep out the chill of night. Even in July the temperature dropped rapidly as soon as the sun set behind the western mountains. Hope pulled her quilted bathrobe closer around her, and tried to find a more comfortable position for her feet.

Hope and Eileen were in the staff sitting room at the far north end of the hall. They had both put in a very long day. A large Coleman-type lamp shed a bright light upon piles of examination papers stacked on the table in front of them. They were busy correcting the examinations that had been given to the eight students that morning. Yacoub had departed for Beirut a few days earlier, so had not taken the tests.

Eileen finished reading her last paper. She totaled the correct answers, scrawled a big red ninety percent across the top of the page and placed it with Christine's pile.

"Mine are finished," she announced. "Can I help you?"

"No, thanks," Hope replied. "I'm almost through."

The teakettle was hissing on the stove. Eileen rose, and gave a groan, as she stretched her long arms above her head. She pulled her bathrobe about her lanky figure.

"It's chilly in here," she remarked. "What we need right now is a good cup of tea." With that she got the teapot and cups from the sideboard.

Hope sipped the hot tea gratefully when it came, and continued with her work. Eileen replenished the water in the kettle and returned to her chair with her own cup. She ran her fingers through her short, dark, curly hair, leaned back in her chair, and surveyed her partner affectionately. After a long sigh, she drew the first pile of papers toward her and picked up her pencil. She jotted down the grades on a scratch pad, made a rapid calculation, then announced, "Christine made an average of ninety-four percent."

"That's only to be expected," Hope commented. She laid a completed paper on Aida's pile, pausing to add, "After all, most of this is just review for Christine. She had almost a year and a half of training at the Mount of Olives Hospital, you know."

"Did you ever learn the real reason behind Christine's dismissal?" Eileen asked. "Of course, I know that she pitched into another girl with a knife in a fit of rage, and refused to apologize afterward. But do you know why she went berserk?"

Hope laid down her pencil and the paper she was correcting.

"No," she answered thoughtfully. "It has often puzzled me. I can't believe that she just went crazy. She and another student were dressing the wounds of a woman patient, when Christine picked up the scissors from the dressing tray and slashed the other girl across the face. I believe the other girl must have given her strong provocation. She swore that she hadn't done a thing. Christine made no defense. The nursing superintendent, Sitt Maryam, couldn't get her to admit that she was even sorry, or to explain why she had done it.

"The worst of it was, that the patient, the only one who might have testified for Christine, died that night. So Christine's fate was sealed, especially since the other girl's father was an influential member of the hospital board."

Hope paused thoughtfully, then continued, "Sitt Maryam was the head nurse in the emergency ward there ten years ago, when they brought Christine in by ambulance. She was so badly burned that no one thought she could possibly live. She was fifteen at the time. Her whole family perished that night in the tragedy that left Christine horribly scarred. She fell over a charcoal brazier while trying to escape from their home in a cave on a hillside near Jerusalem. Sitt Maryam cared for her burns for months afterward. Then she had to return periodically for skin and muscle grafts for over three years."

Hope finished her cup of tea. Then she went on: "It was Sitt Maryam who encouraged Christine to finish her secondary schooling and go into nurse's training. But after what happened, Sitt Maryam was forced by the hospital board to dismiss her without any recommendation. She lost all her credits. No other government hospital would accept her. So we were her last resort. She wants desperately to be a nurse."

"She has the makings of a good one, too," Eileen commented. "I don't have any trouble with her, and I don't expect to. I must admit that she is a bit standoffish with the other students. But she is good to the patients and wonderfully efficient. I never have to tell her twice how to do anything. It is such a relief to have one pupil who isn't scatterbrained, like a couple of others I could mention. There is certainly no nonsense with Christine where the men are concerned."

Hope had returned to her paper. Now she spoke up sharply, "I suspect the reserve toward men you admire so much in Christine stems from her conviction that the disfigurement of her skin is revolting to them and bars her from any hope of marriage. Surely you wouldn't wish such a misfortune on any of the other girls?"

"Oh, Hope, of course not," exclaimed Eileen, shocked. "Anyway, Christine's face isn't disfigured. That scar below her ear and across her lower cheek is hardly noticeable. The little twist at the corner of her mouth gives her a pleasant, interesting look, as if she were about to break into a smile. Her long sleeves and the white scarf she wears around her neck hide most of her other scars."

"You've never seen her chest and shoulders," said Hope grimly.

"No," Eileen admitted. "But it doesn't necessarily take a physical handicap to make a girl discreet where men are concerned. Take Elizabeth Kakeesh, for instance. Now there's a calm, sensible girl. She isn't the most brilliant student in the world, but she is certainly dependable. No nonsense about her."

"No imagination, either," retorted Hope, trying to concentrate on the paper in her hand.

Eileen chose to ignore the last remark. She was figuring Elizabeth's grades. Soon she announced triumphantly, "Elizabeth's grades amount to seventy-two percent. She studied hard for that mark, I know."

"Almost too hard. That girl is getting positively round shouldered from poring over her books and nursing charts. She squints so, and holds them so close to her eyes, that I wonder if she can see any farther than her nose. Remind me to take her to the eye doctor in Jerusalem next week to be fitted for glasses. It would be a shame for a tall, well built girl like that to develop a permanent stoop."

Hope began checking Aida's paper. Eileen resumed her calculations. Presently she announced, "Warda Shaheen is only one point behind Christine with a total of ninety-three percent. If only that girl would take a few lessons from Christine."

Hope made no comment. A little later she pushed Aida's finished paper over to Eileen. "Please calculate this one next. I know Faiza Lateef hasn't a chance, but I hope Aida squeezed through."

Obligingly, Eileen set to work. Meanwhile, Hope skimmed through Faiza's test paper, marking a red zero after almost every answer. Then she wrote eighteen percent at the top. She leaned back, watching Eileen's face.

Eileen carefully checked her figures three times. Finally, she reported, "Sorry, Hope, it's only sixty-three percent, two points shy."

A long silence followed. Eileen leaned back in her chair, studying her superior appraisingly. Hope's cheeks began to flush under that speculative gaze. The pinker they grew, the more the amusement deepened in her colleague's eyes. In vain Hope tried to evade the tender mockery of that glance. At last, she gave up, and whispered weakly,

"I hate to drop her, Eileen. Don't you think . . . that is . . . if she is strong enough in the most important subjects . . . ?"

She floundered. Eileen gave her no help, so she concluded lamely, "Don't you think we might stretch a point in her case, and allow a little leeway in the less important subjects? Let's check her papers over again."

"Softie!" Eileen jeered affectionately. But she separated the papers and passed Hope's subjects across the table without any further comment or objection.

Hope studied the first paper, made a slight alteration in two of the grades, then raised the total a couple of points. She pushed the paper over to Eileen explaining, "She understands how to calculate drugs and dosages well enough to get by for the present.

She manages the medications in the clinic correctly. I will give her some private help right away on the questions she missed."

After consideration of the second paper, she added three points to the total and placed it on Aida's pile with the comment, "She doesn't express herself well in writing, but I believe she understands Materia Medica fairly well, too. It is a very important subject, but sometimes difficult to explain. I am sure she could do better with it in Arabic."

Eileen was still frowning doubtfully over her first paper. Now she spoke up, "I gave her a generous sixty-five percent in nursing procedures to begin with. She barely gets by with her classroom recitations in the subject. She is rather untidy and slapdash in her ward work, too. This mark will have to stand."

She added the paper to Aida's pile; then catching her colleague's pleading glance, she relented somewhat on the next subject.

"I might be able to stretch a point in nursing history," she conceded. "The welfare of patients does not actually depend on a knowledge of that subject. Also, I doubt if a knowledge of chemistry will ever be needed here during the lifetime of these students. They are not likely to ever see the inside of a modern chemistry lab."

"Chemistry isn't needed," Hope replied. "The subject wasn't required in my training course. It has been included in the American training curriculum since then, and I thought we ought to include the beginning principles in the training here."

Eileen raised Aida's grades a little in the two subjects under discussion. But neither of them could, in good conscious, do much more.

"She adores little children and shows a real knack in handling them. I wanted to put her in charge of the children's ward when it opens," Hope said sadly.

Eileen, who had been busy calculating, exclaimed, "We've hit the magic figure right on the nose!" As she spoke, she crossed out the original total of sixty-three percent and replaced it with a large, flourishing sixty-five percent. With the last vigorous downstroke, the point of the red pencil snapped off with a sharp "ping."

"My goodness," Eileen remarked facetiously. "I hope we haven't stretched the point a little too far."

Hope was absorbed in calculating Faiza's total. Finally she laid down her red pencil.

"Well, Faiza's grade is only twenty-seven percent," She announced gloomily. "There isn't the remotest possibility of stretching her points even halfway toward a second chance. She simply lacks the basic education needed for academic work. Even if all the textbooks were in Arabic, she still wouldn't be able to understand them."

"You're perfectly right," Eileen agreed. "She failed in all my subjects, too. She can bathe a patient well and make a neat hospital bed. She can read a thermometer correctly. The nurse's aide examinations are coming up next week. She ought to be able to pass them. Do you think she would be satisfied to stay on here with Azizy and Zacchia as a nurse's aide? We could certainly make use of her services."

"I think she will be glad to," Hope replied. "Of course, if she does stay on, she must understand clearly that she is forbidden to give medications or to perform any of the special duties that are reserved for the students who are qualified to go on with the full course. She doesn't understand fractions or decimals. She could easily kill a patient with an overdose of a drug. Her answers on the subject of drugs and dosages were appalling."

Eileen consulted her completed list. She reported consolingly, "All the other girls did well. Aminah Abdullah made eighty-seven percent. Hanni Milad has eighty percent. And Regina almost tied Hanni with seventy-nine percent."

"Good for Regina," said Hope. "I didn't expect her to do so well."

"Neither did I," said Eileen. She added rather pointedly, "But then, I don't know much about her. She is your headache, not mine. Hanni is of far more help in the men's ward. I only wish that Hanni showed a little more spunk. She is so weak willed and kindhearted that she can't refuse any request. The men patients impose all sorts of extra tasks upon her that they could very well do for themselves. She needs to develop more backbone and stop trying to please everybody. No wonder that she has to spend a couple of days in bed every month."

Hope sighed, recalling with pity the periodic monthly suffering of the frail, shy girl, whose eagerness to serve far outstripped her physical strength. The director pondered the situation while Eileen set about preparing a second pot of tea.

Hanni was the oldest in a large Christian family, whose hard working parents could provide little but love for their brood. Before she was three years old, Hanni was already lugging heavy babies around. Throughout her childhood she constantly shouldered burdens far too heavy for her in order to spare her mother. By the time she reached her teens, her customary sharing of the meager food from her own plate with hungry younger brothers and sisters had taken its toll in producing a frail, undernourished body. Although her schooling was frequently interrupted by her mother's numerous pregnancies, Hanni had managed to acquire a secondary certificate from the mission school in Bethlehem in time to enter the first training class at Beth Hanani.

Within a few weeks, the nourishing food at the hospital and the regular hours of rest and sleep served to round out the girl's thin body. A shy prettiness began to develop. But no one could restrain her burning zeal to expend all her energies in service to others, regardless of her own health. Hope was sure that Hanni had no rest from work at home on the days she visited her family when off duty at the hospital. But there was nothing that anyone could do about it.

Hope waited until Eileen poured the tea and sat down. Then she said, "You are right about Hanni, of course. Undoubtedly, she does overtax her strength trying to do too much for everybody. But we can't change her disposition. Spiritually and mentally she has the makings of a very fine nurse."

"Amen to that," Eileen agreed, sipping her tea. "Still, I'm thankful that meekness such as Hanni's is a rare quality among the Arab people. I much prefer someone with a little more gumption. Aminah, for instance, is always a perfect gentlewoman, just as gracious and sweet and thoughtful of the patients as Hanni. Yet the men would never think of imposing on her. They act like tame lions when she is around. She is lovely to look at, but she seems almost sexless where men are concerned. There is a mysterious detachment about her. I get the feeling that the men regard her almost as if she were a nun, or even an angel."

Hope smiled. "I think I can understand it. Aminah and her father have been very close companions ever since her mother died. Her tie to him is so strong that she just doesn't see other men. Unless some unforeseen incident happens to loosen the strong attachment she now feels to her father, she may never marry."

"Well, this country could use a few Florence Nightingales," Eileen commented. "Being single is not regarded in Arab lands as a blessed state for any woman. Even polygamy is preferable. Perhaps it's the Christian taboo that deters some of the Moslem women from accepting our faith."

"Maybe the men have the same idea," added Hope. Suddenly, she broke into a giggle. She sorted through Faiza's pile of papers and handed one to Eileen. "Read it aloud," she said, settling back in her chair in delighted anticipation.

Obediently, Eileen began reading.

"Medical Definitions: (1) Parasites are bugs what eet of ded people; (2) Bronchioles are brown hols in the stumick; (3) Germs are—Oh, *no*!" Eileen broke off, staring at the page in disbelief. Then she broke into peals of laughter. Hope joined her, saying, "When I came to that definition, I knew she was hopeless!"

In the midst of their shrieks of laughter, the door opened quietly.

Molly Claiborne, trim in cap and uniform, slipped in hastily, closing the door behind her. She stood regarding her colleagues with mock severity. Weak with laughter, they leaned back in their chairs and regarded her with streaming eyes.

"I knocked, but you didn't hear me," Molly announced.

"Is anything the matter?" asked Hope.

"Well," replied Molly airily, "If you are referring to the wards, the answer is no. All's quiet on the eastern and southern fronts, but I can't say as much for the north wing. I could hear your shrieks from the other end of the hall. Tell me, am I working in a lunatic asylum or in a respectable TB hospital, where sane folks are usually asleep at this hour?"

Eileen pushed Faiza's paper over to Hope, saying, "You read it to her. I can't."

Hope picked up the paper. She waved it at Molly, demanding, "Do you know what 'germs' are?" Without waiting for an answer, she quoted from Faiza's paper, "Germs are peeple . . ." she giggled, then rushed on, "are people wot liv eest of Franz!"

Eileen joined her in a final explosion of mirth.

Molly's lips twitched, but she managed to control herself.

"Ladies, do you realize that it is nearly two o'clock? I shall accept no excuse if you oversleep and fail to relieve me on time in the morning." She clicked her heels smartly together, brought a hand up to her cap in a snappy salute, and departed.

"I feel too exhausted to move," sighed Hope, "and much too keyed up to sleep."

Eileen stretched and gave a great yawn.

"I move we have one more cup of tea before we turn in," she said rising.

"Suits me," Hope replied, beginning to yawn herself.

Her companion filled their cups and set the teapot between them on the table. They sipped quietly for a minute. Then Hope began meditatively, "I have been wondering what brought you to the mission field, Eileen. Would you tell me?"

Eileen smiled. "Nothing very dramatic, really, although it seemed so at the time. I am willing to confess if you will."

Hope nodded. "Go ahead."

Eileen kicked off her shoes, wrapped her robe about her long legs, and swung her feet up to rest on the table, tilting back comfortably in her chair.

Eileen reflected a minute, then began her story: "I'll make it short and try to put it in a nutshell. It was about six years ago that I discovered I was in love with a married man. He was the head surgeon in a large hospital, happily married to my best friend. I had been his assistant for five years, and I could never really get interested in any young man, although I didn't know why at the time.

"One afternoon we met accidently in the supply room and our hands reached for the same instrument. It was like an electric shock. I pulled my hand away, but I knew he had felt the same feeling."

Eileen paused, and smiled to herself as she took a sip of tea, then continued. "At this point I didn't know what might happen, but I am convinced that God stepped in and took a hand. I happened to be in church the next week and listened to a missionary from Egypt. He told how much nurses were needed in the hospital there. I knew that if I didn't get away, and sever my relations with the doctor completely, things might really get out of hand. It had to be done quickly and permanently. I signed up for a three-year term of mission work in Egypt. I had no ties to keep me in America, so, less than two months after tendering my resignation, I was on my way.

"I'll admit the doctor was stunned, and I knew his feelings for me went deeper than he realized. But he didn't seem to comprehend our danger. Men never do."

Eileen paused to favor her absorbed listener with a bright smile.

"I am convinced that God had plans for me, because by the end of the second year out, I was heart whole and fancy free again. I knew that what I had felt for the doctor was only physical passion. I knew I was too hard boiled and self-centered ever to be capable of the unselfish love required for a happy marriage. I determined to serve as acceptably as possible in the nursing field. Nothing satisfied me after returning to America. I had been bitten by the 'mission bug.' You know how it gets you?" She looked at Hope, who nodded. "I learned that Dr. Dawson was wanting a teaching assistant here. So I applied and was accepted. Now, here I am, and here I'll stay, as long as you are willing to put up with me.

"I like the climate, the work, and the feeling that God sent me here. I love all my fellow workers, especially you. You have the 'love-giving' quality that I lack. I am praying that some of it may rub off on me before you decide to fire me and get somebody a little more tenderhearted."

Eileen spoke jestingly, but there was a wistful note in her voice. Hope laughed, and replied, "Now you sound just like the chief. He is always buttering me up. I think too much of you to ever fire you. I could use some of your poise and levelheadedness. Perhaps we complement each other."

Hope rose and poured some more boiling water on the tea. She filled both their cups, then began.

"My story is quite different from yours. I am at least fifteen years your senior. Unlike you, I went out to Nigeria on regular assignment almost as soon as I finished nurse's training. I have a brother and sister, both much younger. My parents were living. Family ties were very close. I was terribly homesick during the first year or so. I served in Nigeria about sixteen years altogether, not counting the two furloughs at home. The furloughs were mostly taken up with gaining college credits in teaching and hospital management.

"I started a training school for nurses during my second term. The students were mostly men. They all lacked the education for much academic training. They could be taught to administer first aid. They learned to give injections and medications. But few were capable of assuming leadership or of making decisions on their own. Now that African governments are instituting better national education, the situation is improving. More students are developing leadership qualities. The mission doctor has been able to train some capable surgical assistants."

Hope drank more tea and went on: "There was always much surgery to be done. But hospital maternity care was practically unknown. Occasionally, a woman was brought to the hospital unable to deliver. Sometimes it was necessary to perform a cesarean. But mostly we had calls to far-out villages when women were in difficult labor. The doctor was usually too busy to go. I went whenever I could. But mothers and babies often died before I arrived, or in spite of what I could do when I got there. I taught the few women students all that I knew about obstetrics, and some of the men, too.

"On my second furlough, I stayed home an extra year to take a special course in midwifery. When I went back to Nigeria for the last time, I recruited all the native women I could find and concentrated on teaching them midwifery. There is so much need for it throughout this part of the world that I incorporated it in the first year nursing curriculum here. Of course, at present we can only give theoretical training. But I hope to affiliate with some other hospital so that they can get practice in actual deliveries."

Eileen nodded. "I thoroughly approve," she said.

"Well," Hope resumed, "in my third term I stayed an extra year in Nigeria. By that time the training curriculum was well established. Nurses had come out from America to help. I felt that my work there was finished. I wanted a chance to teach students who were advanced enough academically to achieve a higher level of proficiency, more in line with our American standards."

"So you came here," Eileen prompted, as Hope paused.

"Not at first," she replied. "My parents were both in failing health. I arrived home in time to help mother nurse dad in his final illness, when he was completely bedridden. She died a few months later. After all those years of strenuous mission service, I was tempted to take it easy for a while. You see, there was a boy I went with in high school—"

"Aha!" Eileen exclaimed.

Hope smiled. "Perhaps I didn't mention him at first because he was never really important. I think I was too much like my mother. I believe that neither of us were ever capable of a 'grand passion' for any man. We had all kinds of pity for the weak and crippled folks, anyone who required physical help. Both the young man and my dad were too healthy to rate our pity. As I look back now, I realize that Dad must have often felt lonely and somewhat neglected when Mother devoted so much time to the needs of her children and neighbors. But he was proud of her, and he never complained. In his last illness she cared for him devotedly. So he was finally repaid for all his patient understanding."

Hope drained her cup and continued, "The boyfriend and I went everywhere together all through our high school days. Everyone took it for granted that we would be married. But I wanted to be a nurse. Mother agreed that I should get my nurse's training first. So, while the young man waited, he took a course in architecture. By the time I graduated, he was well established in a good architectural firm. I was still in no hurry, but he finally pinned me down to setting a wedding date.

"Three weeks before we were to be married, a medical missionary from Africa showed slides of his work in our church. When I saw the pitiful condition of the African people, especially the babies, all thought of marriage left my mind. I signed up for mission service. I felt sorry for the young man, but not sorry enough to marry him. My mother was the only one who understood, and she encouraged me to go."

Eileen lifted the teapot suggestively. Hope shook her head, and went on: "Mother wrote a few months later that my jilted beau had married, so my guilty conscience was salved. His wife died when their twin daughters were in their teens. The girls had a double church wedding just before I came home from Nigeria the last time. After my parents died, he came and asked me again to marry him. He was well to do and had a beautiful home. My sister urged me to accept him and settle down. I even considered taking her advice. But I had sense enough to know that neither of us would be happy.

"I was still restless. I wanted to see something of the Holy Land. I had known the Dawsons in Africa. When I learned that Dr. Dawson was starting a mission work in Jordan, I used part of my parent's legacy and came out here for a visit. Dr. Dawson asked me to stay on and start the training program here. While waiting for the clinic and hospital to be built, I accepted a temporary teaching position at the Mount of Olives Hospital. So here I am, and that's the end of my story."

Eileen lifted the teapot. "There is still some left. It's hot," she announced. "Shall we have a nightcap?"

Hope held out her cup. Eileen poured the tea while Hope surveyed her appraisingly.

"You know, Eileen, you are younger then I, but you seem far more mature and levelheaded. I was so imaginative and dreamy in my youth that people constantly asked me when I was going to grow up. Even my dad and my beau did. Dad sometimes asked Mother the same question when she got to worrying over something or somebody. We always imagined the worst consequences from trivial mishaps. My fellow workers in Africa told me that I became too emotionally involved in my students' and patients' problems. They hinted kindly that a leader should be more dignified and not act so much like a sister to them, when what they needed was discipline.

"I tried to act more stern and dignified, but the Africans have a good sense of humor. They saw right through me. Since coming here, I've succeeded in growing up only to the extent of mothering the girls instead of sistering them. Dr. Baxter loves to tease me about it. He can make me feel like a six-year-old child."

Eileen laughed heartily, but Hope remained serious.

"You always manage to keep calm and unruffled. You have far more poise and executive ability than I. You discipline the students far better."

"I may discipline them more," Eileen conceded, " but I don't understand them as well. They respond far better to your love and sympathy. I'd give anything to have the compassion that you and Dr. Dawson display."

Hope chose to pass over this compliment. Instead, she seized eagerly on the praise given to the beloved doctor. "Isn't the chief wonderful?" she exclaimed enthusiastically. "He isn't lopsided like me. He can love the rich as well as the poor. But I find it hard to love rich people."

"He knows how to wheedle money out of his wealthy friends whenever he is in a tight spot," Eileen suggested teasingly.

"Why wouldn't they give it?" Hope flared. "His friends know that he invests it carefully. He can be stern with those who try to cheat and take advantage of him. He can be stern with the patients, too, when they refuse to cooperate. I haven't any judgment in administering discipline. Sometimes I give out too much love, when sternness is needed."

"Nonsense!" her companion contradicted. "There's no such thing as giving too much love. I know that I give too little. So, what do we do about it?"

Hope laughed. She leaned forward to stretch out both hands across the table to her friend, saying, "I suggest that we pool it, and divide it up a little more evenly between us."

"Agreed!" exclaimed Eileen. She grasped the extended hands in a warm grip.

In the stillness they barely heard the hall clock chime three.

"Goodness," whispered Hope in a gruff voice, "if we don't call it a day, Molly will report us to the chief in the morning for getting drunk on tea."

They both chuckled and hurried to straighten the piles of papers and put away their tea things. Then Hope lifted the lamp and prepared to follow Eileen out into the hall.

TEN

A DEW DAYS LATER the nurse's aides were given final examinations. Faiza Lateef took it with them and passed. During the patients' rest period the next afternoon, a short service was held in the chapel to recognize the five graduate aides.

Dr. Dawson delivered a brief message. Hope presented the certificates, duly signed by all four members of the administrative staff. Eileen pinned the white armbands, with the word, "Aide" embroidered in blue, around the left sleeves of the graduates. Dr. Baxter led in the singing of "A charge to keep I have." Then the Reverend James Dyson offered a closing prayer of dedication. The service was over by three o'clock.

The happy graduates dashed off to collect their luggage for a three-day holiday at home. They had each received a bonus of one pound that morning from the hospital funds.

The seven full-course students were already having a respite from classes for two weeks. Now they took over the duties of the aides during the absence of the latter group. They would celebrate their own capping service, after the aides returned, with a Saturday all-day picnic at the Dead Sea. The trip had been planned for weeks by Hope and Eileen, funded by a special gift of twenty-five dollars from an American friend. The sum would cover the cost of a chartered bus for the day.

Temporarily freed from teaching classes, Hope seized the opportunity one morning to wash and starch two of her three nursing caps. They were rather elaborate affairs, designed from the original pattern of her own alma mater cap. She made them herself of heavy muslin. They were like small sunbonnets, lacking the gathered neckpiece in the rear. The bonnet part was gathered on a shaped double band in front, and pleated in the back to perch high up on her braids well above the neckline. After ironing, the front band was folded back upon itself so as to stand up like a coronet, and giving to Hope the needed illusion of height.

The caps were difficult to iron, and she never asked the maids to do them. Now she rolled them in a damp towel and left them, intending to come back and iron them after dinner.

When she returned to the ironing room that afternoon she found Murshdeeyah putting the finishing touches on the second cap. They were ironed beautifully. Hope admired the work and praised Murshdeeyah extravagantly. She protested that the girl should be resting instead of doing extra work for her.

Murshdeeyah grinned.

"I not tired. You tired," she insisted. "You rest. I like to iron caps for you. I iron uniforms, too," she added proudly.

"I wondered who was doing them lately," Hope said. "You iron much better than Nadia. But I don't expect you to iron my caps, too."

"I *like*," the girl repeated, delighted at her mistress's praise.

The director went upstairs to put the caps away. She recalled that Dr. Baxter was doing eye surgery this afternoon. She decided to look in and see how he and Warda were getting

along. As she approached the clinic, a young boy emerged lead-
ing a man with both eyes freshly bandaged. Seeing her coming,
the boy left the treatment room door ajar.

Through the open window of the doctor's office she heard the
sounds of violent sobbing. She quickened her steps and entered
the treatment room in time to hear Dr. Baxter's voice rise in a
sharp command.

"Warda! Get up this minute and stop that blubbering!"

Hope stole to the open door of the doctor's office and peered
within. Warda was crouched on the floor under the far window,
hands covering her face. She was rocking mournfully back and
forth, while loud sobs and wails poured from her lips. The doc-
tor towered helplessly over her. His back was toward the door.
Again his voice rose. There was a note in it that Hope had never
heard before.

"Pull yourself together, girl! Haven't you any pride? Get up
this moment, I say!"

For answer, Warda dragged herself forward and wrapped
her arms about his knees. He bent over, tore her arms from his
knees, and dragged her to her feet. She hung limply in his grasp
like a rag doll, supported only by his vise-like hold upon her
shoulders. Her head fell back. Tears poured with abandon
down her cheeks. Her eyes were fixed imploringly on his face.
The lines of her throat and chin were exquisite.

Even when she cries she is beautiful, Hope thought.

Slowly, seductively, Warda's body swayed forward in the
doctor's grasp, head lolling still farther backward, eyes never
leaving his face, until her body almost touched his chest.

Dr. Baxter was startled, and when her meaning became clear
to him, he pushed her from him in a violent move.

Warda let out a sharp cry of pain as she hit the corner of the
treatment table. Hope winced instinctively.

Like a steel spring suddenly released from tension, Warda's
sagging body snapped erect. A blaze of fiery hate sprang up in

her eyes, quenching the tears. The next instant she wrenched open the door behind her and fled.

Aghast and confused by what he had done, Dr. Baxter stood motionless, hands hanging limply by his sides.

Hope tiptoed to the treatment room door, closed it softly behind her, and sped up the path to the hospital.

As she expected, she found Warda throwing things into her suitcases with fury. Knowing that pleading at this point would be useless, Hope quietly began folding garments as they were tossed helter-skelter into the bags, trying to pack them in some semblance of order. Warda offered no comment and no objection. She seemed to be in too much of a state of shock and inner turmoil to even wonder at Hope's presence.

After a while, Hope cautiously ventured to remark, "I don't blame you for leaving, Warda. I saw what happened."

Warda gave a violent start. She dropped the last armful of clothes she was carrying. Fierce pride and dismayed apprehension replaced her frozen expression.

Rightly interpreting the girl's thoughts, Hope went on quickly, "No one else will ever know, Warda, unless you choose to tell them yourself. I am sure I can promise that for the doctor as well as for myself."

Swift relief flooded Warda's eyes. Without a word, she started picking up the clothes she had dropped.

Hope continued, "I am going to grant you a leave of absence for one week. I hope you will think things over and decide to come back. If you do, I promise that you will never have to work with Dr. Baxter again."

Warda's face set in stubborn lines.

"I will never come back! Never!" she declared vehemently.

Hope did not argue, but remarked in a matter-of-fact tone, "You can't possibly crowd all your things into these two suitcases today, my dear. Even half full, they will be almost too heavy for you to carry from the bus stop. I suggest that you sort out the things you will not be needing right away. Leave them here for a few days until you can send someone or come back yourself to get them."

Her quiet tones had the desired effect. Warda began putting back some of the things in her cupboard and bureau drawers. Finally, she closed and strapped the bags, and changed to street clothes. Her face was set, and she stiffened when Hope came to her and put an arm around her.

"I will come to see you in a few days, dear," Hope said. "The capping service will be a week from this coming Sunday. You should be back a day or two before."

Warda strained away from the encircling arm. She started to pick up the suitcases.

"Those are still pretty heavy," Hope said. "Wait here. I will ask Saleem to carry them down to the highway for you and lift them aboard the bus when it comes."

The girl said nothing. She sat down on the bed to wait. Hope bent down and kissed the Girl's flushed cheek, and added, "I will be praying that you come back. I believe that God intends for you to serve Him in this place and wants you to stay. Your country needs you. So do we."

The girl made no response. She stared woodenly past Hope as if she were not there. So Hope sorrowfully departed in search of Saleem.

After Warda's departure, Hope made her way back to the clinic. She found Dr. Baxter gloomily washing up the instruments he had used that afternoon. He greeted her morosely and went on with his work. She perched on a stool, not offering to help. There was a long silence. Finally, Hope quietly remarked, "You didn't need to push her quite so hard, you know."

He swung around to face her, flushing to the roots of his hair. "She told you?" he asked incredulously.

"No, I saw you," said Hope. "I followed her afterward and found her packing, just as I expected. She left on the bus a few minutes ago."

Dr. Baxter mopped his brow.

"I am awfully sorry. I had no idea that she felt that way toward me. It started when that boy who was with the patient started to tease her. He didn't have any idea that I understood every word he was saying. But she knew that I did. It was most humiliating for her. She just went to pieces the minute they were gone."

Hope thought she detected a hint of disparagement of her own sex in his tone, and flew to Warda's defense.

"Do you think her actions were sufficient excuse to justify your own ungentlemanly behavior?" she demanded.

"Good heavens, no! My humiliation is far greater than hers, I assure you." The flush deepened on his face. He shifted his glance to the floor and continued in a very subdued tone, "The serpent in the Garden of Eden must have been a very beautiful creature."

Hope took time to digest his humble confession, then admitted in a kinder tone, "She really is beautiful, and she hasn't yet learned to control her emotions. It was a difficult situation for you." She went on, "Her pride received the heaviest blow. She would die of mortification if anyone else ever found out. I promised for us both that we would never tell."

"Nobody will ever hear it from me," he assured her. "I am certainly not proud of myself."

"I gave her a week to think things over. I do hope that she will come back. I promised her that she would not have to work with you again."

"Fair enough," he agreed ruefully. "I would hate to think that I was the cause of your losing one of your girls."

Hope began to dry the instruments for him, and their task was nearly finished when Hope thought to broach another dark subject. "Have you noticed anymore money disappearing from the cash box when I'm not around?" she asked.

"Sometimes it seems so." He frowned. "The thief appears to be getting more cautious though. It may be just coincidence, but

I am only conscious of coins disappearing on the days when Murshdeeyah comes down to help the girls clean up, after you have gone up to the hospital early on class days."

Hope was distressed.

"Murshdeeyah is such a faithful worker. Do you really think . . .?"

"I don't know what to think, and I haven't a shred of evidence, but . . ." Here the doctor stopped.

"Until we do find the thief, we will keep on eyeing everybody with suspicion. I've been hoping that it isn't one of my girls, but I would feel every bit as bad if it turns out to be Murshdeeyah. She mothers me, and I have grown fond of her."

"You don't look as if you need mothering," Dr. Baxter said.

"Murshdeeyah wipes the dirt off my face and watches for any specks on my uniforms or shoes. She pins my caps on straight. I found her ironing the caps today. She does them beautifully. When I think how dirty and untidy I must have looked before she took me in hand, I wonder that I wasn't fired long since as a disgrace to the mission family."

She joined in his laughter as he locked the clinic door behind them. They walked together up the path. As they neared the hospital door, Hope said wistfully, "Warda would have made such a wonderful nurse. Do you suppose that she will come back?"

"I am willing to predict right now that she will return in plenty of time to get her cap," the doctor replied cheerfully. "I believe she will be all the better for this experience. I will be eating humble pie for a long while to come. Warda will, too, mark my words."

Leaving Hope at the door of the hospital, he went off down the driveway leading to his home.

As Hope seated herself in her chair at her desk she reached for her nursing schedule and began shifting assignments to cover Warda's absence.

ELEVEN

THE NEXT MORNING HOPE left Christine in charge of the clinic following mid-morning tea in order to catch up with some work in her office. Before long she heard the front door open and close, followed by the sounds of a sharp altercation in the hall. She glanced up from her papers as a shadow fell across her desk.

A tall slender woman stood proudly erect in the doorway, bracing herself against Aida's tugs on her arm. The student nurse was expostulating in voluble Arabic, while she tried to prevent the woman from invading the office.

Hope took in the bare mud-stained feet, the shabby black robe, the ragged brown bundle clutched in the woman's arms, the defiant posture. But when she saw the fierce, frightened dark eyes, fixed with burning intensity upon her own, she rose hastily to her feet.

"Let go of her, Aida," she said quietly. "Tell me what this is all about."

The girl released the woman's arm and tried to squeeze past her. Failing in the attempt, she waved a paper over the intruder's shoulder, explaining aggrievedly, "This is an admittance order for the baby from Dr. Baxter. She is real sick. But her mother won't let me take her. She insists that she wants to see you first."

Relieved of the dragging restraint on her arm, the woman appeared much taller, even regal. The tribal markings on her face proclaimed that she was not a Palestinian refugee, but a Bedouin. She stood motionless, her burning eyes continuing to search Hope's face.

Sensing an anguished appeal for help behind that scrutiny, Hope moved out from behind the desk. The woman warily retreated a step. Hope halted. Aida seized the opportunity to slip in past the newcomer. Hope motioned the girl to stand to one side. A prayer rose swiftly from her heart, "Father, please help me to show this woman Thy love." Then she raised her eyes to meet that searching gaze and quietly waited.

Several minutes passed. The hand on the wall clock reached the quarter hour. A single chime rang out. The tick of the clock grew louder. Once Hope spoke quietly to Aida without turning her head, "Tell her she can come to see her baby next Friday on visitors' day." Aida relayed the message.

The clock ticked steadily on. Neither woman stirred. The eyes of the one questioned. The eyes of the other reassured. The stranger's eyes were beginning to soften. After a while, Hope smiled encouragingly and held out her arms.

Several more seconds ticked past. The minute had arrived at the half-hour. There was a little preliminary whir. Then the first chime rang out loudly in the stillness.

Abruptly, as if the sound had released an automatic signal somewhere deep in the woman's body, she glided forward, placed her ragged bundle in Hope's outstretched arms, turned swiftly, and was gone before the second chime ceased to vibrate.

Hope drew in a deep breath, then quickly exhaled it as the stench from the brown bundle filled her nostrils. She turned her head to one side, trying to hold her burden away from her fresh uniform. "Let me see the doctor's orders, Aida."

Obediently, her student nurse held the paper up before her eyes. The director leaned forward and scanned it. "Hmmmm!" she commented, reading aloud: "Acute malnutrition, suspected advanced TB of the right lung, moderate heart murmur, possible tubercular meningitis . . . well, our first case for the children's ward is certainly challenging." She studied the name at the top.

"Her name is Zoohrah. What does that mean in English?"

"It means flower," Aida replied.

Hope's nose wrinkled. "She smells like anything but a flower right now," she commented. "I can't put her down anywhere in this condition. Have you time to help me for a few minutes?"

"Dr. Baxter told me I should stay and help her get settled," Aida replied.

Hope glanced at the clock and said briskly, "If you run quickly to the laundry, I think you can get a pail of warm rinse-water before they dump it out on the vegetable garden. It will do for her first bath. And, Aida, we haven't any baby clothes ready. Please stop at Mrs. Baxter's. Ask to borrow a couple of Stephen's little diapers and shirts."

Aida departed. Hope shifted the bundle expertly to her left arm. Picking up the order sheet, she mounted the stairs to the second floor. There she unlocked the linen closet, selected towels and a light blanket, and draped them over her right shoulder. Proceeding on to the large bathroom adjoining the women's ward, she laid the odoriferous bundle on one of the long work tables, placing the clean linens at the other end. She set an oval foot tub midway between them, and donned a large plastic apron. Finally, drawing a long breath, she turned to examine the contents of the bundle.

Aida appeared with the baby clothes and a large pail of warm slightly soapy water. She poured the latter into the foot tub, setting the empty pail on the floor nearby.

As the fetid wrappings were removed from the child's body and dropped one by one into the pail, both nurses exclaimed in horror over the pitiful mite exposed to their view. The emaciated body was curled into a tight ball, knees touching a blue-veined forehead. The tiny pointed face was startlingly white below the thick masses of matted black hair. Faint mewling squeaks, like those of a starving kitten, emanated from it.

"Please hand me those scissors from the shelf, Aida," Hope ordered.

Aida did so, then held up the child's head while Hope whacked away at the tangled masses of hair, adding chunks of it to the discarded wrappings, until only an inch or so remained on the little head. Then she lowered the tiny body into the warm tub and began scrubbing away gently at the encrusted filth.

The long black lashes remained tightly closed over the child's eyes, but the mewling ceased. Gradually, the curled-up limbs relaxed sufficiently to enable Aida to straighten them out in the water. When Hope saw the length of the skeletal structure, she realized that the patient was much older than she had supposed.

"What age did the mother give for this child?" she asked.

"She said she was born during the winter of the big snow," replied Aida. "That was four—no, five years ago."

"Then she is nearly five years old!" gasped Hope. "She is no bigger than a year-old baby. She is not only filthy, she is starved! How could any mother treat her child so?"

Too late, she bit her tongue and faced Aida's blazing eyes.

"Didn't you notice the tribal markings on the woman's face? She comes from a Bedouin tribe far south of here. She walked for days across the desert to bring us her baby. Where can you find water on the desert? Where can you find milk for a child in this country, when a mother never has any of her own to nurse it? Most of the Bedouin babies born during that winter died. Many of the women died, too. All the Bedouin were near starving. They lost most of their flocks in the heavy snows. She didn't starve her child on purpose. She had nothing to feed her. We don't have the special baby food, and the milk, and all the fine things you have in America." Aida stopped, then added, "Anyhow, Bedouin and Arab mothers tend to believe that bathing a sick child will kill it."

"I know," Hope admitted meekly, lifting the dripping little body from the tub and wrapping it in a bathtowel.

Mollified, Aida began rubbing lice-killer into the short curls at the back of Zoorah's head while Hope patted the child dry. They started dressing her in Stephen's garments.

"Do you believe that baths are harmful to the sick, Aida? Hope asked humbly."

The Arab girl had scored a victory and could afford to be magnanimous.

"Not any more, thanks to you. You taught me a lot of things I needed to know."

"Thank you, dear," she said. "And thanks for the lesson you gave me. I needed it."

She wrapped the drowsing child in a blanket and handed her to Aida, saying, "Take her to the women's ward. Let Hikmat hold her while you get a crib from the children's ward and put it in the alcove by the nurses' desk. Then please come back here. Take this pail out to the garbage pit before the lice start crawling out of it. I will get the medicines and some milk for her. We may have to use a feeding tube, but I want to try a nursing bottle first."

When Hope arrived at the door of the women's ward with her supplies, a reception for the latest arrival was well under way. Hikmat was holding court in the central bed. Eight other patients were crowded around to get a glimpse of Zoorah. The crib stood in readiness in the hall alcove. The excited patients were teasingly blocking Aida's approach to the child. Aminah was vainly trying to herd the women back to bed.

A sharp "*Imshi!*" from Hope sent the women scurrying back to their beds. Hikmat promptly surrendered Zoorah to Aida's arms. Hope instructed the girl to sit in a chair by the desk, holding the child upright against her chest. Then she produced an eight-ounce nursing bottle filled with milk and pressed the nipple against Zoorah's tightly closed lips.

The black eyes slowly opened and stared unblinkingly, then the lips parted. Hope slipped the nipple between them. Tentatively, then with growing eagerness, the child began to suck. Hope made a motion to withdraw the bottle. A pair of claw-like hands promptly seized it and hung on with unexpected strength. After about two ounces had disappeared, Hope firmly pulled the bottle from the clutching hands and picked up a medicine glass containing four large PAS tablets. She held out one tablet between her fingers. Zoorah's black eyes fastened upon it. She opened her mouth.

"These are big, but maybe she can swallow them," Hope commented. "Get ready to tip her forward and thump her back if she chokes," she warned Aida, dropping the tablet into the child's mouth. There was a convulsive swallow. The tablet was gone. Hope picked up the nursing bottle and allowed Zoorah a few more sucks. Then she offered a second tablet. One by one, they were successfully downed. Finally, Aida took over the feeding. The child was allowed to finish the milk while Hope prepared the streptomycin injection.

Aida bared the child's scrawny buttocks and held her against her own shoulder, shuddering with sympathy. "Oh, Miss Callaway, how can you get it in?"

"Just the way I showed you in the clinic, Aida." Hope swabbed a spot on the bony buttocks, pinched up a long fold of skin, then slid the needle in the full length of the fold before discharging the contents of the syringe. She massaged the site gently as she withdrew the needle. Zoohrah neither squeaked no stirred. When Aida laid her down in the crib to re-pin the diaper, the child was already asleep.

Both women hung over the crib, regarding the sleeping little patient with satisfaction.

Hope thought a moment more, then said, "Aida, I am convinced that this child is too mentally alert to be afflicted with meningitis. In fact, I am willing to predict that in less than six months she will be transformed into a sturdy blooming flower and will really live up to her name!"

Elated by her own prediction, she went on, "Aida, how would you like to transfer from the clinic to the women's ward, and have Zoorah for your special project? You seem to have a knack with babies. I had planned to put you in the children's ward as soon as it was open. With my help, and the help of Faiza, Christine can manage without you in the clinic. If—" Hope hastily corrected herself, "I mean when Warda returns next week, she can go into the men's ward and Elizabeth can go out to the clinic. You can help Aminah here with the women and take full charge of Zoorah. Would you like that?"

Aida's eyes glowed.

"Oh, Miss Hope, I'd love it!" she exclaimed. "Zoorah is so sweet. I love her already."

"I'll arrange it right away," Hope said.

She called Faiza from the women's ward and sent her off to help Christine in the clinic, explaining that she was only to give the medications that Christine prepared, according to the senior nurse's instructions. Aida spoke up hesitantly as Hope was about to return to her interrupted desk work.

"Miss Callaway, I will be off duty on Thursday. We will not get our hospital allowance until Friday. Could you loan me two pounds on Thursday so that I can go into Jerusalem and buy material for a dress for my mother? I want her to have a nice dress so she won't be ashamed to come to the capping service. If I wait much longer there won't be time to get it made."

"I will be glad to loan you the money, Aida," Hope said heartily. "Come to my room before breakfast Thursday and I will have it ready for you."

When Aida appeared Thursday morning, Hope drew her into the room. "I want to show you something." She brought forth a simple dark blue dress of heavy crepe. It had a dainty white lace collar. There was a short matching jacket with long sleeves.

"Do you think that this dress might fit your mother?" Hope asked. "It came in the mission box a few weeks ago, and it is too big for me, and too old for any of you girls."

Aida answered eagerly, "It is much nicer than anything we could make or buy for her. I know she will be glad to wear it if it fits. We Arabs may be proud about some things, but not too proud to accept gifts of useful clothing."

Hope wrapped the dress carefully in a piece of brown paper, tying it with a bit of string. Then she took her purse from the cupboard and handed the girl two one pound notes. "You had better take this along,too," she advised. "If the dress doesn't fit, you will still have time to buy your material. We don't want your mother to miss the capping service for lack of a dress."

Aida accepted the money gratefully. "I won't spend it if I don't have to, Miss Callaway."

It was still an hour before mid-afternoon tea time when Hope glanced out her office window to see the bus from Bethlehem stopping at the hospital gate. She was surprised to see Aida descend. It was far earlier than the girls usually returned after a day off at home or a shopping spree in Jerusalem. The girl came hurrying up the driveway carrying a brown parcel. It looked bulkier than the one she had carried off on the bus that morning. Overcome with curiosity, Hope intercepted her in the hallway.

Aida beamed with delight. Opened her bundle and drew forth a life-sized baby doll made of rubber. It was dressed in diaper, gown, and booties.

"Isn't it sweet?" the girl exclaimed. "I bought it for Zoohrah. I hurt her when I gave her the injection yesterday. She cried. I thought the rubber doll would help. I will tell her the dolly is sick and needs injections. Zoohrah can use an old needle and pretend to give the injections to her dolly to make her well, too."

"But what about your mother's dress?"

"Oh, the dress you gave me fits her perfectly," Aida answered. "She thanks you for it, and promises to wear it to the capping service. I saw the rubber doll in a Bethlehem shop on my way home from the bus this morning. When I didn't have to spend the money for my mother's dress, I went back and bought it. I can't wait to show it to Zoohrah."

Hope accompanied the excited girl to Zoohrah's bedside. She was wondering what Jaleel Yusef would have to say about his daughter's purchase. The students received only two pounds allowance each month. Aida dressed so shabbily that Hope suspected Jaleel of confiscating her allowance as soon as she brought it home. The girl never appeared to have any money except for bus fare. Dolls like this one were imported. It must have cost almost every piaster of her two pound allowance. The director wondered if Aida had returned early in order to escape an unpleasant encounter with her father.

They found Zoohrah wide awake. The first smile they had ever seen broke across the child's face when Aida held the doll up before her wondering eyes. The scrawny arms stretched out to clasp the doll rapturously to her bosom. The tears of joy in Aida's eyes convinced Hope that the girl felt well paid for the sacrifice she had made, and would willingly endure whatever punishment her father might mete out to her for her extravagance.

From that day forward, Zoohrah accepted her injections without a whimper, then bared her "sick" baby's buttocks to apply the needle, admonishing her to not cry because the *ibra* (needle) would make her well and strong, too.

TWELVE

THE 10:00 A.M. PLANE from Beirut came skimming in low over the distant hills. It touched down right on time at the Kalendia airport a few miles north of Jerusalem. Hope and Dr. Dawson were on hand to meet Mrs. Ouida Prinstetter, R.N., who came briskly down the gangplank, a tubby little gray-haired figure in a suit of forest green wool. A long brown pheasant feather waved atop a soft suede "Robin Hood" hat of matching green. She was clutching an amazing assortment of objects: a banjo, a large striped shopping bag, a corduroy covered traveling pillow, a sweater, two coats, a square green overnight bag, and an umbrella. A heavy brown purse and a camera swung on leather straps from her shoulders. In spit of her burdens, she managed a gay wave of greeting as she approached the entrance gate where Hope and the chief stood waiting.

They relieved her of the bulkier items of luggage. She gave them each a hearty handshake, then whipped off the little green hat, held the brim between her teeth, and smoothed down her short, flyaway hair with both hands. Replacing the hat at a jaunty angle, she explained, "I call this operation collecting my wits. My gray thistledown flies in all directions at the least puff of wind."

She delved into her capacious purse, found her claim checks and baggage keys, and handed them to Dr. Dawson. He went off to collect her trunk and suitcases. Hope escorted her to the customs desk to get her passport validated. This done, the two women went on to the baggage room to find the doctor. Mrs. Prinstetter's luggage was already piled high on a cart. A porter was wheeling it out the door to the Dawson car. The doctor returned the keys to Mrs. Prinstetter, remarking casually, "I didn't have to open up anything for inspection."

"You will soon learn that the name of Dr. Dawson is an 'open, sesame' wherever you go in Jordan, Mrs. Prinstetter," Hope explained. "Any friend of his is welcomed with open arms."

As they swung out onto the highway leading to Jerusalem, Hope and Dr. Dawson began pointing out places of interest to the newcomer. They had gone only a short distance, however, when she suddenly cried, "Please! I refuse to answer to Mrs. Prinstetter any longer. Unless you promise to call me 'Misprint' from now on, same as everybody does back home, you can turn right around and take me straight back to the airport!"

The doctor roared with laughter. Hope laughed, "Miss Print," she repeated delightedly. "How wonderful!"

The little woman beside her beamed.

"Glad you like it. I made it up myself when I went back to nursing after my husband died. The other was too long for patients to pronounce. So I made up Misprint,—spelled with only one 's,' you understand, and just one single word, 'Misprint,' a typographical error, that's me!"

"Misprint!" Dr. Dawson and Hope chorused obediently.

Their amazing little companion clapped her hands like a delighted child, then settled complacently back in her seat.

"Now that we have that matter settled, you may proceed with the guided tour, Doctor," she ordered graciously.

Shortly after twelve o'clock, the car turned into the hospital driveway. As they rounded the hedge-bordered curve leading to the side entrance, Dr. Dawson braked sharply to avoid hitting two people standing in the middle of the path. Hope recognized Aida Yusef. Next to her was her father, Jaleel. They were engaged in heated conversation. In the split second before the two saw the car, Hope gained the fleeting impression that Jaleel's arm was raised as if about to strike his daughter. The next instant, they sprang aside, and the doctor drove on.

Hope would have hastened back to Aida's aid as soon as the car stopped, but hospitality required that she conduct Misprint to her room at once. They were already late for the staff dinner. She knew that Saleem must be enjoying his meal right now in the men's dining room. Margaret Dawson was undoubtedly waiting dinner at home for her husband. Suggesting that the chief leave the luggage in the car for Saleem to pick up later, she hustled Misprint upstairs for a hasty wash-up.

It was late afternoon before Hope found time to make afternoon rounds of the wards. She caught sight of Aida in the far corner of the women's ward. The girl kept her back turned as much as possible, evidently trying to avoid her superintendent. Her eyelids appeared quite reddened and puffy. Hope dared not ask questions for fear of offending the girl's pride. She felt certain that Jaleel Yusef would not dare resort to brutal punishment while Aida remained under Dr. Dawson's protection. The mild-mannered doctor would not tolerate cruelty. Upon more than one occasion he was known to have persuaded the Bethlehem authorities to mete out jail sentences for inhumane treatment and injustices that had been brought to his attention. Temporarily at least, Hope dismissed the afternoon's incident from her mind.

Shortly after the noon meal on Sunday, Hope encountered Faiza in the upper hall emerging from the room that she still shared with Aida until such time as sleeping accommodations could be arranged for her on the first floor with the other two aides. The girl was in tears.

"Miss Callaway," she wailed, "The extra pound that you gave me for my holiday last week is gone. My mother helped me to buy some dress material when I was home. I was saving the pound to pay Marika for making two new dresses for me. She is one of the older girls in the youth group at the Bethlehem Church. Mother doesn't have a sewing machine. Marika is bringing me the dresses tomorrow, and I must pay her. I hid the money in the toe of my shoe when I came back yesterday. I locked it in my suitcase. It was there when I went to chapel this morning. The suitcase is still locked. But now the money is gone! Here is the key."

She held up a small key of such ordinary design that exact duplicates could undoubtedly be found in almost every home in Jordan. The souks, or markets, in Jerusalem and Bethlehem were flooded with cheap imported imitation leather suitcases with almost identical locks. Most of the students at Beth Hanani owned similar ones.

Hope tried to recall which members of the hospital staff had been absent from the morning chapel service, but was unable to do so.

Meanwhile, Faiza was sobbing, "I know Marika needs the money tomorrow. My allowance isn't due for three weeks. I haven't any money to pay her."

Hope said, "I think I can find an extra pound in my cupboard that I can lend you." On the way, Hope felt in her pocket for her keys. They weren't there. She always carried them with her. She quickened her steps, recalling that she had donned a fresh uniform for chapel. She probably left them on the bureau or in the pocket of her discarded uniform. But they were not on the bureau or in the uniform pocket. Faiza watched anxiously while Hope searched the drawers of her desk and bureau, and even looked under her bed and her pillow. She tried the handle of her wardrobe. It was securely locked. Puzzled, she escorted Faiza to the door, assuring her that she would find the keys and bring her the pound note before the day was over.

Just then Aida emerged from the women's ward at the end of the hall. She was in full uniform. Hope recalled that she had been left alone on duty during morning chapel services and intercepted her as she was about to enter the children's ward.

"Aida, did you happen to see anyone down at this end of the hall during chapel services? Anyone entering or leaving my room? Or your and Faiza's room? Faiza has lost some money and I seem to have mislaid my keys."

Aida's face flushed in earnest concentration. Then she exclaimed positively, "No, Miss Callaway. I was in the children's ward most of the time. Once I thought someone was on the stairs, so I stepped out to look down into the lower hall. I saw Murshdeeyah going down the lower steps to the kitchen from the main hall. She might have been up here on the second floor. Do you suppose your keys were stolen, like Faiza's money?"

"Stolen is a very unpleasant word," Hope said slowly. Faiza's pound may turn up. Perhaps I have just mislaid my keys. My cupboard door is locked. I wanted to loan the pound to Faiza until she locates hers. I will look further."

"I will help you look," Aida offered. "Maybe you left them in the classroom downstairs. I'll go see." She started for the stairs.

"I don't think I could have left them down there," Hope called after her. "I wasn't in there. Oh, I did stop in the classroom for a minute on my way out to the chapel. But I'm sure I didn't leave the keys."

Aida was already out of earshot. Hope went to the staff sitting room and began searching aimlessly. In a few minutes Aida appeared triumphantly in the doorway and handed her the missing keys. "They were right on top of the desk in the classroom," she announced.

Aida returned to her post as Hope hurried back to her room and unlocked the wardrobe. The contents appeared undisturbed. No money appeared to be missing from her purse. She hastily selected a couple of half-pound notes from her billfold, relocked the wardrobe, pocketed the keys, and went to give the money to Faiza.

The girl thanked Hope warmly. She knotted the money carefully in the corner of a handkerchief and thrust it into the bosom of her dress, remarking, "It will be safe here until Marika comes for it tomorrow."

Hope returned to her room, pondering the mystery of the keys. She could not imagine why she should have placed her keys on the classroom desk and walked off leaving them behind. She decided that she must be getting forgetful. Could it be a sign of advancing age? Now that the thief appeared to be shifting operations from the clinic to the hospital, she would have to watch her step more carefully.

"I wonder who she can be?" Hope whispered, then clapped her hand over her mouth in dismay. Her mind had already leaped to the inevitable conclusion that the suspect must be a member of her own sex. No man, not even the two mission doctors, would set foot in the women's quarters of the hospital, except in dire emergency, such as a fire, without being invited there by a female staff member for a specific purpose. Certainly, no male employee would ever dare risk discovery there, knowing the swift retribution that would be meted out by the Jordanian governmnet. Therefore, this last theft could only have been committed by a woman. But who?

"Dear heavenly Father," she whispered, "please don't let it be one of my precious girls or Murshdeeyah. I don't think I could bear it if the thief turns out to be any one of them."

THIRTEEN

On a beautiful Sunday afternoon in August the chapel was filled with guests. The lecturn, which usually stood on the right side of the low platform, had been removed. In its place stood an oblong table covered with an embroidered cloth. A row of eight chairs occupied the center of the platform, flanked on the left by a small portable pump organ with bench attached.

At two o'clock, Eileen Anderson came down the aisle and seated herself at the organ. Pumping the clattering foot treadles, she filled the wheezy bellows with air and began playing "Onward, Christian Soldiers."

Dr. Baxter rose from his seat in the front row, faced the assembly, and raised his arms in invitation.

"Let us all stand and sing the first verse," he said. "I am sure we are all familiar with the words."

His powerful tenor rang out with compelling clarity and many voices joined enthusiastically in the well-known Salvation Army hymn, singing in a variety of tongues. When they came to the chorus, Hope, who was waiting in the doorway, stepped out down the aisle followed in single file by seven trim young women in crisp blue uniforms.

True to Dr. Baxter's prediction, Warda was among them, having returned two days earlier. There was a new womanly dignity and reserve in her bearing that greatly enhanced the perfect beauty of her features.

Hope had timed their entrance to bring them to their places on the platform at the close of the chorus. But several voices continued lustily on:

"Like a mighty army, moves the church of God . . ."

With scarcely a break, organist and congregation caught up the verse and carried the song through a second chorus. To forestall a third verse, Eileen brought her hands crashing down on the keys in a resounding final chord. There was a ripple of good-natured laughter, followed by a round of applause for the seven students, now standing stiffly at attention before their seats on the platform.

Dr. Dawson led the congregation in the Lord's Prayer, then he thanked God for His grace and goodness in bringing the hospital into existence, and for the happy occasion that had brought the group together this day. He concluded with a short prayer.

From the audience there came a long drawn-out, "Aaah-meeen."

When the bustle of seating was ended, Hope stepped over to the covered table. Waiting until all eyes were upon it, she removed the cloth with a dramatic flourish, revealing a row of seven snowy white caps. A murmur of approval ran through the assembly. She then faced the audience and began her speech.

"Today marks an important milestone in the lives of these young ladies before you. In hospital parlance the ceremony you have gathered to witness is known as a capping service. It marks the successful completion of the first six months of an intensive two-year course in nurses' training. During this period the students have been on probation to determine their fitness for further training. These seven girls have acquitted themselves well in all academic subjects given to date, as well as in the performance of all ward and clinic duties assigned to them. They have learned the first, and perhaps the hardest, rule of nursing—self-discipline. They have experienced some of the trials and heartaches as well as the joys that accompany the practice of the profession they have chosen. They have shown that they are 'able to take it,' as we say in America. We are proud of them. And now, for the benefit of those who may not know them all by name, my colleague, Miss Eileen Anderson, will introduce them to you. She will read their names in the order in which they passed their examinations, the highest first. Each nurse will stand as her name is read, so that she may be recognized by our audience."

Hope sat down. Eileen rose from the organ bench and came forward, holding a sheet of paper in her hand.

"I wish to join Miss Callaway in congratulating our students on their fine record," she stated. "I am proud to present them to you. As I read their names, applause will be in order."

Pausing to allow each girl in turn to rise, be recognized, and to receive her share of applause, Eileen read, "Christine Gomry, first; Warda Shaheen, second; Aminah Abdullah, third; Hanni Milad, fourth; Regina Murad, fifth; Elizabeth Kakeesh, sixth; Aida Yusef, seventh."

Amid continuous thundering applause, Eileen resumed her seat at the organ and began pumping the worn old bellows.

Dr. Baxter rose to announce, "We will now stand and sing number two in the English hymnal, number twelve in the Arabic one. Since you folks enjoy singing, we shall sing all five verses of, "Crown Him with many Crowns."

The anthem ended with an exceptionally prolonged "Aaaaaah-m-eeeen," as though the singers were reluctant to descend from the lofty heights to which they had been transported. All resumed their seats quietly. An expectant hush followed.

Hope went to the table, picked up one of the dainty caps, and held it aloft for everyone to admire.

"Twenty-eight years ago at my own capping service," she began, "our superintendent called our caps cotton crowns which, like a queen's crown, were supposed to invest us with a certain authority and dignity. When we donned our caps we said we were donning our dignity."

She smiled reminiscently. The audience smiled back.

"However," she continued, "I have long since learned that no earthly crown, whether of cotton or of gold, can automatically confer upon its wearer such noble attributes as wisdom, compassion, graciousness, kindness, or even dignity. Unless a queen or a nurse is motivated by the love of God, she will never be worthy of the symbol she wears upon her head. These simple cotton caps, in themselves, are of insignificant material value. It is only when a nurse accepts her cap as a sacred obligation to devoted service and to the welfare of others that her crown becomes something of inestimable value."

Hope nodded to Eileen, who then came to stand behind Christine's chair. Hope turned with the cap in her hands, saying, "As each of you now accept and wear your cap, may you always strive to be worthy of this high calling."

Hope adjusted the cap on Christine's head and fastened the front bobby pin in place. Eileen anchored the cap more securely with two more pins. Thus they continued until the last cap was firmly settled on Aida's dark braids. Then seven girls rose in a body and again stood at attention to receive an ovation from the spectators.

Dr. Dawson mounted the platform and gave a short benediction. Then Hope walked down the line shaking hands with each girl and murmuring a few words of congratulation. She was followed by Eileen and Dr. Dawson. When Hope came to Aida, she was startled by the coldness of the girl's hand. She looked with concern at the girl's face while she held the icy hand in both of her own.

"Don't you feel well, Aida?" she asked kindly.

"I'm all right. But my mother isn't here. She promised she would be."

Hope squeezed her hand reassuringly. "There is such a crowd, perhaps you just can't see her."

Aida shook her head. "No, she isn't here," she asserted. "My father is here and she would be with him. I am so afraid . . ." She closed her lips tightly on the unfinished sentence.

The crowd was pressing in upon them. With a final comforting squeeze, Hope relinquished the girl's hand and moved on.

Halfway down the aisle she caught sight of Jaleel Jusef purposefully pushing his way through the crowd to get to his daughter. She wondered why Mrs. Jusef had failed to come.

As visitors and students streamed out of the chapel into the warm sunshine, a pleasant surprise awaited them. Two white-jacketed waiters from a soft drink parlor in Bethlehem stood at either side of the doorway uncapping and dispensing bottles of iced Coca Cola. Hope wondered who had provided the refreshments. Noting a twinkle in Dr. Dawson's eye, she cornered him and asked for an explanation. He grinned cheerfully, explaining, "A friend sent me a little personal check for my birthday with strict orders that it was not to be spent on anything of a utilitarian nature, but on something purely frivolous, and as typically American as possible. I believe I have carried out his orders faithfully."

"Indeed you have," Hope said.

Seeing Jaleel Jusef emerging just then from the chapel with Aida, she excused herself and joined them. Jaleel greeted her effusively. Aida still looked sullen and unhappy.

Her father explained aggrievedly, "I'm afraid Aida doesn't believe me when I tell her that her mother ate something yesterday that upset her stomach, so that she was unable to come today. She will be all right tomorrow. She always recovers quickly."

Aida looked unconvinced. Hope expressed proper sympathy, then moved on to join another group. The sun was sinking low in the Western sky. With the approach of evening, Hope was faced with a small problem.

Only last evening Dr. Dawson had disclosed to her that he had given Mohammed Abdullah permission several days before to provide a banquet tonight in the staff dining room in honor of the seven students and the four women members of the mission staff. Food was being brought out from a Jerusalem restaurant by special van. Margaret Dawson was in charge of the banquet and of the decorations. The food would be served at seven o'clock. Esther Baxter, who was a graduate nurse, would relieve Misprint in the dispensing of the evening medications and supervision of the aides, who were all on duty tonight, in order to free the newly capped nurses for the rest of the day. The party was to have been a complete surprise to all the guests. But because she and Eileen were needed to keep the seven students away from the dining room until seven, it was found necessary to let her in on the secret. The news filled her with dismay. Her fainthearted remonstrance that the picnic planned for next week was sufficient "partying" for the occasion was met by amused chuckles and a fatherly pat on the head by the doctor.

On the surface, a happy evening appeared to be in store. Lately, Hope had dared to think that the girls were beginning to overlook Aminah's favored position and to treat her more kindly. However, Mohammed's generosity in providing the banquet for tonight might easily be construed as insufferable patronage. If such were the case, Aminah would again be placed in a most unfavorable light.

Meanwhile, she was kept busy shaking hands with departing guests and making appropriate replies to their complimentary remarks and good wishes. Soon only a few stragglers remained. Among them was Mohammed Abdullah. He was talking with

Dr. Dawson. Aminah was beside him. Eileen had the six other students rounded up on the pretext of taking a picture.

Finally, Hope approached Abdullah and requested that Aminah be allowed to have her picture taken with the group, and then to join in a song fest that she and Miss Anderson had planned for the girls.

Mohammed glanced at his watch in amazement. With profound apologies for having stayed so late, he favored Hope with a conspiratorial smile and a formal bow. Dr. Dawson strolled with him down the driveway to his car. As he drove off, Hope couldn't help wishing that the evening were over with.

FOURTEEN

Just as Mohammed's car pulled out on the highway, two large delivery vans from Jerusalem passed him and swung into the hospital driveway. The two nursing directors quickly herded their mystified charges indoors and hustled them upstairs into the private sitting room of the missionary staff. On the way, Hope suggested that the students might wish to stop off in their rooms and exchange their starched uniforms for more comfortable street clothes. Since change of costume would require removal of their newly acquired caps, none of the girls took advantage of her offer.

Eileen Anderson seated herself on the piano bench before the little spinet. She faced the girls with a teasing smile, indicating their caps.

"If you are planning to wear them to bed tonight, I wouldn't advise it," she remarked. "They'd get crumpled, and you couldn't sleep comfortably."

Abruptly, she whirled around on the bench and struck up a lively rendition of "Turkey in the Straw." This was followed by a series of American folk songs, plantation melodies, and cowboy ballads, which were familiar to the students. They sang them now with gusto as Hope led them to Eileen's rollicking accompaniment. When their repertoire flagged, the two women regaled them with snatches from Gilbert and Sullivan. At last the two paused for breath. Their audience applauded vigorously and demanded more.

Eileen was in a capricious mood. Instead of complying with familiar tunes, she started playing selections from the world's most famous composers from memory. The students sat enthralled, as did Hope. She was amazed at her colleague's masterful performance.

For her final number, Eileen chose Beethovan's beautiful "Moonlight Sonata," which never failed to bring a mist to Hope's eyes. Evidently, it had the same effect on the highly impressionable young Arab girls. When the last lingering note died away, the hush that followed was an eloquent tribute to the artist's superb talent.

Eileen swung around on the piano bench. "What is this, a funeral?" she demanded. "I suggest we play musical chairs and cheer everybody up."

The girls sprang to arrange the chairs. They were in the midst of a hilarious game when Murshdeeyah appeared to announce that they were wanted in the dining room at once.

Margaret Dawson met them in the lower hall. They trooped into the dining room with exclamations of surprise and delight. The tables were arranged in the shape of a wide "U" with seats along the three outer sides and at each end, leaving the center free for serving. Pastel-colored crepe streamers decorated the walls and ceiling. Tastefully arranged bouquets were spaced along the center section of the table.

The table was laden with an amazing variety of food, most of which had been cooked earlier in Jerusalem. There were two roast turkeys stuffed with rice and *snobar*. This is the Arabic name for pine nuts, which are used extensively in mid-Eastern

SEVEN COTTON CROWNS   [115]

rice dishes. There were small meatballs, baby lamb chops, fried bean cakes. Hot vegetables and a variety of cold salads, olives, relishes, cucumbers, and jams were served, as well as round loaves of the Arabic "aish," and small, hot American yeast rolls made by Margaret. Truly, it was a feast fit for kings, or in this case, for hungry queens.

Misprint and Molly Claiborne arrived. The four missionary nurses were assigned seats at the base of the U. The students were scattered down each side. Christine and Aminah were seated at the two open ends, with their backs nearest the door.

The girls stood behind their chairs awaiting Hope's signal. She had planned to disclose the name of their benefactor at once. She knew that they were bursting with curiosity. But her courage failed at the last moment.

"Let us sing the 'Doxology' by way of thanks," she murmured.

Following the briefer than usual "Aaaa-meeen" there was a loud scraping of chair legs on the tile floor as all settled down with keen appetites to enjoy the sumptuous repast. The quantity of food that disappeared was astounding. At last all appetites flagged, to be replaced by an increasing buzz of excited conversation. The maids cleared away the main course, with Margaret's and Fatmy's assistance. The kitchen crew then withdrew.

Hope was about to rise to her feet to make the fateful announcement when Margaret appeared in the doorway and pulled the lightswitch, plunging the room into darkness except for the light streaming out from the kitchen across the hall. Then flickering lights moved toward them. Fatmy waddled in bearing an enormous three-tiered frosted cake ablaze with tiny candles. Tamam and Nadia followed with dessert plates and silverware.

Fatmy set the blazing cake in the center of the table. They all admired the beautiful decorations. The candles began to sputter, and were extinguished and removed by the maids. Margaret switched on the lights. Fatmy cut generous slices of the cake.

The maids distributed the plates among the guests. The kitchen crew started leaving and the girls began to eat.

With sinking heart, Hope realized that the dreaded disclosure could be postponed no longer. But Margaret was announcing from the doorway, "There are ice cream bars, too. Fatmy will bring them."

"Margaret," Hope called hastily, "please ask Fatmy to hold the ice cream for a few minutes. I will let you know when we are ready. I have an announcement to make first. Please close the door."

Margaret obeyed instructions. Hope rose slowly to her feet. All eyes were upon her. She tried to speak lightly.

"I am sure you are all wondering to whom we are indebted for this lovely banquet," she began. "He did not ask me to tell you his name, but you will all wish to thank him for his generosity, I know." She paused to swallow, then went on. "Aminah will be just as surprised as anyone else that her father, Mohammed Abdullah, planned this party as a token of his gratitude and appreciation for the love and happiness that Aminah has found in our midst. I believe you will agree with me that he has been most kind."

An indefinable gasp went around the table. Hope sat down in the midst of a most dreadful silence. There was no applause. Six girls choked, slowly laid down their forks, and stared miserably at their plates. No one could have failed to read the guilt written on each face. No one except Aminah. After her first startled glance at Hope, her eyes darted swiftly around the circle. Watching Aminah's face in that awful moment, Hope saw it crumple for the first time in hopeless anguish and despair.

Before Hope could move or speak, there was a sudden screech of chair legs. Christine rose unsteadily from her seat nearest the door and groped toward it, murmuring faintly, "I feel sick. Please excuse me."

"No!" screamed Aminah. "I will not excuse you! I will not excuse any of you! You will stay and listen to what I have to say!"

She flung herself upon Christine and pushed her violently back into the chair she had just vacated. Aminah was white with anger. She placed her back against the door and faced her classmates defiantly. Already, the fire in her eyes was being quenched by tears.

"Now!" she panted. "You will listen to me! I have taken all your insults, but I cannot stand by and let you insult my father. He is kind and good. He never did anything in all his life to hurt anyone. He has always tried to make me happy. He wanted to make us all happy tonight. Is that a crime? Is it a crime to love people and to want to give them gifts? Is it a crime to want them to love you, not for the gifts, but because you love them?"

She drew a sobbing breath. Her voice dropped to a lower tone, full of deep sorrow.

"If this is an example of Christianity, then I don't want you or your Christ!" Her voice broke. She flung open the door and fled weeping down the hall.

Throughout the girl's impassioned tirade, the four missionaries had sat in stunned silence. Now they became aware of another sound, which had been steadily increasing from the moment Aminah began speaking. All the students were weeping. Some sat with hands covering their arms on the table. At length Christine raised her head, wiped her eyes, and struggled to her feet. She looked imploringly at Hope. "Miss Callaway, please believe me," she said. "I didn't mean to insult Aminah. I really was sick. I was sick with shame at the way I had treated her."

The other girls raised their heads and wiped their eyes as they listened. "I do love her," Christine said. "I want to beg her to forgive me."

Instantly, all the other girls began babbling at once. Hope was able to gather that all felt the same as Christine. She had to rap several times on the table to get their attention. Before she could say anything, Elizabeth sprang to her feet, and demanded loudly, "Why are we all just sitting here talking, while Aminah is crying her heart out upstairs? We ought to be up there right now confessing all this to her!" She turned to Hope for confirmation.

"I think it's a perfectly wonderful idea, Elizabeth," Hope exclaimed. The girls were already halfway out the door.

"Do hurry and bring her back as soon as you can," she called after them. "Dessert will still be waiting!"

In later years none of the group was ever to forget Mohammed Abdullah's wonderful banquet and its happy ending. The seven students congregated in Aminah's room when it was all over, trying to outdo each other in expressions of love and friendship. Long after customary lights-out, Hope stuck her head in Aminah's door and firmly ordered them off to bed.

Later, making a bed check with her flashlight, she found the first six sleeping soundly. But when she flashed the light toward Aminah's pillow, the great, dark eyes of the girl reflected its gleam. She smiled as Hope bent over her, and whispered, "I'm just too happy to sleep tonight."

"I want you to know I had absolutely nothing to do with this, my dear," she said. "The girls all felt terrible. They were so ashamed of the way they had treated you. If you hadn't been crying so hard yourself, you would have heard them crying, too."

"Yes, they told me," sighed Aminah blissfully. "Oh, Miss Hope, this is the happiest day I ever expect to have in my whole life."

"Don't be too sure of that," Hope replied, "I predict that many more happy days lie ahead for you."

"But never as happy as this one," Aminah insisted.

Hope switched off the light and sat on the edge of the bed. She took Aminah's hands between her own.

Aminah whispered earnestly, "Miss Hope, please forgive me for what I said about not wanting anything to do with your Christ. I know that you are following His example. Will you please pray that He will help me to be good like you?"

"No, my dear child," Hope said. "I will never pray that you will grow to be like me. I am too full of faults and weaknesses myself." She paused, then added, "If you want to be truly good, you must look to Jesus Himself as the only example of true goodness. Then try to pattern your life after His. I will pray that you will come to accept Him as the Lord and Master of your life. Then you will know a happiness far greater than anything you are experiencing tonight."

She bowed her head and prayed aloud. When she concluded her prayer, a sweet voice in the darkness softly echoed her closing "Amen."

FIFTEEN

As THE FIRST RAYS of the sun topped the distant mountains the following Saturday morning, a chartered bus of ancient vintage rattled to a stop before the hospital. A merry group of hospital personnel clambered aboard, laden with provisions for an all-day excursion to the Dead Sea.

Everything possible had been done for the patients the previous day, including the semi-weekly baths and treatments. None were in critical condition. Eileen Anderson insisted that she could manage alone with the aides' help for one day. The chief elected to stay at home and rest. Margaret was not only keeping him company, but she was baby sitting young Stephen Baxter. Thus Esther would be free to enjoy the day along with her husband and two older children: Timothy, eight, and Fern, six.

Hope added a last blanket to the heap already piled on the wide bounce seat stretching across the rear of the bus. Then she settled down contentedly beside Misprint on the front seat.

With a noisy clashing of gears, the creaking vehicle got underway and headed toward Bethlehem. There it stopped at the Mission Church. A dozen or so of the teenaged Youth

Group swarmed aboard. The Reverend Jimmy Dyson and his wife, Ruth, followed, each carrying various baskets and bundles. Nageeb, the bus driver, helped Jimmy to stow several long poles lengthwise under the seats.

At the last minute, Khaleed Khalil appeared. He swung aboard carrying only a bathing suit rolled in a towel. He appeared bored, and responded only briefly to the exuberant greetings of the young people. Hope knew that he had only come along at Dr. Dawson's insistence. Khaleed was a strong swimmer and the chief felt responsible for the safety of the women in the party, although it was almost impossible for anyone to drown in the briny waters of the Dead Sea. He stalked grumpily to the rear of the bus, cleared a seat for himself amid the pile of blankets, and lapsed into a morose silence.

Not so the young people. Among the squeaks and rattles of the old bus, they began derisively chanting improvised words of ridicule for their decrepit conveyance to the tune of "London Bridge is Falling down." The maligned vehicle rumbled along at a fairly good pace on a level stretch of road, passing Rachel's Tomb on the left. Mar Elias loomed ahead. Here road barriers separated West Jordan from Israeli held territory. They were blocked from further passage along this direct route to Jerusalem and had to swing sharply to the right.

The road was roughly constructed and twisted around the Israeli emplacements on the ridge above. They continued down the precipitous road, around hairpin turns, and they finally reached the bottom in safety. Then the bus began the grinding climb up a steep grade. At the top they would catch their first glimpse of Jerusalem. Soon the city lay spread out before them in a breathtaking panorama beyond the ridge at the far side of a deep, narrow valley. Every detail of the Holy City was sharply outlined by the bright morning sun, now riding high in the sky above the Mount of Olives to the East. The large Moslem edifice, known as the "Dome of the Rock," built many years ago on the site of Solomon's ancient temple, dominated the landscape. The golden dome flashed back the sun's rays with dazzling brilliance.

Nageeb shifted into the lowest gear for a last steep descent that brought them quickly to the bottom of the narrow canyon. A large number of natural caves in the rock formation of the canyon walls on either side furnished comfortable living quarters for many families of the area. A final climb around a couple of sharp curves at the far end of the small valley brought the travelers up through the hillside village of Ras el Ahmound to the termination of the makeshift Bethlehem road. Soon they were rolling smoothly along on the new highway that leads from Old Jerusalem to Jericho and the Dead Sea.

Hope explained to Misprint that between the two cities the road descended from an altitude of 2,500 feet above sea level to 1,300 feet below. She added, "Of course, the descent was far steeper and shorter in Jesus' day. Then people traveled onfoot or on donkeys, and roads were straighter and narrower. There is still a very old road off to our left, which He probably used."

Soon the village of Bethany lay behind them. They were traveling along the edge of a deep gorge between brown hills with huge rock formations and little vegetation. Except for an occasional flock of sheep or goats, herded by a lone shepherd, the country appeared to be totally uninhabited.

Eventually the bus reached the bottom of the mountain gorge and headed out on the flat open plain stretching eastward to the Dead Sea. A few miles farther on, the highway turned abruptly northward toward Jericho and the mouth of the Jordan River. There appeared in the distance the waving fronds of tall palm trees. Green fields stretched out below the palms that surrounded orange groves and banana plantations. The lush vegetation was due to the bountiful supply of sweet water that had been gushing steadily forth from Elisha's fountain ever since the day the prophet healed the bitter waters by casting salt into the spring.

The bus was still some distance from this fertile spot when the driver turned off the highway into a rough, barely defined track. After fully two miles on this bumpy road, they reached the comparative smoothness of the beach. Nageeb continued south along the shore until he came to a large dune jutting out fairly close to the water's edge. He drew the bus up close alongside it and turned off the ignition. It was not yet ten o'clock.

The young folk spilled out of the bus and raced to test the temperature of the water, discarding footgear on the way. Ruth Dyson and Misprint hurried off to chaperon the girls. Esther Baxter was being dragged along rapidly in their wake by her two offspring. Nageeb and Khaleed emerged, each carrying a large pile of blankets. The latter dropped his burden on the ground and made off down the beach with his bathing suit.

Nageeb attacked the side of the dune with a shovel to make a straighter wall. Dr. Baxter and Jimmy brought forth the poles from beneath the seats. Thrusting one end of each pole high up in the side of the dune and the other ends through the open windows of the bus, they formed a frame. Then using the blankets, they fashioned a sort of dressing room for the ladies.

All the masculine members of the group then went off to a private cove. Mixed bathing was still frowned upon in the Middle East. Bathing suits were not even stocked in the West Jordan shops, indeed, swimming was almost an unknown skill. The Jordan River, although deep enough for swimming, was deceptively swift. It widened out in just one spot, not far from Jericho, where it was shallow enough to permit waist deep wading. John the Baptist is believed to have used this place for his historic baptism of Christ.

In anticipation of the outing, Hope had appealed months before to the women's society of her church at home for some used, one-piece bathing suits. Each of the Beth Hanani staff now wore one under her outer garments. They crowded into the narrow dressing room and hastily stripped off their dresses and slips, expecting to beat the teenagers into the water. The lack of bathing suits presented no problem to the younger group. While their competitors were undressing in the tent, they simply dropped their outer garments on the beach and raced into the water clad only in muslin panties and slips. A few yards from shore they lay flat on their stomachs, wriggling along in the shallow water. Gleeful hoots from the latecomers brought them to sitting positions in the warm water. Hope had swum here before and knew that waist depth was still much farther out and none of her charges were in any danger of drowning. However, she warned them that if they swallowed any of the brackish water, it would make them sick.

Ruth Dyson suggested that they all join hands and wade out together. Two chains were quickly formed. Ruth and Misprint acted as end guards on one, Esther and Hope on the other. The four were experienced swimmers. Esther had taught little Fern how to float on her back, and even to paddle a little. The water was so dense and weighted with chemicals that Fern's little legs soon gave out. She floated blissfully on her back, towed along by her mother and Christine. The latter's scarred arms and chest were well concealed beneath a long sleeved blouse.

They were about waist deep when Hope called a halt in order to rest.

"We've come far enough this time," she announced. "I propose that you turn around, join hands again, and start wading back. We swimmers will get in a little practice and then join you."

A short time later, all were stretched out on the beach in the warm sunshine. Swimming attire dried quickly in the heat of the sun and sand. By the time a warning shout from Dr. Baxter announced the approach of the men, all had donned their outer clothes.

Khaleed was with the men. He was now in high spirits, and willingly assisted in unloading the food baskets. The women passed out aish, the pancake-type bread. These were split partially open and used as plates. They were stuffed with slabs of salty white cheese, olives, hard boiled eggs, sliced tomatoes, and cucumbers.

After lunch was over, Jimmy Dyson organized a game of beach ball among the young people. It soon ended, due to the noonday heat. The women and girls betook themselves to the privacy of the bus and dressing room for midday siestas. Jimmy and three of his boys went off in search of wood for the evening fire. The other male members of the party stretched out on the sand under the bus. The gentle lap of waves provided a soothing lullaby and they all slumbered through the midafternoon heat.

Hope woke with a start at four o'clock to find that she and Misprint were the sole occupants of the bus. The latter was still sleeping soundly. Most of the dressing room roof had collapsed. She could see from the bus window that it was deserted. Ruth and Esther must be down at the beach with the girls. As she started to descend the bus steps, she caught sight of Khaleed and one of the girls strolling along behind the sand dunes. His head was close to that of his companion, his hand was on her arm, and he appeared to be talking very persuasively. She wondered how he had maneuvered to catch one of the girls alone, and what had induced her to go off walking with him like this. Such conduct was most indiscreet. The girl certainly knew it. She kept glancing uneasily around in all directions. Suddenly, she broke away from Khaleed's detaining hand and darted off toward the shore. She emerged on the beach. Hope hastened to intercept her. It was Hanni Milad. She was flushed, breathless, and she looked extremely frightened. She accepted Hope's sharp rebuke meekly, then hastened to join the other girls who were wading a few feet from shore.

The male explorers returned with some dry wood, which they dumped beside some blackened stones on the beach. Then they departed to join their comrades at their private swimming cove.

Dresses were again discarded, and again the women swam while the girls waded to their heart's content. The sun drew nearer the western mountain peaks. The girls were heading shoreward when Hanni tripped on a submerged rock and fell face down in the water. She gasped as her head went under, and swallowed a large mouthful of the bitter brine. Tears poured from her smarting eyes as she struggled to her feet. Hope quickly arrived at her side. Instructing two of the girls to hold Hanni by the arms, she thrust her finger far down the girl's throat. Hanni regurgitated. Then Hope led the shivering girl from the water, wiped her streaming face with a towel, and made her lie down on the hot sand until the shivering ceased and a little color returned to her pale cheeks.

Esther and Ruth herded the other girls into the sagging dressing room. There they exchanged wet bathing suits and underclothes for fresh, dry garments. Hope and Hanni were the last ones to dress. Just as they emerged from the shaky dressing room, the tottering poles collapsed.

Now the menfolks straggled in. Nageeb expertly built a fire between the blackened stones. The two American men brought a huge cookpot from the bus and emptied the water jugs into it. They set it on a rusty grill above the fire. Then they dismantled the fallen tent, stowed the poles aboard the bus, and brought the blankets to spread around the campfire for seats. The sand was already cooling fast, but the air would remain sultry throughout the night. Nageeb nursed the fire. When the water in the pot reached the boil, Esther dropped in a cheesecloth bag of tea leaves. By the time Jimmy offered a prayer of thanks and the food was distributed, the tea was nicely brewed. Cups were dipped in and passed around again and again, until the fire went out and only a few drops of tea remained in the pot.

Just before complete darkness descended, a bright glow appeared beyond the hills of Moab. The glow rapidly increased in brilliance. Suddenly a sliver of light silhouetted the top of Mount Nebo, followed by the bright orange orb of a full moon. Its beams spilled down the western flanks of the mountain, and swiftly spread a shimmering golden path across the sparkling waters of the Dead Sea. There was an awed silence. Then Dr. Baxter's voice rose reverently in a simple hymn. All joined in. Several more hymns followed. The moon rose higher and Hope relaxed under its mellow radiance, drowsily conscious that she ought to bring the party to a close, yet reluctant to break the spell.

Suddenly, as if an alarm clock had rung in her brain, she realized that she had not heard neither Hanni's voice nor Khaleed's for some time. She rose and moved quietly among the shadowy figures behind her. Recognizing Christine, she whispered, "Have you seen Hanni?"

"Yes," Christine replied. "She said she wasn't feeling well. She went up to the bus to lie down."

Hope was becoming slightly alarmed. She made her way over to Dr. Baxter and Esther. They were sitting together in the center of the circle with Fern and Timmy curled up in their laps, sound asleep. Hope bent over and whispered to the doctor, "Where's Khaleed?"

Dr. Baxter turned to look behind him. "I don't know," he whispered back. "He was here a little while ago. What's up?"

"Hanni isn't here," she whispered. "She is probably asleep in the bus. I'm going to see. Isn't it time to go, anyway?"

"Right ho!" he responded. He raised his voice to announce cheerfully, "Ladies and gentlemen, the zero hour has come. We must prepare to go over the top of yonder mountains. Look sharp now, and collect all your belongings, including a few moonbeams to tuck under your pillows tonight."

His booming voice carried on the clear air all the way to the bus, which loomed up sharply in the bright moonlight. Only the far side, next to the dunes, was still in shadow.

While Hope was still some distance away, she thought she saw a darker shadow slip down the steps and disappear behind the nearest dune. She dismissed the thought as a trick of the moonlight, and climbed aboard, calling softly, "Hanni."

A soft voice responded drowsily from the rear seat of the bus, "I'm here." The girl sat up, rubbing her eyes.

Relief sharpened Hope's tongue. "Hanni! I was worried about you. Why did you go off alone like this?"

"I told Christine where I was going," Hanni replied faintly. "I was so tired. I must have fallen asleep."

Hope's voice softened. "I hope you are feeling better now. Do you need help to collect your things?"

"No, thank you," Hanni replied. "I brought all my things from the beach and put them with the others on my seat before I went to lie down." She rose and moved tiredly down the aisle. Lifting the bundle from her seat, she sat down quietly with it on her lap.

The others began to arrive. They stowed away bundles, baskets, blankets, and clothes. Dr. Baxter and Jimmy made a final tour of the campsite with flashlights, while Nageeb warmed up the motor. At the last minute Khaleed arrived quite out of breath. He explained he had gone for a walk and was some distance away when he heard the motor start. He retired to the rear of the bus, and they started off.

Nageeb used the headlights to illuminate the uncertain trail leading across the dunes, but as soon as they reached the highway he dispensed with the lights. There was never any traffic at this late hour. The moon's gleam made it almost as bright as day on the highway before them. Soon the lowlands were left behind. The road wound steadily upward like a wide silver ribbon.

The singing began again, ranging from hymns to old ballads to Arabic chants. The boisterousness of the day had spent itself. The voices were hushed to a dreamy sweetness by the beauty of the night. Hanni's voice alone was silent.

Hope felt the peace and contentment of the day move through her body. In the years to come she would look back in gratitude to this one perfect day. She leaned back and closed her eyes with a sigh, never dreaming that even now shadows were beginning to close about the Beth Hanani Mission hospital.

SIXTEEN

Eileen was waiting in the doorway with a lamp when the bus rolled up to the hospital steps at the scandalous hour of midnight.

"I was beginning to get a little anxious," she said. "Did you have some bus trouble?"

"No," Hope admitted, "It was my fault that we stayed so late. It is such a beautiful night that I hated to break up the party. How did everything go here today?"

"Just fine, no problems," replied Eileen. "The patients are all asleep."

She turned to the students, who were tiptoeing up the stairs behind them, and called softly, "Girls, I had Murshdeeyah save some rinse water from the wash today so you could rinse off some of the brine. You will find two buckets of it in your bathroom."

The girls hurried off. Eileen linked an arm in one of Hope's and ushered Misprint along with her lamp. "I burned an oil cake in our bathroom geezer," Eileen whispered. "There will be enough warm water for a couple of quick baths."

At Misprint's door, Hope gave her a little shove. "You go first." Misprint smiled and disappeared.

Eileen hastily drew Hope into her own room across the hall and shut the door.

"Hope," she said urgently, "I believe the thief must be Murshdeeyah."

"Oh, no!" Hope said. "What makes you suspect her?"

"She was the only one up here today," Eileen said. "She brought up the pails of water about eleven o'clock. Last evening Aida wanted change for a pound note, so she could take along a few piasters to treat the girls today. It was just before supper. The office was closed for the day, so she asked me if I could change it. I brought her up here and got the change from my purse. It was locked in my cupboard. For some crazy reason, I slipped Aida's pound note under the paper lining of my drawer, right here." She pulled the drawer open to show Hope. "I intended to take it down and get some small change from the office this morning. I forgot it until noon today. When I came up to get it, it was gone."

"You haven't told anyone else yet of your suspicions?" Hope asked.

"Of course not," was the quick reply. "I know as well as you do that we must have positive proof before we dare make any accusations. Even then, it would be up to you to handle the situation."

"The joys of being a superintendent." Hope sighed. "Do you know, I suddenly realize how much I have grown to care for Murshdeeyah. Behind that gargoyle of a face is one of the keenest minds and tenderest hearts that God ever put into a human body. Somehow, I just can't believe that she would ever stoop to thievery."

At breakfast next morning, Hanni's roommate, Christine, reported that Hanni was feeling too weak to get up. She had gone to the bathroom several times in the night. Hope well knew that even a small amount of the Dead Sea water could act as a violent purge. So she was not surprised at Christine's news. She went up to see Hanni after breakfast. The girl was sleeping soundly. Hope did not disturb her, but went off to rearrange the nursing schedule to cover Hanni's absence for the day.

On Sunday Hope was surprised to see Jaleel Yusef mounting the steps of the chapel. They were both late. Dr. Baxter was already in the midst of the opening prayer. Hope nodded a silent greeting to Jaleel. They stood with bowed heads in the doorway until the prayer was ended. Then she invited Aida's father in to the service. He refused apologetically, explaining that he could not stay. He had just come to bring something to his daughter. Hope pointed Aida out to him. She was sitting in the front row with some of her classmates. He looked distressed. Hope smiled and held out her hand, saying, "I will be glad to give her whatever it is that you brought."

Jaleel recoiled, thrusting his hand deep into his pocket as if to protect his gift from her. "No, no, thanks," he stammered. "I must give it to her myself."

She nodded understandingly. Naturally, if it were money he had brought, he would wish to give it to Aida personally. She made her way down the aisle and whispered to Aida that her father was waiting to see her at the door. Hope relieved her of the hymnbook and took her place in the row. The girl was back before the hymn ended. Her hand was thrust deep into her skirt pocket, as if guarding some precious treasure.

Hope wondered uneasily how much money Jaleel had given his daughter. With the thief still at large, Aida stood in danger of losing it unless she could be persuaded to entrust it to the safety of Hope's own strong wardrobe.

Aida darted out the door as soon as the chapel service ended. She was nowhere in sight when Hope reached the entrance. Fear for the safety of the girl's funds lent Hope courage to risk another rebuff. She hastened to the nurses' quarters and knocked on Aida's closed door. After a long silence within, the door opened a crack. Aida peered out with a distinctly unfriendly expression on her face.

"What is it?" she asked warily.

Taken aback, Hope blurted out, "Aida, did your father give you very much money?"

The girl's eyes flashed defiantly.

"What if he did?" she countered.

Hope hastened to explain.

"Faiza isn't the only one who has lost money around here lately, Aida. I thought you might like to keep yours locked up in my . . ." she broke off abruptly. Murshdeeyah was gliding silently by them on bare feet. Hope called after her sharply, "Murshdeeyah, what are you doing up here? Where are your shoes?"

Murshdeeyah turned respectfully and answered, "Regina tell me I can borrow her English book. She tell me get it from her room. No shoes. Off duty today."

Hope sighed. "You may get the book, but you really ought to wear shoes all the time."

"*Nam*," agreed Murshdeeyah, proceeding on her way. Hope waited. Murshdeeyah returned with the book and went off down the stairs. Hope wondered how much of their conversation the maid had overheard. Evidently, Aida had been wondering, too. She spoke up eagerly, "Do you have a good strong lock on your *dulab* (wardrobe), Miss Callaway?"

"It should be," Hope answered. "It's a respected American make and the only duplicate key is in Dr. Dawson's safe."

Aida came to a swift decision.

"I thank you for offering to keep my money. My father earned some extra money this week. He brought me a whole pound today. He gave me one for a present at the capping service, too. Miss Anderson changed it for me Friday, so I could have some money to spend at the picnic, but there wasn't anyplace to spend it there. I will give you the two pounds now to keep for me."

She went over to her bed and pulled a cheap suitcase from beneath it. She took from her pocket a small key, similar to many others used by the Arab residents of the hospital. Then she opened the suitcase with it and brought forth a knotted handkerchief from the toe of a shoe. "I was putting this away when you knocked," she explained.

She accompanied Hope to her room, where they counted out the contents of the handkerchief at the desk. Hope put the money in an envelope and wrote Aida's name on the outside. Then she produced her key ring from her pocket. Aida watched with great interest as Hope unlocked the door, placed the envelope on the shelf inside, relocked the door, and pocketed the keys.

"It must be terrible to be a thief," she observed slyly. "They must have to sneak around with their shoes off, like Murshdeeyah, so nobody can hear them."

"That will do, Aida," Hope ordered sternly. "I am sorry I told you about the thief. I want you to promise me right now that you will not repeat what I said to anyone else."

Aida promised glibly. There was a cunning gleam in her eye that gave Hope little assurance that she would keep her word.

By Monday morning Hanni was back on duty. She was wan and pale, but she asserted that she felt better. Margaret Dawson came to Hope at noon with a note from Sheila Dobson, wife of the American vice consul in Jerusalem. She had been to the embassy to visit Sheila and her new son, Kendall, that morning. Their daughter, Karen, now two years old, was a small baby, and had caused Sheila no difficulty. The boy was very large. There had been complications at his birth. Now, three weeks later, Sheila was still very weak. Her note to Hope was urgent. She asked if Hope could spare one of her students for a week to help with the care of the two children. Sheila had a cook and housemaid, but she could not trust them with the formula and feeding of a new baby. She would be glad to pay a student three pounds for her services.

Hope thought immediately of Hanni. She was experienced in the care of babies. The Dead Sea experience had been weakening. The work at Sheila's would be far lighter than that of the hospital ward. Three pounds was a munificent sum. Hanni would be glad to earn that for her family.

She went in search of Hanni. As she expected, the girl was eager to go. That very afternoon, Margaret returned with Hanni to the Dobson residence in the embassy building.

Tuesday morning Regina reported the loss of half a pound. She had hidden it in the toe of a shoe in her own locked suitcase. Hope went with her to examine the bag. As she expected, the lock was of such cheap construction that the simplest key would turn it.

The situation had reached a crisis. After conferring with Eileen and Dr. Dawson, Hope called a meeting of all female resident employees and students. There she broke the unpleasant news that several thieveries had taken place lately in the hospital residence quarters. It appeared certain that the thief must be one of their own number. A shocked silence followed. Then, like the disciples at the Last Supper, they all began casting suspicious glances at each other. Instinctively, Hope looked at Aida. She was gazing fixedly at Murshdeeyah, who was standing in the doorway with her mother. Murshdeeyah was bent over interpreting the announcement to Fatmy. Hope's glance swept around the circle of other faces. All eyes were beginning to follow the direction of Aida's pointed gaze. Doubtless, the girl had already confided her suspicions to several others. Now the subtle poison was having its effect. Murshdeeyah finished talking to Fatmy. In the midst of an accusing silence, she raised her head to encounter a barrage of unmistakably hostile eyes. She stared at the group in puzzled bewilderment.

"I warn every one of you now that I will not tolerate any unfounded suspicions among you," Hope said sharply. "They are cruel and unjust. Anyone who points an accusing finger without first having positive proof of the thief's identity, is liable to immediate dismissal. Is that clearly understood?" She waited until there was a unanimous murmur of assent. Then she continued, "It appears that the simplest key will open most of your suitcases. My wardrobe is strongly built. It is equipped with a special lock and key. I can keep any money you might have in it for you. You can draw the money out whenever you want. I suggest that each one bring me your money for safekeeping until we can get you new locks for your own wardrobes.

"For the present, none of the domestic staff will be allowed to enter the nurses' living quarters upstairs at any time for any reason, unless accompanied by one of the mission directors. This means that the students must clean and mop their own bathrooms. A schedule will be posted by tomorrow. Is all that clear?"

There was another murmur of assent. Hope was satisfied that sane and sober judgment would prevail. "Thank you all very much," she said. "The meeting is over."

She looked toward the doorway. Murshdeeyah and Fatmy were no longer in sight.

By suppertime Hope's wardrobe was filled with several more deposits. Although the amounts varied from a few piasters to two or three pounds, Hope carefully counted the money with each depositor, wrote down the amount on each envelope, and had the owner sign her name. As a further precaution she detached the wardrobe key and hung it around her neck on a cord. Several days went by without incident.

Early Saturday morning, Hope was dressing when a knock sounded on her door. She slipped into a robe and opened the door to find Tamam and Nadia confronting her. "We found the thief, Miss Callaway," Tamam announced.

"It's Murshdeeyah," Nadia added.

Hope put a warning finger on her lips and hastily drew them into her room, closing the door. "Now tell me how you know?" she asked.

For answer, Tamam exhibited a knotted square of bright yellow flowered cloth. She untied the knot and produced two fifty piaster notes, explaining, "This is my money, and my handkerchief. I missed it right after I woke up this morning. Nadia helped me look. We found it under Murshdeeyah's mattress." Hope looked at Nadia, who nodded confirmation.

"Where was Murshdeeyah?" Hope asked.

"She and Fatmy were in the kitchen starting breakfast," Tamam answered. "When we opened the door, we saw a corner of my handkerchief hanging down in plain sight under her mattress. I knew it was mine as soon as I saw it."

"Does Murshdeeyah know that you found it?" Hope asked.

Nadia spoke up. "No, not yet. I told Tamam we should bring it straight to you before we said anything. So we did."

"You did the right thing," said Hope approvingly. She opened the door a crack, saw that the hall was deserted, and whispered, "Girls, please wait out here a minute for me while I dress."

When the three of them arrived at the kitchen, they found Murshdeeyah stirring a pot of cereal at the range. When Hope called to her from the doorway she came forward eagerly. A look of hurt bewilderment crept into her black eyes when she saw the two maids standing behind Hope. Without a word, Hope took her by the arm and led her into the small ironing room. The maids followed and closed the door.

She held out Tamam's knotted handkerchief. "Have you ever seen this before, Murshdeeyah?" she asked.

The girl glanced at it indifferently, and replied, "Nam. It is like Tamam's."

"It is Tamam's," corrected Hope, "and it has money tied in it. Tamam missed it early this morning. It was found under your mattress."

Murshdeeyah showed no surprise. She stood gravely considering the matter. Then she said flatly, "So, that is it." She turned her mournful black eyes on the two maids and favored them with a long, level look. Their gaze did not waver. Then she turned to Hope with a sigh of resignation, saying simply, "They will not believe me. Maybe you will not believe me. I did not take Tamam's money. I am not a thief." There was a deep sadness in her voice and a great dignity in her bearing. In spite of the evidence, Hope began to wonder.

"Girls," she said, "Please show us just where you found the money."

The maids led the way to Fatmy's and Murshdeeyah's room. The beds were neatly made. Nadia lifted the head of one of the mattresses and placed the knotted handkerchief on the springs a few inches in from the edge. The corner of the handkerchief hung down so that it was in plain sight from the doorway. Nadia lowered the mattress into place, then raised it again. The handkerchief promptly slipped off and dropped to the floor. Tamam picked it up, remarking, "It fell down just like that before."

Murshdeeyah's eyes flickered with amusement.

"Am I a fool?" she asked. "No thief with brains enough to steal would hide anything where it would be found so easily. Unless," she added significantly, "they wanted it to be found."

"Murshdeeyah is quite right," Hope said. "Whoever put the money here wanted it to be found right away. Anyone could have done it. Somebody wanted to throw suspicion on Murshdeeyah to divert it away from themselves." Hope paused and looked at Nadia and Tamam. "They succeeded in fooling you two into believing that Murshdeeyah was guilty. Do you still think that she is the thief?"

The maids hung their heads and looked foolish as they replied, "We didn't want to believe it, Miss Callaway," said Tamam. "We like Murshdeeyah and Fatmy."

"We hope that Murshdeeyah will forgive us," added Nadia.

For answer, Murshdeeyah's lips parted in a wide smile of joy. She gathered the two girls into her long arms with a loving hug of forgiveness.

The loud ringing of the first breakfast bell by Fatmy brought all four back to the realization of their morning duties. Tamam and Nadia made for the door. Hope issued a parting warning, "Girls, don't breathe a word of this to anyone. The thief must be getting desperate. If we keep quiet, I think she will be caught soon."

Hope was about to follow the two maids, but the dark skinned girl blocked her mistress's exit. With long fingers she tilted Hope's chin and looked fondly into her eyes.

"Missy Hope," she said, "you believed that I was not a thief. Shukran." (thank you) Her fingers reached up caressingly to tuck a few loose hairpins into Hope's soft locks. Then she stepped aside and let Hope precede her out of the room.

The next day, for the third successive Sunday, Jaleel Yusef was present in the morning chapel services. Aida came to Hope's room soon afterward. She was very excited. She had another pound that she wanted to deposit for safekeeping. Hope obligingly unlocked the wardrobe.

"What are you going to do with all your wealth, Aida?" Hope asked teasingly.

The girl hesitated, then stammered in confusion, "Actually, my father is only letting me keep it for him. He gambles. When he wins he can't trust himself to keep the money for fear he will lose it again. He wants to save thirty pounds to buy my mother a fine sewing machine. You have such a good lock on your *dulab* that I told him it would be safe here."

"But, Aida," protested Hope. "I am not running a bank. I cannot assume responsibility for your father's money. He will have to put it in a bank. The new locks for the wardrobes arrived yesterday. They should all be installed by the end of the week. Then each of you will be responsible for your own money."

Aida looked startled, and quite dismayed. "The locks are here already?" she asked in surprise.

"Yes, they came much sooner than we expected. You don't need to worry, Aida," Hope added kindly. "I'll keep your father's money here this week, but you will have to take it to him on your day off, or else put it in your own wardrobe by the end of the week. By then you certainly ought to have your own new lock."

Aida thanked her halfheartedly. Then she left the room with a look of such acute distress on her face that Hope wondered if she were anticipating some kind of punishment from her father because of the failure of his banking scheme.

The next evening Hope was preparing the lesson she would present to the girls in another hour. She was at her desk in the classroom. After a few minutes she found herself in need of a medical dictionary. She had one in her bedroom upstairs. Just as she emerged from the door of the classroom to get it, she caught a glimpse of a familiar red flowered skirt whisking up the stairs leading to the second floor. She reached the foot of the stairs in time to see the tail of the skirt disappearing in the direction of the forbidden nurses' living quarters. She raced soundlessly up the stairs.

Murshdeeyah was gliding stealthily down the hall like an animal stalking its prey. She was barefooted. Hope followed with equal stealth, wondering that the girl never once turned her head to look behind her. Murshdeeyah arrived at Hope's door, swiftly turned the knob and entered. Hope was close behind.

A sudden shriek sounded from within, followed by the sound of scuffling and the thud of a chair being overturned. Hope entered to see a blue clad figure struggling in Murshdeeyah's strong arms. The tall maid had evidently sprung upon the intruder from the rear, pinioning both arms to her sides. Now Murshdeeyah was wrenching at the girl's tightly clenched right hand. As the two figures swung around in the struggle, Hope saw the white nurse cap clinging precariously by one pin to the side of the dark braids. The girl's face was hidden for the moment. As wildly as she fought, she was no match for the dark skinned girl who held her. Relentlessly, Murshdeeyah pried at the clenched fist.

A moment later a small metal object fell clattering to the floor at Hope's feet. Automatically she stooped to pick it up. It was a wardrobe key. Hope knew, without looking, that it was a duplicate to the one around her neck. Slowly she straightened up. Her eyes sought the face of Murshdeeyah's opponent.

It was Aida. Her face was contorted with rage. The two girls stood gasping for breath, warily eyeing each other. Aida was the first to find her voice.

"Miss Hope," she panted shrilly, "I caught your thief! It's Murshdeeyah! She had that key and was trying to unlock your *dulab*!"

"No, Aida," Hope said sadly. "I know better. You were here first. I followed Murshdeeyah down the hall. It was you who had the key."

"No!" screamed Aida. "I swear it was Murshdeeyah. Didn't she try to steal Tamam's money? Didn't she take the pound from Miss Eileen's drawer? Didn't she take the money from the clinic and steal Faiza's pound? She is the thief, I tell you!"

"Aida, please stop," Hope commanded wearily. "Everything you say only involves you more deeply. I want to know just one thing. Where did you get this key?"

Aida flung back her head and snapped her lips stubbornly together in a sneer of hatred.

Hope regarded her silently for a long moment, then said quietly, "Very well, Aida. You will please go to your room and start packing at once. You will leave this hospital tonight."

As Aida flounced sullenly out the door, Hope turned to Murshdeeyah.

"Please find Miss Anderson," she said. "Ask her to come here at once. Please come back too, *also*. I will need you."

Murshdeeyah glided away on her errand. Hope closed the door and leaned against it, staring at the key in her hand. Her mind refused to grasp the fact of Aida's guilt in spite of the evidence. Surely, the cunning scheme must have been devised by Jaleel. Hope moved slowly to the wardrobe and inserted the new key in the lock. It turned easily. She opened the door. All the deposit envelopes appeared to be in place on the upper shelf. She rapidly checked their contents with the amounts listed on each envelope. Nothing was missing. Her heart was too weighted with sorrow over the defection of one of her students even to feel relief that all the money entrusted to her care was safe.

A light tap sounded on the door. Eileen entered, followed by Murshdeeyah. A group of chattering students were coming down the hall behind them. Hope hastily instructed Murshdeeyah to stand guard inside Aida's room and to let no one enter while the girl was packing. Then she closed her own door and gave Eileen a rapid account of what had happened.

"Aida is packing now," she concluded. "I want to have a talk with her before she leaves. I didn't have time to consult with Dr. Dawson, but I have told her that she must leave here tonight. I am sure he will agree with me. Will you go tell him what has happened? Ask him if he will arrange transportation into Bethlehem for Aida. Perhaps both the doctors will go. Someone will have to deal firmly with her father, or he may beat her unmercifully." She was talking distractedly.

"Now, don't worry," Eileen admonished. "I am sure Dr. Dawson will know what is best to do."

"My class is due to meet in ten minutes," Hope added anxiously.

"I'll take care of them, too," Eileen promised.

The two separated at Aida's door. Hope knocked. The door opened an inch or so. Then, seeing who was there, Murshdeeyah allowed Hope to enter.

Aida gave her a brief glance and went on with her packing. Her expression discouraged any attempts at conversation. The forgotten nurse cap, held by a single pin, swung crazily back and forth above one ear as she moved to and fro collecting articles from bureau drawers and wardrobe. Hope felt an overwhelming pity for the girl who had forfeited the right to ever wear that cap again. Out of a heart wrenching concern for Aida's future welfare, she finally ventured to speak.

"Aida, you must know that I love you. I am so sorry and grieved over what has happened," she said.

Aida deliberately turned her back and jerked some dresses from their hangers. Sweeping the things off the bureau top into her bag, she slammed the lid shut.

Hope tried again.

"Aida, won't you let me be your friend? I'm sure your father is behind all of this." Still no answer. Then Hope became desperate. "Hasn't your nurse's cap meant anything to you at all?"

For the first time Aida seemed to become aware that she was still in full uniform. Her hands flew to her head and found the dangling cap. She tore it loose from the last pin. Without uttering a word, she whirled to face Hope, threw the cap on the floor between them, and stamped on it with both feet.

With a cry of anguish, Hope covered her face with both hands and fled to her room. A few minutes later Eileen found her face down on the bed sobbing wildly into her pillow.

Eileen managed to quiet her long enough to give her the report from Dr. Dawson. He concurred with Hope's decision that Aida should leave the hospital that night. Both he and Dr. Baxter were preparing for the trip into Bethlehem. "I told the other students what happened," Eileen added. "They will all stay in the classroom and study quietly until Aida is gone."

"Do you know what Aida did with her cap, Eileen?" Hope wailed. "She threw it on the floor and stamped on it. Her cap! She stamped on it with both feet! Oh, how could she?"

There was a rising note of hysteria in her voice. Eileen wisely made no comment. She took Hope's shoes off and got her into a nightgown and then into bed. She brought a cool wet washcloth and bathed her tearful face. Hope was still shaking. Eileen took her pulse. It was racing.

Eileen stepped across the hall to Misprint's room and asked her to sit with Hope while she went to call Dr. Dawson. In a few minutes his cool hand was upon Hope's hot forehead and he was checking her erratic pulse.

"Young lady," he announced firmly, "you are completely worn out. I am going to give you a sedative and a sleeping cap-sule. I order you to stay in that bed for twenty-four hours." Hope started to protest, but the chief continued, "Hold out your hand." He produced a small medicine case from his coat pocket, shook two white tablets into Hope's hand then turned for the glass of water Eileen had gotten. Hope popped the tablets into her mouth and swallowed the water. The chief repeated this procedure with a second bottle, then giving Hope a big smile he turned to the door. "Have a good rest," he said.

Eileen went to refill the water glass. When she returned with it, Hope was propped up on pillows with her Bible on her lap.

"You won't need to stay any longer," she said. "I will just read a little and then turn out the light."

There was a sound of wheels on the gravel driveway.

Eileen went out, leaving the door slightly ajar.

Hope glanced down at her Bible and began to read. She grad-ually began to relax and a deep peace filled her heart.

Eileen checked back half an hour later to find her sound asleep. She carefully eased the extra pillow out from under Hope's head, closed the Bible and put it on the table. There were tears on Hope's cheeks. One hand lay on the coverlet, palm upturned.

Eileen dropped to her knees and laid her cheek against that soft palm.

"Father," she whispered, "please keep watch over her tonight. Give her the rest and strength that she needs. She is so vulnerable to hurts. This has been a cruel blow. Help me to ease her burdens in whatever ways I can. Teach me to be less harsh with the people around me. I ask all this in Thy precious name. Amen."

As she rose, two bright tear drops fell from her eyes into Hope's outstretched palm. The fingers curled together in an eager, grasping motion.

Satisfied that her prayer had been heard and answered, Eileen switched off the light, and quietly withdrew.

SEVENTEEN

HOPE WAS ROUSED BY a beam of bright sunlight glinting through a slit in the window drapes. She raised her arm and peered groggily at her wristwatch. It was ten-thirty. She turned her back on the sunbeam and drifted off to sleep again.

At three o'clock in the afternoon she was roused again by a fumbling at the doorknob. There was a clatter of dishes as the door swung open. Murshdeeyah entered, bearing a large teatray. The girl set it down on the bedside table. Seeing that Hope was awake, she drew back the blinds, remarking, "You sleep long time, Missy Hope. You hungry now, maybe?"

Hope looked listlessly at the tray. She shook her head.

"No, Murshdeeyah, I don't want anything, thanks," she murmured.

Wearily she closed her eyes, wanting nothing more than to escape back into the painless oblivion from which she had just emerged. Murshdeeyah would have no part in the escape. She shook Hope's shoulder.

"Missy Hope," she said urgently, "Listen. I tell you something. Aida cries after you left last night. Cries much."

Hope's eyelids flew open. "Are you sure, Murshdeeyah?"

Murshdeeyah nodded delightedly and repeated with great satisfaction, "*Nam,* you leave, she cry. She tell me go stand out in hall. Proud. Not want me to see. But I hear, okay. I see plenty, too. She leave uniform on bed. She not leave cap." The girl swooped down as if to snatch up something from the floor, then made a motion as if thrusting an imaginary thing into her bosom.

Hope was sitting bolt upright in bed. Her eyes were glowing. "Are you sure, Murshdeeyah?" she asked eagerly.

"*Nam,*" replied Murshdeeyah. "She think I no see. I see, okay. She hide cap here." Again the girl indicated her bosom. Then, chuckling, she seized Hope's pillows, fluffed them up, and propped them behind her mistress's back. This done, she lifted the teapot persuasively, "You hungry now, maybe?" she suggested.

"Oh, yes, please," cried Hope. "I am starving."

Murshdeeyah poured a cup of tea and settled the tray on Hope's lap. Then, with another significant gesture toward her bosom, she departed, chuckling with satisfaction.

A short time later Eileen entered to find Hope finishing off the last crumb on the sandwich plate. Taking note of the empty tray and Hope's bright eyes, she began teasingly, "Well, Miss Lazybones, are you rested enough? If so, the chief will allow you to join the mission staff at dinner and a meeting in his home tonight at six-thirty."

"I never felt better in my life," Hope declared.

Eileen closed the curtains at the window, pulled the pillow from behind Hope's back, and shouldered the tray. "You have two hours more to sleep," she said. "I'll tell Margaret she can put another potato in the pot."

It was always a privilege to dine at the Dawson home, for the food was invariably excellent and the conversation merry. Tonight the entire mission staff was present, including the Dysons from Bethlehem, who were staying the night. As the latest arrival, Misprint occupied the seat of honor at Dr. Dawson's right. Even Molly Claiborne was present. The early evening medications were being dispensed by Christine and Aminah. Regina was baby sitting the Baxter children. Everyone was in a lighthearted mood.

When the party rose to adjourn to the sitting room for coffee, the chief whispered in Hope's ear, "You certainly look rested and happy tonight. Did my pills really have that much magic?"

Hope smiled, and whispered back, "The pills did help, doctor, but Murchdeeyah worked most of the magic. That girl would make a wonderful nurse."

His eyebrows lifted skeptically. Then he laughed, and said, "You may be right, at that. The sight of that comical face ought to be enough to cheer a corpse."

When Maryam had collected the coffee cups and retired to the kitchen, Dr. Dawson opened his well-worn Bible. All listened attentively as he read a portion from the Book of Isaiah. Then he closed the Book and prayed simply, "Father, we are gathered here in Thy presence to ask guidance in the discussion and in the decisions we are to make this hour. We pray that any plans made may be in accordance with Thy will for the future welfare of this work. In Jesus' name, Amen."

"You all know that a tragic event occurred here last evening. One of our student nurses was caught in the act of stealing. She has been dismissed. We also have business to discuss. But first, perhaps Miss Hope will satisfy our curiousity as to why she is bubbling over tonight, when less than twenty-four hours ago, she was in the very nadir of despair." He turned inquiringly to Hope.

Hope gave the chief a radiant smile and then began to relate the story about Aida's cap and of Murshdeeyah's disclosure.

"So the cap really means something to her, after all," she said. "I am convinced her father instigated the whole plot and forced her to take part in his scheme by threatening her with some dire punishment."

Jimmy Dyson spoke up: "Jaleel Yusef is known around town as a gambler and a bully. I learned today that he has been losing heavily. He is suspected of thievery. He used to beat his son unmercifully. The boy turned out to be a coward and a weakling. One night he killed a man with a knife. He claimed self-defense, which it probably was, for the boy wasn't really vicious. The court gave him ten years in prison. It is well-known that Jaleel beats his womenfolk, too. I suspect that he didn't dare beat Aida as long as she was under Dr. Dawson's protection."

"I can add another little item to the man's record of misdeeds," remarked Dr. Baxter. "He makes duplicate keys, for a price, which is illegal in this country. But so far, no one has informed on him."

"That explains how Aida got a duplicate key to Hope's wardrobe," Eileen exclaimed.

"Jaleel engineered the whole thing, of course," said Hope. "To think how cleverly he schemed for her to deposit the money she was stealing from us right back here in my wardrobe, so that she couldn't possibly be suspected when the money was stolen."

The case continued to be discussed until finally the chief broke in with, "Suppose we get on to more pleasant business. I believe each mission family has entertained Misprint at least once since her arrival. Now we wish to welcome her as a group. I'm sure you'll all agree that she is a very valuable addition to our staff."

There was hearty applause. Misprint arose and bowed deeply several times. Then she began modestly, "Thank you very much. I haven't much to say, except that in the few weeks since I came, I already feel that I have known and loved every one of you all my life. If God can use me even a fraction as much as He is using all of you here, I shall be most happy." With that she sat down.

"Thank you, Misprint," said the Chief. "Now I have a new item of particular interest to Miss Claiborne. She is due to go on duty soon, so we had better get it on the agenda right now."

Molly was in full uniform, ready for work. "I still have a few minutes." she said. "Please don't keep me in suspense any longer, Doctor."

The chief's eyes twinkled, and he continued, "As you all know, Miss Molly has an impatient fiancé awaiting her in Georgia. He has completed his medical studies and wants her home. She was due to leave six months ago, but kindly overstayed her time until we could find a replacement. I have good news. The young lovers will soon be reunited. Deaconess Marta Krueger and her nephew are flying from Germany. They will arrive within the week."

He was interrupted by Molly, who flew across the room to bestow upon him an ecstatic hug and kiss. Then the women crowded around her. An excited babble of laughter and congratulations followed. Suddenly, Molly consulted her watch.

"Oh, my goodness!" she exclaimed. "I must be off or I'll get fired for sure." She paused in the doorway to say, "Thanks a million for the lovely dinner, Mrs. D, and thanks for the wonderful news, Dr. D. Goodnight, everybody!"

The chief settled back in his chair with a sigh of satisfaction. "Now I have another piece of good news," he continued. "A large gift has arrived from a private donor in America that will enable us to start construction on a nurse's residence immediately. I have consulted the contractor. He can arrange to begin construction in two weeks. It may be possible to have the side walls up and the roof poured before the heavy rains start in December. I think we can plan for the ground breaking ceremonies to take place a week from this Saturday."

There was enthusiastic applause, together with a "Rah, Rah!" from the irrepressible Dr. Baxter.

"Is there anything more to add before we begin our season of prayer?" the chief asked.

Misprint spoke up.

"I don't know if this is the time and place to speak of flannelgraphs. Some of you know that I brought a large number of

Bible flannelgraph figures with me. Most of them I made myself.
You place the figures on a board as you tell the story. I thought
they would be an effective witness to the patients in the wards,
if I could find time to teach the student nurses how to use them."

"I am very familiar with their use," said Ruth Dyson.

"The storebought ones are very expensive. I brought just a
few from America. I wish I could have brought more."

"I think you have brought along an excellent project,
Misprint," the chief said. "With two more nurses due this week,
perhaps our nursing directors can work out a schedule for you
to teach the students. Now, is there anything else?"

"Yes," said Hope. "I visited Rose Zaki in the hospital this
week. The doctors will remove her body cast in a few days. The
bones have knit well. She will need to walk with crutches for a
while. She is anxious to spare us any further hospital expense. If
her home were not on such a steep hillside, with no level area out-
side for exercise, she could go home right away. Could we bring
her out here to recuperate? There is plenty of level ground out-
side where she can exercise. We could put two beds at one end of
that large sewing room. Her daughter, Lydia, could stay here to
help her. She could commute to school in Bethlehem on the bus.
If the Mennonites will take Daoud to board in their boys' school,
Rose could rent her house and use the money to pay his expenses.
She could do enough around here to earn a salary, too. The linen
room is stacked high with mending that she could be doing. We
will be taking in another class of students as soon as the nurse's
residence is finished. We will double the number of women
patients. My time will be completely taken up with nursing and
teaching. Rose will make an excellent housekeeper. She can plan
meals, order supplies, and supervise the domestic help far better
than I." Hope stopped and looked eagerly at Dr. Dawson.

He smiled, saying kindly, "It isn' necessary to plead, Miss
Hope. You deserve such help. God will provide the where-
withal."

Ten days later, Regina returned from a visit to her home in Bethlehem, with the news that Jaleel Yusef had married Aida off a few days earlier to an older man from Nablus. He was twice a widower and lived on a tract of farmland some distance from the town.

"There was no betrothal party, no celebration at all," Regina said ~~mourn-~~. "Aida left in a taxi with her husband. She wore an old dress and carried just one shabby suitcase. Mother thinks her father owed the man a gambling debt, and got him to cancel it by letting him marry Aida. She thinks he got money, too."

Hope was greatly disturbed by the news. She could only pray that Aida's husband would be kinder to her than her father had been.

EIGHTEEN

THE MONTH OF SEPTEMBER was crowded with many events, beginning with the arrival of Sister Marta Krueger and her nephew, Rolf Reinhoffer. The two were quite a contrast to each other. Sister Marta was a large, cheerful woman, who performed her duties in a firm, capable manner that brooked no nonsense. Rolf was a slight, unprepossessing individual. A pair of thick lensed glasses did not entirely conceal the quiet friendliness of his blue eyes. He was somewhere in his mid-forties.

In less than a week Molly Claiborne turned over her night shift to the deaconess, and flew off to meet her long-suffering bridegroom in New York.

Rolf took on a number of tasks. He assisted Dr. Baxter in the clinic on men's day. He helped with eye surgery two afternoons a week and relieved the male attendants on their weekly nights off duty. He spent every spare moment gardening, which was his hobby. The Arab gardener, Issa, took to following him around like a devoted slave. He learned how to care for the seedlings and small evergreens that Rolf had brought from his homeland. Everything in the garden bloomed and flourished under his expert care.

With the lightening of her duties in the clinic, Misprint began developing the flannelgraph project. She also started some simple handcraft therapy in the wards. Her presence was always hailed with delight. The patients laughed at her amusing misuse of the Arabic words they tried to teach her. The morale in the men's ward, was considerably improved. Compulsory confinement to bed for any length of time can be very trying on the masculine Arab temperament.

The ground-breaking ceremonies for the new nurse's residence took place as scheduled. Thereafter, six days a week from dawn to dusk, the clang of hammer and chisel could be heard throughout the hospital compound.

The thirty-six beds in the men's ward were now filled. The women's ward contained eighteen women patients, besides Zoorah and a merry little seven-year-old girl named Salamy. Rose Zaki was happily installed in the sewing room with her daughter. She was doing well on her crutches and managed the greater part of her household duties with little assistance.

Hope and Eileen were considering an early opening of the children's ward, when a Bedouin mother, named Leika, was admitted with her four-month-old baby boy, Nabeel. Both were in the acute stages of pulmonary tuberculosis. The child wailed incessantly, keeping everyone awake in the ward except the two children. Nabeel occupied the same bed as Leika. Native custom decreed that no child of his tender age should be separated from his mother. In spite of strict orders to the contrary, the other women patients picked him up at all hours and walked the floor with him.

On the third day, the two nurses cheerfully threw native customs out the window and moved the three children into their own pleasant ward just down the hall. The two little girls were delighted with the nursery pictures on the walls, and with the child-sized table and chairs. With Dr. Dawson's permission they were allowed out of bed long enough to eat their meals at the table. Zoorah always brought her doll along, propping her up in a separate chair and offering her food from her own spoon.

Relieved of the care of Nabeel, Leika immediately began gaining strength. The grumbling of the other women over the American nurses' hardheartedness soon ceased. They settled down to enjoy their required rest.

Regina was put in charge of the children's ward in the day-time. She cared for Nabeel devotedly. The other nurses slipped in at odd hours to help whenever possible. Nabeel failed to ben-efit from the change. He grew steadily weaker, until he was no longer able to swallow the baby formula containing the crushed tablets of medicine that he needed so desperately. Dr. Damson had to resort to feeding him through a stomach tube. The doctor took spinal tests on Nabeel, and more X-rays. They revealed a positive tubercular meningitis, as well as extensive tubercular involvement of both lungs. In all his medical practice, the chief had never known of anyone who had recovered from such an unfortunate combination. At the regular staff prayer meeting that Sunday night, he stated that unless God saw fit to inter-vene, he was certain that the child would not last another week. The missionaries knelt and joined in fervent petition to the One who loves all little children, that the life of this one small child might be spared.

The very next morning there was a perceptible change in Nabeel's condition. Sister Marta reported that he had slept more naturally during the night and his temperature had improved. Within two days he was able to take his food and medicine without the aid of the tube. By the following Sunday night, they knew that their prayers were granted and the "mira-cle baby" was well on the way to recovery.

Work continued rapidly on the new building. By the time the rains came, the nurse's residence was safely roofed against the heavy storms of late December. The hospital was completed in February and the doors were opened to admit patients in early March.

The clinic had already been in operation for a year. During that year an appalling number of those who sought medical help were found to be suffering with tuberculosis in such advanced stages that the chances of a cure seemed very slim.

When the hospital was opened, the kind doctor was forced to the painful conclusion that older tubercular patients must be denied admission, as well as any of the costly medications. Funds and beds were so limited that they must be conserved for the young. In most cases, the relatives of those who were admitted were not able to pay the full cost of their food, nor for the large quantities of expensive drugs needed for successful treatment. Although generous gifts came from America, they were never adequate to provide free care. Monthly payments by relatives dwindled as time went on. The financial burden grew heavier and heavier. Many heartbreaking choices constantly had to be made. The doctor often lay awake at night, haunted by the faces of those whom he had to turn away. To the young and hopeful patients, charity was always stretched to the very limit, for the chief's trust in God's provision never faltered, though sometimes it was sorely tested.

Several days after the last bed in the men's ward was filled, the chief rose from a restless sleep and drove to the metalsmith shop in Bethlehem. He ordered a dozen more bedframes constructed, and then went to the souk in Jerusalem. Here he ordered an equal number of mattresses to be made. When they arrived, he coaxed Hope into squeezing six more beds into the men's ward. The other six beds were stored in one corner of the screened porch at the far end of the ward. Soon the six beds were filled. Then those on the porch were set up. One by one, six convalescent patients were moved out onto the porch to make room in the ward for six others. Thus, the ward originally built to accommodate thirty-six patients now housed forty-eight. The porch screens were replaced by windows before winter closed in.

One morning Hope came upon the chief standing in the open doorway of the tiny isolation room. He was eyeing the vacant bed speculatively. Hope reached past him and closed the door in his face. "The answer is no, Doctor," she said firmly. "I insist that this room be left free for isolation or emergencies. We never know when it may be needed."

"Very well, Miss Hope. I yield." The doctor sighed.

During her morning class the next day, Hope received a request from the chief to join him immediately in the X-ray room. She passed a pretty little Negro women and a small toddler in the hall. The woman appeared to have been crying. There were four men squatting on the floor near the door. A rude sort of stretcher leaned against the wall. The chief was studying some X-rays when Hope entered. He called her over to look at them.

"This fellow's lungs aren't in nearly as bad a shape as I judged by his appearance," he remarked. "He is too weak to walk. Four fellows brought him in on a stretcher from some little village near Hebron. Thats at least fifteen miles from here. Did you see his wife out in the hall?"

Hope nodded. They moved to stand on either side of the X-ray table. The patient lay motionless, with eyes closed. His dark face had a peculiar grayish pallor. Hope placed her hand upon his forehead. It was moist, but not as hot as she had expected. "He doesn't seem very feverish," she murmured. Her fingers felt his temples. "His pulse is very weak."

"I'm afraid he is far too sick to travel the fifteen miles back home," the chief stated quietly. Hope caught the wistful implication in his voice. She glanced at the patient. His black eyes were wide open. They were fixed imploringly on her face. His lips began to move.

Drawn by a strange feeling, she bent her ear down close to his lips. Faintly she heard the one word, "Yesuah." Startled, Hope raised her head and looked searchingly into those dark eyes. Their gaze never wavered. She smiled and nodded reassuringly. The weary eyelids closed and a look of peace settled down upon the ravaged features.

Hope turned excitedly to the doctor. "Did you hear him?" He said, "Yesuah," she exclaimed. "This is the man we have been holding that special bed for. He has come in the name of Jesus."

The doctor's eyes were moist as he placed a hand affectionately on her shoulder.

"Thank you, my dear," he said. "I am sure there will be much blessing in this for us all."

It was almost dinner time when Hope dismissed her morning classes. Regina shyly asked her to come see something in her room that she had brought from home. Hope accompanied her. Regina flung her door wide open, and proudly pointed to a large sheepskin lying on the floor beside her bed. "I saved up my money and bought it last week," she said. "Come feel how soft it is."

Hope obligingly sat down on the bed beside Regina and leaned down to stroke the soft wool.

"It is lovely," she said. "But isn't it full of fleas?"

Regina looked hurt.

"Oh, no," she assured Hope earnestly. "My mother washed it very carefully. I am sure she got rid of all the fleas."

"In that case, Regina," she said, "I wish you much pleasure in your rug. It will be wonderful for tired feet."

"I bought it to use for a prayer rug," Regina explained shyly. "I don't mind the bare floor for my feet, but it hurts my knees when I pray."

Hope gave her a loving squeeze. "A prayer rug should be standard equipment for every Christian," said Hope. "Do you remember that you will soon have to take a turn in the men's ward?"

Regina sighed.

"Yes, I do know Miss Hope. I pray about it. But it hasn't seemed to help me get over my fear."

"It will, my dear," replied Hope confidently. "The Lord is preparing you, whether you know it or not. When the time of testing comes, you will not fail Him."

NINETEEN

As soon as the patient's rest period was over, Hope began making afternoon rounds with the chief. They started in the women's ward. Christine was taking temperatures. The doctor strolled the length of the ward, stopping beside each bed to shake an eagerly outstretched hand and to say a kind word. Then he glanced through the charts. Christine brought the temperature report. He surveyed it with great satisfaction. "Even Leika's temperature is well stabilized now," he remarked. "I hope that the men patients are doing as well."

They went on to the children's ward. Regina was cuddling Nabeel on her lap while she fed him his afternoon nourishment. The doctor moved into the child's line of vision. The black eyes began shuttling back and forth between the chief's face and the spoon, never missing a mouthful. The doctor laughed heartily. "Just keep stuffing that little fellow, Regina," he ordered.

"I'll do my best, Sir," she replied demurely.

Zoorah and Salamy finished eating their yoghurt. They began beating their spoons on the table by way of attracting the chief's attention. Obligingly, he walked over and patted their heads, while they hugged his knees.

Then he turned his attention to the latest arrival. She had been admitted that morning. The cup of yoghurt stood untouched on her bedside table. She lay motionless on her side, face turned to the wall. The doctor bent over her, thinking she was asleep. To his surprise, her eyes were wide open. She was staring unseeingly at the wall. He consulted the chart that Hope brought, then bent over and called her by name, "Lateefa!" Only the girl's eye muscles moved. She glanced at him indifferently, then turned back to the wall.

Hope noted by the child's chart that she was twelve years old. She was exceptionally tall for her age, but painfully thin. Right now she was flushed with fever.

The chief explained that she was the daughter of a Bedouin chief. The tribe had broken camp only that morning some distance north of Jerusalem. They were headed for a better pasture site far to the south. They passed close by the hospital soon after dawn. A few miles farther on, Lateefa became too ill to walk. Her father placed her across the back of his own donkey and brought her back to the hospital. Khaleed was able to interpret his strange dialect. He agreed to leave his daughter behind for treatment when X-rays revealed tubercular lesions. The doctor delicately mentioned the matter of payment for food and medicines. To his surprise, the Bedouin chief produced a well-filled money pouch and counted out the sum suggested by Khaleed. He talked earnestly with Lateefa for a few moments, then left. He would return for her when the caravan came north again in the spring. He promised he would pay whatever more was owing at that time.

Regina laid Nabeel down in his crib and came to stand beside them.

"She won't let me do anything for her," the little student said worriedly. "She refuses to eat or to take her medicines. I think she is homesick. She just doesn't understand me."

Moved with pity, Hope slipped her arm gently under the thin shoulders, and attempted to turn the girl toward them. Unexpectedly, Lateefa lashed out fiercely with both fists. Hope barely managed to escape a smashing blow aimed at her nose.

"Whew!" exclaimed the chief. "Better leave her alone until morning. By that time she may be hungry enough to cooperate a little. I thought her father made everything clear to her. Perhaps she didn't take it in. We will have to find somebody who can speak her dialect to explain things to her."

Hope accompanied him down to the men's ward. On the way, they stopped in the isolation room to see the Negro patient. His name was Farouk Mahmoud. Although he was now flushed with fever, he seemed much more alert than he had been in the X-ray room.

The chief studied his chart for some time, particularly the lines on the graph sheet. He called Hope's attention to them. "This isn't the usual TB pattern," he observed. "At this hour his temperature ought to be more than ninety-nine six. His pulse is low, too."

Hope felt the man's hot forehead. Then she reached for the thermometer. She carefully placed it in Farouk's mouth. The doctor was counting his pulse. "His pulse is pretty weak, but not alarmingly fast. Now, let's see what the thermometer registers." He whistled as he read it, then handed it to Hope.

"One hundred five point two," she read aloud. "That last temperature was taken less than an hour ago. It seems to have shot up much faster and higher than a tuberculosis temperature."

The chief's face was grave. He said, "I will get a blood count on him as soon as I finish rounds. I want a stool specimen, too. If Rolf isn't on duty, please find him. I don't think we should trust this job to an attendant. Ask Rolf to use a cool enema to get the specimen, and then to follow it with a cooling sponge bath. Use isolation precautions. Miss Eileen can continue making rounds with me. I saw her in the men's ward as we came down the hall."

Hope went in search of Rolf. She found him in the garden. He went at once to change into his white hospital uniform.

On her way back to Farouk's room, Hope recalled that the mercury in the thermometer had registered far higher than the ninety-nine six, before she had shaken it down. The fact was puzzling.

When she left Rolf in charge of Farouk, she went to the desk just outside the men's ward door. Elizabeth was seated at the desk busily charting temperatures. Hope sat down in the chair across from the girl and watched idly as Elizabeth marked the dots indicating temperature, pulse, and respiration, on each of the patient's graph sheets. Hope noticed that the work went very slowly. Elizabeth squinted badly. Suddenly, the mystery of Farouk's thermometer dawned on Hope.

"Elizabeth," she asked, "where are your glasses?"

The girl started, flushing guiltily. "They are in my room," she admitted.

"Why aren't you wearing them?" Hope demanded. "The eye doctor told you that you must wear them all the time."

"But I can see all right, Miss Callaway," Elizabeth protested. "Really I can! I use them every night to study. You can ask Warda." Warda was her roommate.

"Please go get them at once."

Elizabeth cringed as if she were slapped. "Oh, Miss Callaway," she implored, "please don't make me wear them in the ward. It is a disgrace for Arabs to ever wear glasses unless they are blind. Please! Everyone will think I am blind."

Hope stared at the girl in amazement. It had never occurred to her before how rarely she ever saw an Arab wearing glasses, unless they were the dark ones that indicated blindness. She realized that this was a deeply rooted Arab prejudice. For centuries, they had taken pride in their keenness of vision. In this twentieth century, however, eye diseases were taking a heavy toll among the Arabs. Excellent visual aids were obtainable at low cost in modern eye clinics throughout the area. The tragedy was that many people with poor vision, refused to wear the needed glasses.

Hope knew that she must convince the girl of the necessity for wearing glasses, or else her future usefulness as a nurse would be an utter impossibility.

As Hope thought about the problem, her eyes lit upon the tray of thermometers. She picked up a handful; checked to see that the mercury was properly shaken down in each, and rinsed them under the cold water faucet. Then she prepared a basin of warm water. One by one, she carefully dipped the glass bulbs in the water, raising the mercury to various levels. Elizabeth was completely mystified. Hope glanced at the mercury in the first thermometer, and held it out to the girl. "Read it for me, please, Elizabeth."

Elizabeth peered at it and announced, "Ninety-nine point two."

"Ninety-seven point two," Hope corrected. She handed the girl a second thermometer. Elizabeth scrutinized it more closely, then proclaimed, "One-o-three point two."

"One-o-three point five," Hope corrected. She handed Elizabeth three more in the same way, and each time her answers were incorrect. She began to wilt. The perspiration was streaming down her face.

As Hope held up the last thermometer, she said, "Can't you see it, Elizabeth? It is clear up to one hundred seven. A patient would never survive such a high temperature unless it were brought down very quickly."

She shook all the thermometers down and replaced them in the tray, leaving the troubled girl to ponder the matter, Finally, she asked kindly, "Did you take Farouk's temperature at three o'clock?"

"Y—yes," the girl faltered.

"You charted ninety-nine six," Hope told her. "Dr. Dawson and I both questioned it at four. I took it again. It was one hundred five point two then, which is dangerously high. You had forgotten to shake the mercury down at three, and I noted it was far higher than what you had recorded." She paused, then asked very gently, "Do you still think you can see without glasses, Elizabeth?"

The girl's eyes were gazing down at her tightly clasped hands. She humbly shook her head.

"Do you still want to be a nurse, Elizabeth?" Hope pursued in an even gentler tone. Elizabeth's head rose and bowed once in a positive gesture of assent.

Hope spoke with deep earnestness.

"Elizabeth, a patient's very life may depend upon a nurse's integrity. The doctor relies on her for correct information. Farouk is a very sick man. Would you want to be responsible for his death?"

Elizabeth raised her head and stared at Hope in horror.

"Oh, no, Miss Hope," she gasped. "I didn't know . . . I never meant to lie. I really thought I could see the thermometers."

"Now that you know otherwise," Hope persisted, "which means more to you, your Arab pride, or your Christian service?"

Elizabeth rose to the challenge. She lifted her head. Her honest brown eyes met Hope's squarely. She replied bravely, "I wish to be a good nurse, Miss Hope. I will go fetch my glasses now. I promise to wear them faithfully from now on." She marched resolutely down the hall.

At supper time, Hope hurried through her meal and excused herself early to prepare for the evening classes. She was mounting the stairs to the main hallway when she caught sight of a small white-clad figure slipping out the big glass door at the main entrance. It was Lateefa. With a sharp cry of alarm, Hope sprang to the door, flung it open, and started running after the child. Lateefa turned left at the foot of the steps and sped by Dr. Dawson's house at the end of the driveway. She headed for the open fields beyond. Just past those fields was an old caravan trail leading through mountain passes toward Gaza, far to the south. Lateefa was making unerringly for that distant cleft in the hills through which her father's caravan had passed many hours before. The sun had already set. Hope could feel the bitter chill of the approaching night descending as she ran after the girl. She soon saw that she was losing ground. Lateefa was as fleet as a deer. Though in a weakened condition, the child's fever gave her a false strength. In the thin muslin gown she would never survive a night of exposure in those cold mountains. The caravan had been gone far too long for Lateefa to overtake it either that night, or the day following.

Too late, Hope realized that she should have sounded a general alarm. If she turned back now, Lateefa would be swallowed up in the gray twilight before she could summon aid. Her one hope lay in keeping the child in sight, on the chance that Lateefa might stumble, or drop from sheer exhaustion.

The runaway reached the loosely piled up rock wall that marked the boundary of the mission property. Without pausing, she climbed nimbly to the top. Some instinct made her hesitate and look back. Hope gained a little on her. The next moment, Lateefa caught sight of her pursuer. She sprang from the rock wall to the field below, and was off again at a faster pace than before.

Hope reached the wall and tried to clamber up the loosely piled fence. The rocks gave way, and she fell to her knees with a groan of despair. She was struggling to rise when two huge bare feet suddenly sailed over her head in a magnificent leap that landed them on the very top of the wall. Another leap to the ground below, and they went bounding off in pursuit of the small white figure, now just a blur in the distance. Even in the half light, Hope recognized those big, bare feet, and the brightly flowered red skirt tucked into the waistband above the long black legs.

It was Murshdeeyah, running like a great Olympic racer. Hope sent up a prayer of thankfulness. Then she settled down confidently to nurse her bruised knees while she awaited Murshdeeyah's return.

Some time passed. Then Murshdeeyah loomed up in the darkness. Lateefa was on her shoulder. She set her burden down on the top of the wall. Hope held the child while the black girl clambered over. The tall girl chuckled as she lifted her burden again.

"I mama now," she said. "Good ears. I hear you call out on stairs. I run. Get Murshdeeyah a baby." She cuddled Lateefa against her shoulder.

An anxious group approached them from the hospital, carrying lanterns. Lateefa's absence had been discovered. They were starting out to find her. Murshdeeyah carried the child upstairs, bathed her dusty feet, and tucked her into bed. At a word from Hope, Regina brought her pills and an injection. Murshdeeyah addressed the Bedouin girl in a strange dialect, and turned her over, face down, for the injection. Then she sat her up in bed, handed her the pills, and held a glass of water for her. Lateefa obediently swallowed the pills. Then Murshdeeyah placed the untouched supper tray across the girl's knees, and fed her every bite of food. Tucking the blankets around the child, she shouldered the tray, and started for the door. Lateefa pulled the covers up, and resolutely shut her eyes.

Murshdeeyah chuckled, and said, "She go sleep now. No run away any more. I promise her I come back in the morning. Okay?"

"Okay," Hope replied thankfully, departing to teach her waiting class.

TWENTY

Hope and Eileen were at breakfast next morning when they received an urgent summons from Dr. Dawson. They found him in the laboratory examining slides under a high powered microscope. His face was drawn and haggard. He wasted no words.

"Ladies," he announced, "Farouk Mahmoud's tests show a well advanced case of typhoid fever."

The two nurses exchanged apprehensive glances.

"We have begun a typhoid regime," the chief continued. "Rolf has a partial isolation set up. Had we known yesterday in the X-ray room that the primary TB was complicated with typhoid, we would have sent the man on to a government hospital at once. We are only licensed to care for tubercular patients here. I must report the case to the government officials today. They may decide to move him immediately. He has failed considerably in the night. I feel that another move just now would prove fatal. If he survives the next few days, he may have a fighting chance. I should like to ask permission to keep him here. I need the opinion of our own mission staff first." He paused, then asked, "When did the staff and employees receive inoculations last, Miss Hope?"

"I will have to check their medical records for the dates," replied Hope. "Each one received one soon after they arrived here."

"Please bring them to my office," the chief requested. "everyone in the hospital has already been exposed to some extent. All the patients will need to be inoculated, for their own protection. All those on your list who have not had boosters recently, should certainly be given them. Miss Eileen, will you please find Dr. Baxter and ask him to join us for a conference in my office?"

Within a few minutes the four were gathered around the chief's desk. Their faces were sober. Not only were lives endangered by Farouk's presence in the hospital, but medical officials might choose to close down the mission work altogether for infraction of government rules. However, there were as yet so few hospital facilities available elsewhere in the country to handle tubercular patients, that the latter prospect seemed hardly likely.

Hope had checked all her records and made a report on the inoculations. Most of the employees, patients, and staff would need booster shots. When a count was made there were ninety-six in all.

The chief had two full cartons of 20 c.c. vials on his desk. He pushed one over to Dr. Baxter saying, "This will be more than enough. We will get started in a few minutes. First we must decide what is best to be done for this man, Farouk."

Hope was the first to speak. Her eyes were shining.

"Doctor," she said eagerly, "you told us that he may have a chance to survive if we keep him here. Perhaps we can't save him. But it doesn't seem right not to give him that chance. So, it appears to me that the best thing we can do for Farouk is to keep him right here, if the medical officials will let us. Whether or not he lives, I believe that God will bless us if we try to help him, and will honor our faith by keeping the rest of us safe from typhoid infection."

There was a long silence while the other three pondered Hope's statement. Then Eileen ventured dubiously, "Have you considered the fact that Farouk will need special nursing care day and night? That means at least two nurses, maybe three, would be tied up caring for him. Sister Marta has the whole hospital to handle at night. She wouldn't have time to do it. That leaves only four of us. Even if our student nurses knew the technique required, we do not dare expose them to the danger of close contact. Inoculation does not guarantee complete immunity, does it, Dr. Dawson?"

"No," the doctor said. "But attacks are very rare when it is given. When typhoid is contracted while the immunization shot is still in effect, the severity and duration are considerably lessened. However, you are quite right about the student nurses, Miss Eileen. We cannot risk exposing them to the danger."

Hope had been studying the medical records. Now she asked, "Doctor, do you remember that Regina had a severe reaction to her initial typhoid shot last spring? You asked if she had ever had typhoid. She told me a few weeks ago that she had suffered a very prolonged attack six or seven years ago. Wouldn't that attack make her immune to ever contracting it again?"

"I believe so," the chief replied, looking questioningly at Dr. Baxter. The latter turned to consult the medical books on the shelf behind him. He selected a volume, turned to the chapter on typhoid, and ran his finger down the pages, pausing to read portions to himself.

"Ah, here we are!" he exclaimed, raising his voice to read aloud: "'As a general rule, one attack confers a lifelong immunity.'"

Hope regarded them all triumphantly.

"Well, then," she said, "with the reaction Regina had last spring, it seems certain that she does have an immunity. It would be safe, then, for her to work with Farouk. I can teach her the isolation technique. We could manage a long day shift together for at least twelve, or even thirteen hours, with each of us taking rest periods for an hour or two when Farouk is sleeping."

Hope turned to Dr. Baxter, and continued, "If you are willing to release Rolf from clinic duty, I think he could carry on an eleven or twelve hour night shift. He could get some rest in a chair during the night. Misprint could help again in the clinic on men's day. We can shift the students and aides around to cover the wards. I might even be able to manage my classes. Eileen would have to do most of the nursing supervision and other hospital duties."

"I am willing," said Eileen. "But will Regina be willing to do it? We both know what a scaredy cat she is around men."

Dr. Dawson leaned forward.

"Of course, the girl must be consulted first as to her willingness," he said. "Coercion is not to be considered in a case like this."

He turned to Hope, and said, "Your plan sounds plausible. We all know that expert care is needed, which means that one of our staff must share the work with a green student while giving her instructions in typhoid care. Rolf is the logical choice for the night shift. But why not ask Miss Anderson or Misprint to take the day shift?"

Hope answered hastily, "Dr. Baxter needs her. It wouldn't be fair to ask him to give up both Rolf and Misprint."

"What about Miss Eileen, then?" the chief persisted. "She is younger and more strongly built than you."

Hope flushed with embarrassment. She looked helplessly at Eileen and was silent.

Eileen spoke for her. "She isn't going to tell you herself, so I will. Regina and I do not work well together. I lack Hope's patience and understanding of the girls. There was a slight matter of insubordination when Regina was in the men's ward, under my supervision. I lost my temper. If Hope had not poured oil on the troubled waters, we would have lost a student then and there. Regina would do anything to please her. But she would not accept from me the strict supervision and exacting teamwork that this case requires. I am sorry, but that's the way things are," she concluded honestly.

The chief's bushy brows were drawn together in a thoughtful frown. "What do you think, Dr. Baxter?" he inquired.

Dr. Baxter thought a moment and then replied, "Government officials may take their time about moving the fellow. I think Miss Hope's selection of a team is the only possible solution. However, I suggest that she be relieved of all other duties for the time being. She has already pointed out that the physical strain of typhoid nursing is tremendous. We must not permit her to get overly tired."

"Exactly," said Dr. Dawson. He turned to Hope. "We will agree to your plan on one condition: that you drop your classes and all supervisory work, and let the rest of us handle the problems of this hospital as long as you remain on special duty. Those orders are not to be disobeyed."

Hope nodded her head meekly.

The four scattered to their various duties. Hope went first to the isolation room to talk with Rolf. He had placed a screen a few feet in from the doorway to provide a "clean" area. A small table with a call bell on it stood at the entrance. To the right stood another small table with a basin of disinfectant solution, alcohol, soap, and a scrubbing brush upon it. Clean towels were on a lower shelf. Some isolation gowns were folded upon a chair nearby. The screen hid the patient's bed from the view of passersby. Hope peered around the screen at the patient. His eyelids were half closed. He appeared to be resting comfortably, although he was muttering incoherently to himself. His fingers plucked aimlessly at the bedclothes.

Rolf rose wearily from a chair behind the screen. He shook his head doubtfully at her inquiring look. "He had morphine about three hours ago. His pulse is steadier," he reported. "I gave him his morning bath and medicines, but . . ." His voice trailed off.

"Rolf," Hope said, "Dr. Dawson is not at all certain that we can save him. But we must keep him until the government officials decide to move him, unless he dies meanwhile. Only two of us can be spared for special duty. Are you willing to undertake the night shift? It will mean eleven or twelve hours on duty. You may be able to get some rest here in a chair."

"Sleep is unimportant when one can serve a fellowman, Miss Callaway," he said simply. "I will be happy to do anything I can to help Farouk."

"Thank you, Rolf. I knew I could count on you," Hope replied gratefully.

As Hope stepped out into the hall, Eileen emerged from the men's ward, carrying some bottles of serum. Falling in step with her superior, they climbed the stairs in silence. At the top, Eileen laid a detaining hand on Hope's arm, saying apologetically, "I wish there were some way I could take your place on this case. I am so sorry that I never got to first base with Regina. If you can persuade her to tackle this job with you, I have a feeling that it will either make or break her. I want you to know that I am praying hard that you may succeed."

"Thanks, Eileen," replied Hope. "We will both need your prayers."

They walked on to the children's ward. Hope asked, "Can you spare Christine from the women's ward to relieve Regina . now? I want to talk with her in private. If Regina accepts this assignment, you will have to arrange for someone to take her place in the ward right away."

"Don't worry about a thing," Eileen responded crisply. "We will manage somehow without you for a while. I am not hankering to take your job permanently."

She found Regina engaged in her favorite occupation, feeding Nabeel. The baby's rapid improvement was a constant source of amazement to Hope. Regina held Nabeel up so Hope could see how fat he was getting. Hope smiled at his happy face.

Christine poked her head in the door just then and said, "You sent for me, Miss Callaway?"

"Yes, I want you to take over here for a while," said Hope. "Regina, please put down your baby and give Christine a report. Then come with me. I want to talk with you about another assignment."

Regina's eyes widened with interest and apprehension. Obediently, she laid Nabeel in his crib, gave Christine a brief report, and followed Hope out of the ward. Hope led the mystified girl to the room she had been occupying alone since the departure of Rehab. The sheepskin rug was carefully rolled and lying on the foot of Regina's bed. Except for the time when she had been called to admire it, Hope had not had a private talk with the girl.

Now, if ever, the time had come for the girl to face the test that could free her forever from the bondage of fear of physical contact with men. Without such freedom, she would regain forever shackled, and would be eventually barred from the ranks of professional nursing. Hope was determined to put Regina to that test. She drew her down to sit beside her on the bed.

"Regina," she began cautiously, "tell me why you want to be a nurse?"

As one who recites an answer to the catechism, Regina replied glibly, "Because I love Jesus, and I want to follow His example by helping to heal the sick people."

"Did Jesus heal just women and children," Hope persisted, "or did He heal men, too?"

"He healed men, too," Regina admitted in a small voice.

Hope proceeded, "Regina, our new patient, Farouk, has typhoid fever. He is very ill. He needs constant care. Rolf has agreed to care for him on the night shift. I will take the day shift. But I cannot do it alone. I need an assistant. You are the only student that I can ask to help, because you have had typhoid. You have acquired an immunity to it. Are you willing to do this?"

Regina's eyes were desperately seeking an escape. Her hands were tightly clasped in her lap. She could not answer. Hope took the trembling hands in both her own and held them firmly. Her voice took on a note of urgent pleading.

"Regina, I am certain that God is offering you this opportunity to escape from the chains of fear that bind you. You can become the kind of nurse He wants you to be. Perhaps Farouk is an angel unaware that he has sent for this very purpose."

The hands she held ceased their trembling. Hope continued, "My own heart weeps when I see the disease ridden condition of your unfortunate people. Regina, your country needs you. Farouk and I need you. Most of all, God needs you in His work." She rose and stood before the girl. "Regina," she continued softly, "I will leave you to decide for yourself if you still want to be a nurse. I cannot force you to make the decision. I can only pray that Jesus will help you to make the right one. If you do, He will give you the strength and courage that you need to carry it through."

The dark head sagged low on the sturdy little shoulders.

Hope twitched the rolled sheepskin from the foot of the bed and dropped it at Regina's feet. "If you decide to help me," she said, "you will find me in the isolation room. Leave your cap here. Get an aide's white headscarf, and tie it securely around your hair before you report on duty."

When Hope glanced back from the doorway, Regina was already kneeling on the rug at her bedside, head buried in her arms.

An hour went by, while Hope busied herself with caring for the patient. At last, she heard a faint stir in the doorway. She

looked up to see Regina standing beside the screen that parti-
tioned the "clean" from the "contaminated" area of the room.
She noted with joy that a white triangular scarf was tied around
the girl's head, covering her hair like a turban.

"Here I am," Regina announced with false brightness. "Now,
what can I do?"

"Don't do anything right now," Hope warned. "Just stand
there and watch. Don't touch a thing. This is the contaminated
area. Watch how I do Farouk's mouth care, so you will learn
how."

Hope wrapped a gauze square around a swabstick and
dipped it in a medicine glass containing a clear liquid. Using a
second square, she held Farouk's lips apart with the fingers of
her left hand and began a vigorous scrubbing of his teeth, gums,
and the inside surfaces of both cheeks. Farouk offered no resis-
tance. He appeared to be dozing. She shook Farouk's shoulder
gently until his blurry eyes opened and focused with difficulty
on her face. To Regina's amazement, Hope promptly stuck out
her tongue. Slowly, Farouk followed her example. Immediately,
she seized the swollen tongue between the folded gauze in her
fingers, and set to work on the brownish coating. Dropping the
swabstick and gauze into a trash bucket, she picked up a cotton
tipped applicator, which was soaking in an oily solution, and
passed it gently over Farouk's cracked lips.

"Glycerin and mineral oil," she explained. After rinsing her
hands in a small basin of solution, she came to stand before
Regina without allowing their garments to touch.

"Now," she began briskly, "You already know the isolation
technique for tuberculosis. You know that the tubercle bacillus
is easily killed by soap and water, and by exposure to sunlight."
She continued with impressive emphasis: "*None* of these precau-
tions are effective in destroying the typhoid bacillus. It is far
more virulent, and very difficult to destroy. It attacks many
areas of the body, chiefly the entire intestinal tract and kidneys.

All discharges from the patient's body are dangerous sources of infection."

Hope gestured toward Farouk, who was beginning to mutter incoherently again, and to pluck feverishly at the bedclothes.

"As you can see," she continued, "The patient becomes so weak that he is unable to cooperate in any way. So, for the safety of everyone in this hospital, you must learn to maintain the strictest isolation technique. The least slip would render all precautions useless. The technique requires constant vigilance and faithfulness in every detail. You must learn it well, and never forget it for one instant."

Hope waited until she was satisfied by the grave expression on her listener's face that her words had made the desired impression. Then she stepped over to peer at her wristwatch, which was taped to the bedside table.

"Farouk's temperature and medicines are due in about five minutes," she announced. "Whenever his temperature rises above one hundred three degrees, a tepid sponge bath is to be given. We must get you into a gown, so that you can help me. Will you please step back to the other side of the screen, Regina."

The girl obeyed. Hope advanced to stand in the spot that her pupil had just vacated. "The screen is our dividing line," she said. "The side toward the door is clean. The side toward me is contaminated. Nothing on my side must leave here without proper disinfection. You will notice that I am leaving my watch in here for us to use. Please remove yours now, and put it in your uniform pocket. You can leave it in your room later. May I see your hands."

Regina held out both hands for her inspection. "Your nails must be clipped as short as possible," said Hope. "You will find a pair of manicure scissors on that high shelf. When you finish, put on the clean surgical gown lying there on the chair. Then, before you join me, please tap the call bell there on the table. I want to order nourishment for our patient."

Regina tapped the bell, and began trimming her nails. In a moment Elizabeth appeared at the door. She was wearing her glasses, which only partially concealed a pair of very reddened eyes.

"Elizabeth is here, Miss Callaway," Regina reported.

Hope called from behind the screen, "Elizabeth, will you please ask one of the maids to beat up an egg in a glass of milk and bring it right away? Tell them not to come in past the screen."

Elizabeth departed on her errand. Presently, Regina stepped hesitantly past the screen, wearing the isolation gown. The thermometer was in Farouk's mouth. Hope was counting his pulse. She looked up with an encouraging smile.

"Farouk won't bite you," she said with a smile, "Try to get his pulse. It is soft, so don't compress it much, or you will lose it. You will notice that each impulse has a double beat. That is what is known as a 'dicrotic' beat. It is quite typical of typhoid."

She was talking easily to help overcome the tension in the girl. Regina advanced obediently and placed her fingers gingerly on Farouk's wrist. The sick man became dimly conscious of a second presence beside him. He raised his suffering dark eyes to Regina's face. The look in them was very like that of a sick, fretful child seeking the comfort of his mother. The deep compassion that lies in the heart of every woman for all helpless creatures stirred within Regina in response to that mute appeal. She bent over and spoke soothingly to Farouk in Arabic. His eyes brightened. Hope removed the thermometer, and Regina bent down to catch Farouk's faint whisper. She raised glowing eyes to Hope.

"He wants me to pray for him," she reported in an awed voice."

Hope was preparing an injection. She nodded.

"Go ahead, dear."

Regina placed her cool little hand on the man's hot forehead, bowed her head, and began *"Abana"* (Our Father) . . .

Hope watched breathlessly. The miracle was beginning to happen.

At half-past eleven, Hope went to eat an early dinner so that Regina might eat with her classmates at the regular time and then go off for the first rest period of the afternoon. She stopped at the kitchen door and asked Tamam to bring her a plate of food. As she was entering the dining room, Elizabeth came hurrying toward her from the men's ward. The big, ordinarily phlegmatic student was in a state of great agitation. Behind her glasses, she looked as if she had been weeping all morning.

"Oh, Miss Callaway," she burst out, "Can you ever forgive me? If Farouk dies I will never forgive myself. You told me yesterday that I would be responsible for his death."

Hope took the distraught girl by the arms and looked deep into her troubled face.

"My dear," she said, "I don't remember my exact words, but if they gave you the impression that you are responsible for Farouk's present condition, it is I who need to beg your forgiveness. I merely used him as an example of what could happen. If there is any fault, it would be due to his friends' delay in bringing him to us, not to your misreading of the thermometer. I am truly sorry that my words distressed you so much. Please believe me when I tell you that the present situation is not your fault."

Elizabeth wiped her eyes with a sodden handkerchief, and managed a wan smile.

"That's better," said Hope. "Now, go bathe those eyes and get a dry handkerchief, and get back on duty."

Elizabeth departed. Hope bowed her head over the plate of food. While she ate, she mused for perhaps the thousandth time, on how carefully Westerners must weigh their words lest they unwittingly offend.

By the end of the day a routine was established whereby the two nurses spelled each other in the matter of mouth care, medications, and feeding of the patient. Once during the afternoon Farouk's temperature rose above one hundred four, necessitating a cooling sponge bath. This was given mostly by Hope. Although Regina trembled a little when her hands came in contact with the man's bare flesh, she managed to hold him well over on his side while Hope applied the cooling water and rubbed his back. His abdomen was now quite distended and his thirst and restlessness increased. He swallowed with such difficulty that he could only manage a small sip at a time. His dry, hacking cough added to his general discomfort.

The chief visited once in midmorning and twice in the afternoon, but left no new orders. Since Farouk was already receiving the strongest medications that could be given him, he urged that efforts be redoubled to increase the intake of liquids.

It was in this field that Regina proved her nursing worth. She hung over Farouk, crooning, coaxing, wheedling spoonful after spoonful past the cracked lips.

Regina was given an hour's rest following the dinner at noon. Hope managed to snatch a brief half-hour in midafternoon. She went to an early supper, so that Regina could again eat with her classmates at the regular time.

She returned to the sickroom in time to witness a touching tableau. Farouk's hands were clasped on his chest. Regina's right hand was upon them. Her left hand rested on his forehead. She was murmuring softly close to his ear. Although his eyes were closed, he appeared to be listening intently. Occasionally his lips shaped a word. The lines of suffering on his face seemed less deeply etched. His expression was almost peaceful.

Regina glanced at Hope, then back to Farouk. She continued her soft murmuring. Hope realized that she was reciting Bible passages. She did not attempt to interrupt her. At the conclusion Farouk's lips soundlessly shaped the word, "Ameen," then added, "Shukran." His eyes opened to gaze wonderingly into the tender ones above him. Although bright with fever, there was complete understanding in their depths. Then the lids closed wearily, and the sick man slept.

Regina came eagerly toward Hope.

"Farouk loves to hear me talk about Jesus," she exclaimed. "He seems to know the twenty-third Psalm. His lips formed some of the words with me. Do you suppose that he is a Christian?"

Hope smiled at her eagerness.

"Well, you may be right, dear, but he does have a Moslem name," Hope said. You must be careful not to tire him by asking him any questions."

The supper gong sounded. Hope gave the girl a gentle push toward the screen, and ordered, "Now take off your gown and get scrubbed. Then go enjoy your supper. Get a good sleep and come join me in the morning. You have done a good day's work."

That evening the chief came to inform Hope that he had finally received word from government officials granting permission to keep Farouk at the hospital for treatment. The die was now cast. However long the duration might turn out to be, the three members of the nursing team were committed to the task they had undertaken. Whether it would be for better or for worse remained to be seen.

A horrible stench greeted Hope's nostrils as she entered the door of Farouk's room the next morning. She found Rolf in the bathroom adding some soiled towels to a pile of linens in a round, shallow washtub standing in a corner. They had not been soaked in disinfectant as yet.

Rolf faced her apologetically.

"I didn't know what to do with them, Miss Callaway," he explained. "It would take rivers of water and buckets of disinfectant to rinse and disinfect these enough for boiling in the washroom. Farouk had two large involuntary spells of diarrhea in the night. I thought the only thing to do was to burn these linens. I have a packing box in my room. I can put them in it, soak them with kerosene, and burn them out back."

They looked at each other ruefully, each thinking how much worse the situation was apt to become. Hope blamed herself for not having stopped to consider the hospital's inadequate water supply and the primitive facilities they actually had here for the isolation of typhoid cases.

"I am afraid you are right, Rolf," she said. "This batch will have to be burned. But we can't afford to keep on burning up good linens. I will have to think of something else right away."

Regina was standing in the doorway holding her nose, listening.

Rolf stripped off his gown, scrubbed his hands, and departed. He soon returned with a large packing box. Hope placed the bundle of soiled linens in it. He carried it off to be burned. The two nurses then set about scrubbing the washtub and refuse buckets to remove the odor.

Rolf had bathed Farouk thoroughly at six o'clock. As soon as temperature taking, mouth care, and medications were out of the way, Hope left Regina feeding Farouk while she went in search of some answers to the linen problem.

First she went to the supply cupboard and obtained a large rubber sheet. Next, she stopped at the sewing room. Rose helped her gather some old worn sheets and some cotton for pads. Leaving these in the hall she headed for the Baxter home. Here she informed Esther about her problems. Esther gathered up all of Stevie's old diapers.

"These are far too worn to serve another baby," she commented. "You are most welcome to them."

Hope thanked her and hastened back to the hospital with a growing sense of guilt at having left Regina alone so long.

She stopped by the sewing room and dumped the diapers into a carton along with the pads and sheets. Then she dragged the box down the hall toward the isolation room. As she neared the open door, she smelled the stench emanating from it, and heard from within the sound of loud sobbing. Hope left the carton in the doorway, seized her isolation gown, and pushed past the screen, tying the strings as she went.

Regina was backed up against the screen, wringing her hands and sobbing hysterically. Fearing the worst, Hope sped past her to the bedside.

Farouk had slipped far down on his pillows. Hope checked his pulse. It was fair. She slipped her arm beneath the little man's frail shoulders and lifted him to an easier position. Then she turned to Regina.

"Don't be afraid, Regina, Farouk isn't dead. He just had an accident, that's all. He can't help himself. He is like a baby now. We must clean him up."

Regina shrank back in horror.

"We?" she echoed faintly. "You mean we have to bathe him — down there?"

"Of course, Regina," she answered as she removed the unsoiled top covers. "When Nabeel soils himself, he has to be cleaned up, doesn't he? Same thing with Farouk. Try to think of him as just a helpless baby, like Nabeel, and it won't be so hard."

Hope moved past the girl to drag the carton of makeshift linens into the contaminated area. She paused and tapped the call bell with a fold of one of the clean diapers. When Elizabeth answered, she asked her to bring several large safety pins. Then, selecting pads and sheets from the carton, she carried them to Farouk's bedside. Regina had not moved.

"Will you please bring a basin of water from the bathroom now, Regina?" Hope asked pleasantly.

The girl began to wring her hands.

"Oh, Miss Callaway," she whispered desperately, "Can't we call Rolf?"

"No, Regina!" Hope's voice was as sharp as the crack of a whip. "Rolf is carrying far more than his share of duty now. You cannot ask him to do your work, too!"

Hope realized she was only adding to the girl's fright by shouting at her. She forced herself to speak quietly, praying for just the right words.

"Regina, the first duty of a nurse is to make her patient comfortable, no matter how distasteful the task may be. She may want to turn away and run, but she must steel herself to take that first step forward and do what she can. Every nurse who ever became a nurse, has had to learn to take that first forward step at some time or other. If you turn your back now, you will never be able to stop running."

Regina's eyes were fixed on Hope's face. The fear in them was receding, but her feet appeared to be rooted to the floor. Hope held out her hand. All the compelling love of her loving heart was in her eyes and voice.

"Come, Regina," she urged softly.

Slowly, as if drawn by an irresistible magnet, Regina's right foot moved forward. Then the left. On the third step, she was moving purposefully, resolutely, toward the bathroom. She filled the basin and brought it with steady hands to the bedside, and began her duties as a complete nurse.

When Regina returned from her rest period that afternoon, she carried several squares of soft sheepskin.

Hope cried out when she saw them, "Why, Regina you have cut up your lovely rug!"

"Farouk needs it more than I do," replied the girl sturdily. She turned the covers down and began unpinning Farouk's diaper, explaining, "You showed me the pressure spots on his buttocks this morning. You said they would become open sores if we didn't take good care of them."

She slipped one of the sheepskin squares under Farouk's buttocks, next to his skin, and began repinning the diaper. "The

lanolin oil in the sheepskin is very soothing for pressure sores,"
she explained. "We can burn these up when they get soiled."

Hope stared at the girl in amazement. "Some of the doctors in
America are beginning to prescribe sheepskin pads for bedrid-
den patients," she said. "But wherever did you hear of it?"

Regina assumed an air of superiority.

"Oh, we Arabs have known about it for centuries," she
replied. "All good ideas don't originate in America, you know.
We have a few of our own."

"Indeed, you do," Hope agreed heartily.

Toward noon the next day word came from the office that
Farouk's wife and baby were there. She wanted to see her hus-
band. Hope sent Regina to escort her to the sickroom, then she
moved the screen aside, so that the woman could view her hus-
band from the doorway. He was now beginning to hemorrhage,
and was failing fast. His wife held the child high for his father to
see. Farouk was in a deep stupor. Hope could not rouse him to
look at the boy.

Regina took the baby from the arms of the weeping woman
and led her away. The girl was gone for some time. When she
rejoined Hope, she was brimming with excitement.

"His wife's name is Suweylah, Miss Callaway," she reported.
"Just the same as my little friend who disappeared one day. She
told me that Farouk was born in Abyssinia, only his name was-
n't Farouk then. He went to a Christian mission school there,
and he never forgot about Jesus. He loved to tell Suweylah
about Him. His real mother and father both died when he was
about eleven.

"A Moslem family took him, and gave him their name. When
he was only fifteen, some wicked leaders got the family to go on
a holy pilgrimage to Mecca. But they were slave traders. As
soon as they got the pilgrim group across the Red Sea, they
were seized to be sold as slaves. Farouk was a good swimmer
and managed to get away to the shore. The slave trader thought

he drowned. Farouk said he knew it was Jesus who saved him."

Regina paused for breath, then continued, "He kept along the coast, heading north, and finally got to Aqaba. A few years later, he came to Hebron, and found work as a stonecutter. Everyone thought he was Moslem. He saw Suweylah one day. He began to bargain with her father for her. Because she was so pretty, her father asked a high price. Farouk worked hard and finally saved enough money to marry her. She says they have been very happy. When Farouk dies, she is afraid that her father will sell her again. Her new husband will not want the boy. He will beat and starve him to death if she keeps him. She begged me to take him, but I told her I couldn't."

"I think we could get the Mennonites to keep him in Hebron for her. Then she could see him sometimes," said Hope.

Regina wiped away a sympathetic tear, and smiled.

"Then I won't worry about them anymore," she said. "But Miss Hope, you see I was right. Farouk really is a Christian. God must have sent him here so we could help him get back to Jesus."

Hope smiled at the eagerness in her assistant's face.

"I think so, too, Regina," she said. "I also think that God had another purpose. He knew we needed Farouk."

The girl nodded emphatically.

"I know that I needed him," she said. "Oh, isn't God wonderful, Miss Hope?"

Farouk died about two o'clock the following day. All medications except morphine had been discontinued several hours earlier. Dr. Dawson himself administered the morphine at ten o'clock. He visited again at one, glanced briefly at the chart, and checked Farouk's fluttering pulse. The man was in a deep coma.

"No need to give him another shot, unless he seems to be in pain," the chief said quietly. "Morphine often stimulates the heartbeat for a time, and unnecessarily prolongs the normal course of death. This man's life has run its course."

He stood for a time at the foot of the bed, sadly regarding the pitifully shrunken black man from Abyssinia, who had wandered so far from his homeland to die.

"Only thirty-three," he mused. "Just the age of Jesus when He died. And I am nearly seventy." He sighed heavily, and turned away.

Rolf had refused to rest, and stayed through the morning to help. Hope would never cease to be humbly grateful for the selfless devotion of this servant. Never again would she consider him plain, or odd looking, for she had seen the beautiful soul within the insignificant body.

Hope sent Regina out to dinner at noon, but she did not leave the sick room for food herself. She stood by the screen and drank the tea that Murshdeeyah had brought.

The end came surprisingly quick. Regina was wiping the clammy sweat from Farouk's brow when his eyes suddenly opened. He stared fixedly upward. His eyes began to glow. His lips parted as if about to speak. An instant later, the glow vanished, to be replaced by the blank stare of death.

Regina looked up eagerly at Hope, whose fingers were on the lifeless pulse.

"Did you see the light in his eyes, Miss Hope?" she whispered in awe. "I believe he saw Jesus."

Hope took the washcloth gently from Regina's hand and laid it across the sightless eyes.

"Farouk has gone to be with Him, Regina," she said quietly.

Tears started running down the girl's cheeks. Hope put her arm around her and led her away from the bed. Her own eyes were moist as she said, "Don't cry, Regina. Farouk's suffering is over." She was untying the strings of the girl's gown. "Now," she said, "I want you to scrub your hands and go upstairs. Take a good bath, change all your clothes, and catch the bus for

Bethlehem. You are to spend three full days at home. You have earned a good rest. What is more, my dear, you have earned your crown."

Regina looked up from her scrubbing with a radiant face. "Oh, thank you, Miss Hope," she said. "I will really try to be worthy of it from now on. "Do you know what I am going to do when I see my father?" she asked. "I am going to walk straight up to him and give him a big hug and kiss. Do you think he will like it?"

"Like it?" Hope said. "Why, he'll love it!"

TWENTY-ONE

HOPE AND ROLF STOOD surveying the small pile of linens soaking in the washtub. The room behind them was stripped.

"Thanks to the pads and diapers, and to your heroic efforts, Rolf, we have been able to save most of the hospital linens," Hope remarked with satisfaction.

"I used the last diaper and the last piece of Regina's wool this morning," he replied. "From what you told me, that sheepskin was her dearest possession. Yet she gave it up so gladly and unselfishly. She is a lovely girl, Miss Callaway."

He added, "You will be on duty tomorrow, yes? You need rest. Now you must let me finish. I will get everything scrubbed, and fumigate the room. Then I will take your advice and go to Christ Church Hostel in Jerusalem for two days' rest. This room can be left in fumigation until I return."

"Thank you Rolf, I will go," said Hope, stripping off her gown and adding it to the pile. "May you have a good rest."

Eileen came from the men's ward and caught up with her colleague at the foot of the stairs, inquiring, "Going up to your room?"

Hope nodded, feeling too weary to speak. They mounted the stairs in silence. At the top, Eileen blurted out, "Hope, I know that you are completely worn out. But there is something I must tell you right now. I'm afraid it can't wait."

"In that case," said Hope, "come into my room where we can sit down and talk."

She opened the door and ushered Eileen in. The latter perched uneasily on the edge of a chair. Hope dropped into her big chair, kicked off her shoes, and smiled at her assistant's distressed expression.

"Don't look so serious," she teased. "Are you about to confess to some terrible crime you have committed during my absence?"

Eileen did not smile at the facetious remark. Instead, she came to the point without preamble.

"Hope, Christine has been sulking in her bed for two days."

"Sulking?" Hope echoed in astonishment.

"Yes, sulking," Eileen repeated. "I assure you, I use the word advisedly." She held up her hand imperatively as Hope was about to speak, and continued swiftly, "Please try not to interrupt me until I have finished. I had hoped the matter would be settled before you were released from your case. Since it isn't, I have to tell you now."

Hope forced herself to remain silent. Eileen continued.

"Christine left the children alone, completely unattended in the ward at noon two days ago. She just stalked off to her room and went to bed without notifying anybody. No one discovered her absence until Dr. Dawson and I made rounds at three o'clock. We found the two little girls chasing each other around the room. Lateefa was trying to sleep. Nabeel had kicked off his blankets. He was sopping wet. He was happily sucking a spoon. He was a sticky mess, with food smeared all over him and on the bars of his crib.

"I went to find Aminah in the women's ward. She recalled that Murshdeeyah mentioned when she came to collect the noon trays, that Christine was not in the children's ward. They both thought she had stepped out for just a minute. Aminah was busy at the time getting a new woman patient settled. She never thought to check on Christine later. She came right away to take care of Nabeel. I went looking for Christine."

Eileen moistened her lips, then went on: "I found her in bed pretending to be asleep. When I asked her what was the matter, she said she felt sick. I called Dr. Dawson to check her. He could find nothing wrong. Her temperature and pulse were normal. He ordered lab tests. They were completed yesterday morning. They revealed nothing. She kept insisting that she felt sick and refused to get up. Murshdeeyah brought her breakfast and supper and said that she ate well both times. I had Murshdeeyah put on a hospital gown to help with the children's beds. Aminah gave their medicines.

"Just before noon, Murshdeeyah came and told me that Zoohrah and Salamy had explained, with giggles, what had happened at noon the day before. The two little girls finished eating and came over to watch Christine feed Nabeel. She was holding him on her lap. Nabeel reached up, caught hold of Christine's collar, and ripped the buttons of her uniform open clear down to her waist. Zoohrah and Salamy began to giggle. Christine dumped Nabeel in his bed, pulled her gown together, and ran out of the room. When she didn't come right back, Nabeel started howling for food. The two little girls reached through the bars of his crib and took turns holding him up while they fed him. That's why the bars are so sticky. They finally gave him the spoon to suck on. They thought it was very funny."

Hope could keep silent no longer. "Oh, Eileen, how awful for Christine!" she cried. "How cruel of the children to laugh at her scars. They should apologize to her. I hope you made them do it."

"I did not. I don't intend to," retorted Eileen crisply. "I am sure they didn't even notice her scars. They were giggling at

Nabeel. They thought he was very funny. There is certainly no reason to expect them to apologize. I had already begun to suspect that Christine was sulking over something and was only shamming illness. Now that I was sure of it, I told Murshdeeyah that neither she, nor anyone else, was to bring Christine anymore food. Then I went and told Christine what I had learned. I pointed out to her that her conduct in leaving the ward without notifying anyone was absolutely inexcusable, that there was no room in the nursing profession for personal feelings to take precedence over the welfare of patients. One such breach of ethics in a young, unseasoned novice might be overlooked, but she was old enough, and experienced enough, to know that she had no right to indulge personal hurts at the expense of those around her. I told her it was about time that she got over being so sensitive about her scars."

Hope gasped and pressed her hand over her mouth.

"She just pulled the sheet over her face and didn't answer," Eileen continued. "Then I told her she would get no more food brought to her room. If she wanted to eat, she would have to dress and come down to the dining room. I also said that I expected her to be at her post in the children's ward this morning."

"Was she?" Hope inquired anxiously.

"No," said Eileen shortly. "As far as I know, she has had nothing to eat since yesterday morning, unless Hanni sneaked her something. She is softhearted and devoted to Christine."

There was a conciliatory note in Eileen's voice, as she went on hesitantly, "Believe me, Hope, I didn't ask for this job. You know it was thrust upon me. You were not to be bothered with any hospital problems while you had Farouk on your hands. There was no telling how long you would be tied up on the case. Since I had started this thing, it was up to me to finish it."

She swallowed hard, then continued more rapidly, "When Christine didn't appear this morning, I went to Dr. Dawson with the problem. He approved of my plan and gave me full authority to carry it out. At noon, when I learned that Farouk was still alive, and might linger on for several hours, I went to Christine's room and delivered an ultimatum: Either she would report on duty promptly in the children's ward tomorrow morning, or she would be dismissed from the hospital."

Hope sprang to her feet, gazing at Eileen in horror.

"Oh, Eileen, you can't do that!" she exclaimed. "Poor Christine has suffered so much. I will go talk to her myself. I'm sure she will listen to me."

She was halfway to the door before she realized that her tall young assistant had her back braced against it and was holding the knob in a firm grip. Hope stared at her in bewilderment.

"Don't you understand, Eileen?" she asked. "I must talk to Christine at once." She lifted her chin imperiously as she spoke.

Eileen flinched at the gesture, but stood her ground.

"It is you who do not understand, Hope," she said firmly. "This is my business. I have Dr. Dawson's full authority to finish it myself. I beg you not to interfere. I shall be only too happy to step down when this is settled, and surrender all further authority to you."

"I demand that you step aside and let me pass," said Hope icily.

A spasm of pain swept across Eileen's face. She drew a deep breath, then said sadly, "I was hoping you would understand my position, and that it would not come to this. Now, I must give you an ultimatum. If you interfere and go to Christine, I shall be forced to commit an unforgiveable breach of nursing ethics myself. I shall leave this hospital without notice tomorrow, and depart from this country as soon as possible."

Hope stared at her. She knew by the look on Eileen's face, that she meant every word she had said. Hope's shoulders sagged.

"Eileen, please," whispered Hope. "I love her so. Don't force her to leave."

"She is free to make her own choice," Eileen replied grimly. Her voice softened, as she added huskily, "You may not believe me, Hope, but I love her, too."

With that, she turned and swung the door wide open. Hope took one faltering step forward. Eileen stood tensely erect. The knuckles on her hand whitened as her grip tightened on the doorknob.

Hope buried her face in her hands, turned, and flung herself on the bed. There was a long moment of complete silence. Then the door closed softly behind her.

Hope lay there on the bed for some time, without moving. Her mind was in a turmoil. Had she gotten so puffed up with her own importance, that she really could not believe anyone else could take her place? This thought was not to be overlooked, considering Eileen's strong feelings about Christine's case. Hope wondered if she was getting too involved with the girls and not seeing the overall picture.

Some time later, she became aware of footsteps in the adjoining bathroom. There was the sound of a fire being built in the geezer.

These economical contraptions, with the queer name, are still used extensively in parts of Europe, the Near East, and in Africa. They are round iron stoves with tall metal tanks fitted to their tops. The tanks are piped to showers or bathtubs. A minimum amount of fuel is required for a hot bath. The tank heats rapidly. At the same time, the fire serves to warm chilly bathrooms. To conserve plumbing, as well as expensive firewood and oil cakes, only one geezer and shower had been installed for the use of the missionary staff. Misprint and Sister Marta shared a smaller bathroom between their rooms across the hall. It only had a washbasin and toilet. This larger bath, between Hope's and Eileen's rooms, could also be entered by a door from the hall when their associates desired a shower. Hope wondered who was preparing a hot one now.

The question was settled when a tap came at her door. Murshdeeyah called, "Missy Hope, I fix you nice hot bath."

"Thank you, Murshdeeyah," Hope called back. She struggled wearily to her feet. She hadn't realized just how tired she was. She discarded her soiled clothing and wrapped a robe about her. Then she laid out clean clothes on her bed. She eyed these with distaste. She felt utterly incapable of facing anyone in the dining room tonight, least of all Eileen. On impulse, she swept the garments into a drawer, and got out a nightgown instead. With the feminine logic that seeks comfort in unwonted luxuries, she shook out a pale blue nylon gown. It was a Christmas gift, as yet unworn. With this over her arm, she headed for the hot shower.

It was dusk when she roused from a fitful slumber. The bedside clock told her that the supper hour was over. Although she was not hungry, she wondered idly why no one had brought her a tray. A fleeting thought occurred that Eileen might be subjecting her to the same discipline that was being meted out to Christine. She dismissed the idea immediately, knowing that Eileen was incapable of such pettiness. She wisely concluded that Eileen knew she needed rest more than food. She thought about reading, but she was too drowsy to focus her thoughts. Soon, she switched off the light, and slept soundly until morning, never dreaming that beyond the walls of the adjoining bathroom, her young assistant was spending a sleepless night.

At the first sound of the rising bell, Hope was on her feet. She dressed rapidly and made her bed. When the last breakfast bell sounded, she marched resolutely down the hall. On the threshold of the dining room her eyes were drawn irresistibly to the student's table. A fierce pang of joy seized her chest when she saw Christine, clad in full uniform, sitting calmly in her place at the head of the table.

Hope seated herself at the head of the staff table. Soon, Eileen appeared. Her hands reached out to the doorposts for support, then dropped, as she, too, caught sight of Christine. Unable to bear the expression of naked relief that swept across her assistant's face, Hope looked down at her plate. Eileen quietly took her accustomed place at Hope's right. Under cover of the tablecloth, Hope groped for her hand, whispering, "Eileen, I was wrong. Please forgive me."

Eileen's pale face flushed with sudden joy. She covered Hope's small hand with her own, and whispered back, "There's nothing to forgive."

She stood up suddenly, and raised her voice, "Girls, I move we sing the doxology in thanksgiving for the return of our superintendent."

Hope felt an immense surge of exultation, as she listened to the singing, and to the hearty applause that followed in her honor. She thought she was rejoicing in Eileen's success with Christine. She was quite mistaken. Her happiness actually stemmed from appreciation of the ovation to herself. It was like soothing balm poured on her sorely wounded pride.

TWENTY-TWO

It was three days later when Hope looked out an upstairs window to see Murshdeeyah draping a freshly washed sheepskin over the clothesline to dry. Consumed by curiosity, Hope went out to ask her where it had come from. The black girl flashed Hope a knowing grin, then sobered, and replied gravely, "Missy Hope, I promise I no tell. *Abbadab* (never) by Allah!" Her black eyes rolled heavenward as she spoke. "You think I should tell you, maybe?"

"No, of course not, Murshdeeyah, not if you promised," Hope replied hastly. "But I will make a guess that you are washing it for someone else, aren't you?"

The girl nodded, grinning widely.

The next day Rolf appeared at her office door carrying a rolled up raincoat. He had returned the day before from a forty-eight hour rest in Jerusalem. Already he had put the isolation room back to its former state of readiness.

Seeing that Hope was alone, he unrolled the coat, revealing the sheepskin that she had seen the day before. He shyly asked

Hope to give it to Regina for him in the place of the one she had sacrificed for Farouk.

Hope hesitated, then informed him as tactfully as possible that native Arab custom would never permit Regina to accept it from him. In his own country, such a gift from a gentleman to a lady would be permissible, but not in this land. Rolf was crestfallen. He smoothed the beautiful skin lying across his knees, and said mournfully, "It is so lovely, and I have no use for it myself."

Suddenly his face brightened as a new idea occurred to him.

"Miss Callaway," he said, "could you not take it as a gift from me? Then, if you do not wish to use it, you could give it to Regina as a gift from you. She could accept it from a lady with no embarrassment, could she not? Of course, if you wish it for yourself, you are very welcome to it."

He placed the rug on Hope's lap as he spoke, and looked at her pleadingly. She hadn't the heart to refuse.

"I already have a full-sized Oriental rug, Rolf, so I have no need of this," she said. "It doesn't seem quite right for me to accept Regina's thanks for your gift. But it would make Regina very happy. So I will accept the rug as a gift to me. Then I can give it to Regina in all honesty as something which is mine to give."

Rolf thanked her profusely, and left with a beaming face. Hope sensed that his feeling for Regina went far deeper than mere friendship. However, he impressed her as a humble and sensible man who would not entertain any romantic ideas regarding a closer relationship between himself and a girl who was young enough to be his daughter. She was confident that he would be satisfied to worship his goddess from afar.

Hope took the precaution of swearing Murshdeeyah to absolute secrecy by Allah before presenting the rug to Regina. She was greatly relieved when the latter asked no questions, merely hugged the sheepskin with delight, and exclaimed,

"Oh, how good God is to me! First, He set me free from my silly fears. Then He let you know how much I missed my prayer rug, and laid it on your heart to give me a far lovelier one."

When Hope repeated Regina's words verbatim to Rolf, his nearsighted eyes sparkled. He exclaimed joyfully, "Ach! God is so good! She is so young, and already yet she has such a love for the Father in her heart!"

His words dispelled the last vestige of doubt in Hope's heart regarding the propriety of their mild deception.

On the last day of October, before starting her morning routine, Hope stopped by Dr. Dawson's office to consult him on a minor problem. She was surprised to find him already deep in monthly accounts with Khaleed. The latter did not ordinarily arrive until an hour later.

Apologizing for the interruption, she stated her errand briefly. Equally brief instructions were given her by the chief. She evinced no curiosity regarding the accountant's early presence, but Khaleed evidently thought an explanation was required. He proceeded to offer a lengthy one. He had private business to transact in Jerusalem before noon and would be unable to return to Beth Hanani again today. Since he must cash Dr. Dawson's check to meet the next day's payroll, he had come early to go over the accounts. Usually, Khaleed was far from garrulous.

The next morning, she again needed Dr. Dawson's advice on a trifling matter. She arrived at the open door of his office in time to see a nattily dressed young Arab leaning over the doctor's desk, talking and gesticulating emphatically. She caught the words, "I swear by Allah. I am telling you the truth. I saw him board the four o'clock plane for Beirut yesterday. He had two big *shantas* (suitcases). His cousin, Ahmed Khalil, was there to see him off. When the plane left, I asked Ahmed where his cousin was going, and he said, 'To Brazil.' "

Hope gave a start of alarm. Her first thought was for the chief. She pushed past the visitor. The doctor was slumped down in his chair. His face was ashen, and he gasped for breath.

She turned furiously upon the intruder.

"Get out!" she commanded furiously. "At once! Can't you see what you have done? He has a bad heart!"

The cocky smile left the young Arab's face. He backed hastily toward the door, mumbling. "I didn't mean — I thought he knew. I am an expert bookkeeper. I only came to ask him for Khaleed's job."

Hope didn't even hear him. She had rushed to the aid of the stricken doctor. He did not move, only whispered haltingly, "They are . . . right . . . the desk drawer."

She found the bottle of nitroglycerine tablets and placed one under his tongue. Then she sat down beside him and put her fingers on his pulse. He leaned back and closed his eyes. Slowly, the breathing eased. Color returned to his face. After a moment he said slowly, "I'm all right now. Don't tell Margaret."

He pulled himself together with an effort and sat erect. "You heard what he said?" he asked. Hope nodded. "I am afraid it is true," he continued heavily. "That fellow came out early to ask for Khaleed's job. He thought Khaleed had left with my knowledge and blessing." He smiled wryly. "I am not a good actor. I couldn't conceal my surprise. The whole countryside will soon know that I have been a trusting fool."

There was no bitterness in his voice, only a deep sadness. He continued, "Khaleed left on the four o'clock plane yesterday. Had we known by evening, he might have been detained by Beirut authorities at the airport. All transoceanic flights leave there around six o'clock each morning. By now he is well beyond our reach. That check I gave him yesterday was for two hundred forty-five pounds. He padded the accounts as much as he could. We have less than fifty pounds left in the bank. Barely enough to cover household salaries for the month.

Nothing for the workers on the new building, or for current bills."

He bowed his head in his hands, resting both elbows on the desk. Hope remained silent, realizing that he was praying. After a moment he raised his head and looked directly at her. His smile, though wistful, was indescribably sweet.

"Miss Hope," he said, "I prefer to believe that God is able. He has never failed us yet. Please help me over to the couch, then gather the clan here."

Soon the entire mission staff were gathered in the chief's office, all except for Rolf and Sister Marta, who were sleeping. The chief sat on the edge of the couch. Margaret was beside him holding his hand. They had heard the news of Khaleed's defection. All listened quietly as the chief outlined their immediate financial needs. Then, with equal quietness, they knelt and joined in the doctor's simple plea to God.

When they rose from their knees, Misprint asked, "Just what is our need in American dollars, Dr. Dawson? I don't quite understand the pounds and piasters system."

"Roughly, about six hundred dollars," the doctor replied.

"I have a thousand dollars in savings at home," Misprint said half apologetically. "Sort of an emergency 'nest egg.' I could cable for it today. How long would it take to get here?"

"Three days, maybe. A week at the most," he replied. "I am not going to refuse your generous offer, Misprint. I believe God has laid it on your heart to make it. However, we will accept it only as a loan. Six hundred is enough to tide us over. We will repay it as soon as possible."

"I'm not worried in the least," she replied serenely.

The chief smiled at her warmly, then rose, saying, "Well, since you have decided to be our fairy godmother, Misprint, I suggest that you and Margaret get ready for a trip to Jerusalem with me. I believe the bank manager will be willing to advance me a loan on a promissory note until your money arrives. Dr. Baxter, will you please meet with the employees and workers at noon, and tell them that all salaries will be paid at noon tomorrow?"

Shortly before noon, Hope received word that Hanni had fainted in the downstairs hallway. By the time she arrived, Hanni was sitting at the nurse's desk by the men's ward. Eileen was holding a sponge of aromatic spirits of ammonia under her nose. The two directors helped her to the room that she shared with Christine. They ordered her to rest for the remainder of the day.

The Dawsons returned from Jerusalem with Misprint in time for afternoon tea. Hope was glad to note that Margaret was at the wheel of the car. The two women came straight to the tearoom, explaining that the doctor had stopped at the office safe to deposit the cash for the payroll. When he appeared, he looked none the worse for the shock he had undergone that morning. But he was less talkative than usual. He let Margaret give an account of the day's happenings.

First, they had stopped at Ahmed Khalil's home in Bethlehem. Ahmed freely admitted he had known Khaleed's plans for some time. He said his cousin made the required deposit on his airplane ticket two weeks ago, and paid the balance in cash when he picked up his ticket yesterday. He said that he thought Dr. Dawson was fully aware of Khaleed's plans all along, and that he had been too busy at the hospital yesterday to see Khaleed off at the airport. The fact that Ahmed was palpably lying was of no help.

Mr. Accad, the bank manager in Jerusalem, was genuinely distressed to learn of his countryman's dishonorable conduct. He hastened to offer a far larger loan than was needed, for as long a period as necessary. It was figured at a low rate of interest. The note was drawn up for a month, with the privilege of extension.

Misprint's cable for funds went off at noon. The three had lunch in the Arab National Hotel. On the way home, they stopped in at the Dysons. The Reverend Jimmy was an expert accountant. He would be out in the morning to prepare the payroll and to audit the books. He would bring a young Christian woman, Marika Johar, with him. She had been looking vainly for office work since taking bookkeeping in secondary school. She would be glad of the job at the hospital.

Hope was relieved when Margaret Dawson took her husband home for a rest right after tea.

Later, making ward rounds after supper, Aminah told her that Hanni had come to the door of the women's ward requesting an aspirin for a headache. Aminah was busy with the new patient. She told Hanni to help herself from the cupboard. "Our new patient, Jameela, is coughing a lot," Aminah continued. "Dr. Dawson ordered Elixir Terpin Hydrate. I can't find the bottle. We use it so seldom that it may have been thrown away."

Hope brought Aminah a fresh bottle of the cough syrup from the pharmacy, feeling slightly puzzled. It was not prescribed very often, and yet she thought she had issued a fresh bottle to the women's ward only a few days before. Perhaps she was mistaken.

For some reason, Hope could not get to sleep that night. She read her Bible long after the generator had shut down. She used the coleman lamp then, and at one-thirty she rose and put the teakettle on to boil. After an aspirin and a hot cup of tea, she was just about to turn out the lamp when her keen ears caught the sound of running bare feet. She quickly donned her slippers and robe, when an urgent knock came at her door. The next instant it burst open.

Christine stood on the threshold in her nightgown.

"Miss Hope," she gasped, "come quick! I think Hanni has swallowed poison!"

Hope sped down the hall after Christine, pausing only to fling open Eileen's door and call out her name as she dashed by. She could hear the sound of heavy breathing before she arrived at the room shared by Hanni and Christine. Christine had a candle lit. By its flickering glow, Hope saw Hanni lying flat on her back in a deep, snoring stupor. The girl's face was flushed. ~~The girl's face was flushed~~. There were brownish stains on her lips, and down the front of her gown.

"Get the lamp from the stair landing, Christine," Hope whispered. "Try not to waken the other girls." As she spoke her fingers sought Hanni's pulse. Although weak and very slow, it was thumping steadily.

Christine was back in a moment with the lamp. She was followed by Eileen, yawning and tying her robe about her.

"I heard you call, but I didn't know where you were until I saw Christine," Eileen said. "What's up?"

"Poison!" whispered Hope. She had her arms under Hanni's shoulders. "Help me get her into our bathroom," she panted. "We have to make her vomit. Christine, see if you can find the drug bottle she used."

Eileen's strong arms helped to lift Hanni's limp figure. Between them the two nurses half carried, half dragged the unconscious girl down the hall and into their bathroom. There Eileen held her upright on a chair, slapping her face and trying to rouse her. Hope fetched her coleman lamp and the teakettle.

"Thank heavens the teakettle is still warm," she said. She poured all the water into the washbasin. Dropping in a cake of toilet soap she swished the water into suds.

Eileen was sniffing the brown stains on Hanni's face and gown. "Smells like Elixir Terpin Hydrate," she stated.

"That's just what it is," said Christine's voice behind them. She held up a sixteen ounce brown bottle. Hope noted that the girl was now wearing a high necked bathrobe and slippers.

"It's empty," said Christine. "It was in the wastebasket."

Hope scooped up a large glassful of the warm soapy water. "Stand behind the chair and hold her arms so she can't struggle, Christine," she ordered. "Eileen, you hold her head back and pinch her nostrils together to make her open her mouth and swallow. Get ready to duck her head down over the toilet when she starts vomiting."

She began pouring the soapsuds down Hanni's throat. The girl choked, swallowed, and struggled violently, bringing up a large quantity of brownish liquid. Again and again Hope poured the soapsuds down her throat, while she fought wildly, moaning, "Let me die!" between regurgitations. At last all the soapy water was gone. The regurgitations came back with no trace of brownish color. Hope poured a final glass of clear water down Hanni's throat, and let her rest. Almost at once the girl lapsed into snoring slumber. Hope looked doubtfully at Eileen. Both checked Hanni's pulse, while Christine held her upright. The pulse was slightly stronger, but they could not rouse the girl.

"There was a lot of codeine in the bottle," Eileen observed.

"I'm afraid we shall have to call Dr. Dawson," Hope decided regretfully. She had told no one of his heart attack, and felt very concerned at having to disturb his rest. But he must be called.

"I'll get him," said Eileen. She was already halfway to the door.

Hope and Christine failed in further attempts to waken Hanni. They managed to get her stretched out on Hope's bed. She lay there snoring steadily as before. Her roommate stood eyeing her speculatively. Hope began checking Hanni's pupils. The reaction to light was very sluggish. Suddenly, Christine uttered a sharp exclamation in Arabic. She leaped upon Hanni and began beating her about the face and shaking her violently. Hope had to drag the girl forcibly away from the bed. Christine turned on her wildly.

"Don't you see, Miss Hope," she cried fiercely, "she is pregnant! She has disgraced us all! We are ruined!"

With sinking heart, Hope realized that Christine had hit upon the truth. She recalled the night of the picnic. She had not imagined that shadow slipping down the steps of the bus in the moonlight. She groaned and cast a swift glance at the tightly closed hall door.

"Hush, Christine," she implored. "The other girls will hear."

"They will all hear soon enough," retorted the girl bitterly. "Then our training days will be over, finished!" She collapsed in a chair and began to weep.

The door opened. Dr. Dawson entered, followed by Eileen. He was clad in bathrobe and slippers, with trousers pulled on over his pajamas. He sat down beside Hanni, counted her pulse, and lifted her eyelids.

"I don't think she is in any immediate danger now," he said reassuringly. "She got a good jolt of codeine in that bottle of cough syrup. She wasn't used to it. Luckily you ladies got a lot of it out of her. That was quick thinking. Good thing she was discovered in time." He stared inquiringly at Christine. She was vainly struggling to check her tears.

"Cheer up, girl!" he admonished. "Are you the one who found her?"

"Yes, Doctor," Christine managed to reply. "I am her roommate. She was snoring so loudly that she woke me up. When I couldn't rouse her, I lit a candle. Then I noticed the brown stains. So I called Miss Callaway."

"Good thing you did," said the chief heartily. He picked up the empty brown bottle from the table and regarded it with a reminiscent smile. "This takes me back to my army days," he remarked. "The fellows who were booze hounds used to haunt the pharmacy with bogus coughs. The enlisted pharmacist was a generous soul. He used this stuff himself to get a jag on. As I remember, it took quite a lot to work up a mild one in his case."

He indicated Hanni. "Now this girl didn't need very much to send her off on a binge very similar to an alcoholic one. She will sleep it off eventually. It will take several hours. A stimulant would help. Suppose we give her an ampule of caffeine sodium benzoate."

"I'll get it," Eileen offered. She left the room.

The chief studied Hope's troubled face, then the weeping Christine.

"Well, Miss Hope," he finally said. "It looks as if you both know the answer, but I will put the question to you. Why did she do it?"

Hope looked at him sadly, but could not speak. Christine sprang to her feet and spat out the words venomously.

"It's that snake who ran off to Brazil. He ruined her. He ruined us all. The mission is finished. I've lost my chance to ever become a nurse now. I hope the wretch burns in everlasting hell!"

"Hush, girl!" the doctor thundered, leaping to his feet. "God is his judge, not you. Forget yourself and consider how to help this poor girl, lest you be condemned also!" He placed firm hands on Christine's shoulders and forced her down into her chair. He sat down himself and stared broodingly at the floor.

Hope surveyed the frail form of the helpless young girl before her with mounting pity and indignation. It just didn't seem fair for Hanni to be forced to endure this cruel trial while Khaleed escaped scot-free. Fierce rebellion surged up within her. Furtively, she began calculating on her fingers. She glanced swiftly at Christine, who was absorbed in her own grief. Then she leaned across the bed and whispered, "Doctor, she can't be more than two months, ten weeks at the most. Couldn't you . . ." She could not go on.

The chief's keen, kindly eyes held hers. The dreadful question was too shameful to utter. It died unspoken.

"You know the answer, Miss Hope," he stated quietly. "We both have our vows. That way would never solve this girl's problem."

Eileen came in carrying a syringe swathed in an alcohol sponge. Hope pushed Hanni's sleeve up and Eileen administered the injection. Eileen sat on the bed and took Hanni's pulse.

After a few minutes, she announced brightly, "It is picking up a little already."

No one else spoke or moved.

Eileen stared at the chief. Her gaze wandered to Christine. Suddenly, her eyes widened with dawning comprehension. She glanced inquiringly up at Hope and spread one hand expressively across Hanni's abdomen. Hope nodded sadly. Christine's sobs were lessening. She started to wipe her eyes on her sleeve. Eileen plucked a Kleenex from Hope's box. She handed it to the girl. Christine thanked her and blew her nose vigorously.

The sound roused the chief from his reverie. He stared intently at the girl, then demanded abruptly, "Young lady, do you believe in God?"

Startled, Christine stammered, "Y-yes, sir, I do."

"Do you believe that anyone who takes an oath on the Bible should consider it sacred and binding?" he pursued.

Christine nodded and looked frightened.

He reached for Hope's Bible on the nightstand and hitched his chair closer to Christine. "Now, Christine," he said, "I want you to place your right hand upon this Bible and solemnly swear that you will never reveal to anyone what has happened here tonight. Furthermore, swear that you will never reveal by hint, word, sign, or in any other manner, what you know, or think you know about this girl, Hanni. Will you so swear?"

Christine met his eyes steadily as she laid her hand upon the Bible. Her voice was firm as she whispered, "I swear as God is my witness."

Christine removed her hand from the Bible.

"Oh, Dr. Dawson," she implored, "do you think it will be possible to help Hanni? To save the hospital and the training school from disgrace?"

The chief rose and patted her shoulder encouragingly.

"It is in God's hands, my dear," he replied. "If He intends for His work to go on here, and to help this unfortunate girl, then I am sure He already has a plan. Now let's get Hanni back into her own bed, so that we can get back to ours. I want Miss Callaway and Miss Anderson to join Mrs. Dawson and me in our home for a few minutes after Hanni is settled. Christine, I trust you to guard her with your life. Stay with her until someone comes to relieve you in the morning. Do not let anyone in to talk to her without my permission. She is in no danger, and will not waken tonight."

The hall clock in the Dawson residence chimed half past three as Margaret admitted the two nurses. The doctor rose from the sitting room couch as they entered. The women took seats on a small sofa close by. Margaret sat down beside her husband.

The doctor cleared his throat.

"A few hours ago we thought we were in deep financial trouble. God graciously undertook for us. But that was a small thing compared to this. Aside from our pity and concern over the plight of a poor unfortunate girl, I believe we all realize that this may very well mean the end of our mission in Jordan. The very fact we have failed to guard one of our students from disgrace is an unforgivable offense to Arab parents. It is an insult to the whole Arab race. If this becomes universally known, even if the government allows us to continue, we could never get native recruits to train. Even among national Christians, our Christian witness would be ineffectual." His voice faltered. He cleared his throat again, and said, "We have never needed God's help as much as we do at this moment. Let us pray."

TWENTY-THREE

Twelve hours later Hope carried a tea tray to Hanni's room and relieved Misprint from duty. Hanni was now awake, bathed, and in a fresh gown. She was lying between clean sheets, propped up on pillows. She protested that she was not hungry, but Hope prevailed upon her to drink a cup of tea.

There was a knock. Dr. Dawson entered. Hope had not seen him since early that morning when they had prayed together in his living room. He and Margaret had driven off right after breakfast. They left no word as to where they were going. Disregarding her reproachful look, the chief seated himself on a chair beside Hanni and checked her pulse. The girl hung her head and would not meet his eyes. After a moment, he took both her hands and held them firmly between his own.

"Hanni," he said, "I am sure you know that what you tried to do last night was a terrible sin." The girl's head dropped lower. He continued, "You love your parents. You could not bear the thought of disgracing them. You would have broken their hearts if you had succeeded in what you tried to do."

Hanni pulled her hands from the doctor's kindly grasp. She covered her face with them and started to cry. After a moment he wiped her eyes with his own clean handkerchief, and spoke more sternly.

"Hanni, when we are willing to face up to a situation, God is able to help us. Are you ready to swear that you will never again attempt to take your life?"

Something in the tone of his voice made Hanni lift her head and stare at him with dawning hope. Finally, she whispered, "Yes, Doctor, I swear I will never do that again."

"Good," he said, reaching for the Arabic Bible on her bedside table. "Now, with your right ~~band~~ on this Bible, I want you to take a solemn oath that you will never tell anyone, not even your mother, about what happened here last night, or why you did it. No one in this country must ever know, besides ourselves, that you are pregnant." He let Hanni make her own statement and was content.

Hope replaced the Bible on the bedside table. As she did so, Hanni clung to her and began to sob out a broken confession.

"Oh, Miss Hope, I didn't know what to do when Khaleed asked me to walk with him at the picnic. I knew it was wrong. I didn't know how to refuse. He started to tell me that he loved me, and wanted me to go to Brazil with him. I was frightened and ran off. He followed me to the bus that night and began making love to me." She buried her face in Hope's bosom, shuddering, then went on in a muffled voice, "I tried to call for help, but he covered my mouth."

Dr. Dawson abruptly pushed back his chair. He rose with fists tightly clenched, and began pacing the floor. Hope held the girl close, whispering, "Hush, Hanni, you don't need to tell us anymore."

After a few turns around the room the doctor came to a halt at the foot of the bed.

"Hanni," he called. The girl raised her head from Hope's bosom and stared at him. "When did you tell him?" he asked.

Her face flushed crimson with shame.

"I . . . about three weeks ago," she stammered. "He said not to worry. He would take me to Brazil with him."

"Did you want to go with him, Hanni?"

"Oh, no!" she whispered. "But I . . ."

The chief's eyes began to twinkle. "You thought there was no other way to escape," he finished for her. "You can thank God that he didn't want you to go to South America." He smiled broadly as he asked, "How would you like to go to North America instead?"

"To the United States?" Hanni asked in bewilderment.

Hope's eyes shown with excited anticipation. "Out with it!" she exclaimed. "What have you and Margaret been up to all day?"

He laughed heartily, and sat down again beside Hanni. Now he addressed his remarks to Hope. "After you left us this morning, Margaret informed me that she met Kendall Craig Dobson in front of the American Consulate yesterday. He told her that Sheila had been in such poor health ever since the baby was born, that he applied for stateside transfer about a month ago. The transfer came through this week. Their flight to America is booked for one week from today. Sheila doesn't know how she is going to get packed and manage the children on the plane. She was wishing she could find a good maid to help right now, to accompany them to America, and to stay with her for a while afterward. Margaret remembered the conversation while we were praying. She told me as soon as you left. She recalled that Sheila took quite a fancy to Hanni when she helped with the children a few weeks ago. So . . ." he paused to chuckle again, "we went to Jerusalem today."

Hope regarded him with admiration.

"I am way ahead of you, Doctor," she said, "I expect you already have Hanni's passport and ticket right there in your pocket."

"Well, not quite," he admitted. "There is still the little matter of Hanni's consent. We can't drag her aboard the plane, you know. Margaret has already gotten the signed consent of her parents, which is needed for her passport and immigration papers."

He paused to smile at the wide-eyed girl, and to say, "Yes, Hanni, Mrs. Dawson painted such a glowing picture of America to your whole family that I almost bought a seat for myself on that plane." He returned to addressing Hope, "Ken Dobson made reservations for another plane seat immediately. Sheila says she will be glad to keep Hanni with her in America as long as she wants to stay. When her time comes the Mennonites will care for her and her baby in their maternity shelter until she is able to care for herself. Being in the consulate service, all Kendall Dobson needs now to complete Hanni's immigration papers, is her own consent. What do you say, Hanni?"

Faced with the sudden realization that she would be severing ties forever with all that she knew and loved, the timid Girl was seized with panic. Again she burst into tears and covered her face with her hands. It was the doctor's gentle arms that encircled the frail shoulders this time. He held her and soothed her as tenderly as if she were a small child. With unerring instinct he chose the words that struck a responsive chord in the heart of the frightened girl.

"Courage, Hanni!" he whispered. "God is giving you this chance to make a life for yourself and your baby."

At the mention of the baby, Hanni's sobs quieted. She raised her head and bravely brushed away the tears.

"Thank you, Doctor," she said. "I know God will take care of us. I am willing to go."

"Good!" he said, patting her shoulder. "Sheila wants Hanni to come tomorrow." He rose and turned to Hope. "She understands the need for complete secrecy. She will see that Hanni rests properly. It is best to get the girl away from here before suspicions are aroused and tongues start wagging. She will be allowed a short, chaperoned visit at home the day before they go. Margaret will take her to the embassy right after breakfast in the morning."

Everything worked out smoothly according to plan. In the interval remaining before the plane left, Hope lived in constant dread lest Hanni's secret be discovered. As it happened, she learned on the very next morning after Hanni left the hospital that one other in the institution shared the dangerous knowledge. Murshdeeyah waylaid her in the lower hall just before noon. With an air of deep mystery, the maid drew her into the small ironing room, and closed the door.

"Missy Hope," she whispered urgently, "Hanni okay now? Baby okay, maybe?"

Hope's heart sank to the bottom of her shoes. In spite of herself she glanced anxiously at the door.

"Nobody come now. Nobody hear," Murshdeeyah assured her.

"What do you know, Murshdeeyah?" Hope asked fearfully.

"I know. I see. Much," the girl replied, nodding her head wisely. "I hear Khaleed go Brazil. Tell Hanni. She faint. Sick. Drink bad medicine that night. I clean room this morning, wash sheets, clothes, like you tell me. I see. I know. Much."

Hope groaned at her own stupidity. She wondered how many others knew. "Did you show the sheets to anyone else, or tell anyone about them?"

The girl saw the apprehension in her mistress's eyes. "I not tell nobody, Missy Hope," she assured her quickly. "*Abbadan —* by Allah!" She stuck out her long tongue. This she held with the fingers of her left hand while she drew her right hand across it with a swift, cutting motion. Her face was so comical that Hope laughed with relief.

"Hanni is okay Murshdeeyah," Hope said. "But we must not say anything about a baby. If other people find out we might have to lock the doors of the hospital and go back to America. There would be no more work here for you or Fatmy. You understand?"

"*Nam,*" the girl replied. "I not tell. *Abbadan.* But Khaleed very evil man. Very big. Maybe baby big. Too big. Maybe Hanni too little. Maybe Hanni die."

"We must pray to Allah for Hanni, Murshdeeyah," said Hope.

"*Nam,*" said the girl. "I pray Allah. You pray Yesuah. He make little baby. Help Hanni. Yesuah love babies."

"How do you know that?" Hope asked.

The black girl lifted the thick pad of the ironing board beside her and produced a colored page from an American calendar, showing Jesus blessing the little children. She regarded it fondly. "See?" she said. "Yesuah love babies."

Hope pointed to the small black child standing at Jesus' knee. "See, you are there, too, Murshdeeyah," she said.

The dark eyes widened with childish delight. The girl's grin spread from ear to ear as she studied the picture. "You think that little girl me, maybe, Missy Hope?" she asked.

"I know so," Hope replied with deep conviction.

On the day that the Dobson party left, Hope was the only one from the hospital who was free to see Hanni off. She rode out to the airport with the travelers in the taxi provided by the tourist agency. The Jerusalem bus was very late in arriving. It drew up in front of the airport entrance just as the loud speaker was calling for all passengers to board the plane. Hanni's mother and father were on the bus. They had time for only a quick kiss and a tearful embrace from their daughter. Then she was running after the Dobsons to the plane.

Hope rode back to Jerusalem on the bus with the Milads, trying to cheer them with tales of the wonders of America. In the case of Mr. Milad, she met with some success. But Hanni's mother remained downcast and withdrawn. Suspecting that they had not eaten lunch, she took them to a little tea shop on a side street. She bought them some cakes and tea. Then she left them boarding a Bethlehem bus, and found a seat for herself in a service taxi going beyond Bethlehem to Hebron.

Supper was in progress when Hope arrived back at the hospital. Feeling too weary to eat, she went directly to her room. Here she undressed and climbed into bed. She was utterly exhausted by the suspense and emotional tensions of the past week.

She was awakened by a faint glow on the wall of her room. It took her a few minutes to realize that it was the dawn light shining through her window, which faced the east. She had forgotten to draw the drapes the night before. She wrapped a blanket about her and knelt at the open window. A faint rosy glow was spreading along the rim of the distant hills. A deep sense of peace and certainty regarding Hanni's future welfare swept over her. In that distant land to which she was being carried, the frail little fledgling who had tumbled out of the nest too soon and come to grief, would be sheltered and strengthened by her heavenly Father.

Hope bowed her head.

When she raised it again, the bright morning sunlight was flooding the room. All the dark shadows that had dogged her footsteps throughout the difficult past week were gone. She rose. Briskly she set about preparing herself to meet the challenges of another day.

TWENTY-FOUR

ON HER WAY TO tea that morning, Hope encountered the chief and Mohammed Abdullab coming out of the doctor's office. Mohammed regretfully declined their invitation to tea, explaining that he had been away for several days in Beirut and had much business awaiting him in Amman.

Misprint was the only occupant of the tearoom when the too entered. The doctor pulled a check from his pocket. He saved it triumphantly before the nurses, saying, "Now we won't need your loan, Misprint. Mohammed heard of our loss when be returned from Beirut last night. He couldn't get out here fast enough this morning to apologize for Khaleed's disgraceful conduct, and to write a check fully covering the amount he had stolen."

The two nurses stared at the check in amazement. It was for two hundred and fifty pounds.

"But Mohammed is a leader in the Moslem Brotherhood," Hope gasped. "I never dreamed that he would ever support any Christian work in this country."

The chief smiled.

"You underestimate our friend, Miss Hope," he replied. "Mohammed realizes more than most Moslems that we are helping his countrymen. This isn't the first time he has come to our rescue. He is generous to many causes, but he never lets his left hand know what his right hand is doing. I am sure he does not wish me to publicize this gift. However, Misprint is entitled to know why we will not need her loan. She may wish to have the money returned to her bank in America when it arrives, which should be any day now."

"No, Doctor," said Misprint thoughtfully. "I believe I will leave it in the bank here for emergencies. I may be needing it myself before long."

November sped swiftly by. Misprint and the students were hard at work on the flannelgraph Christmas story. It was to be presented in the chapel the Sunday before Christmas, then in each of the three wards on Christmas Day. Lots were drawn by the five students for the five scenes. The first scene fell to the lot of Aminah. Being the only Moslem, Aminah had to study her passages more diligently than the others. Her knowledge of the Bible was more limited.

On the morning of December 15, the rising bell brought Hope to her feet. In the chill darkness, she lit her Coleman lamp, dressed rapidly, and made her bed. There was a gentle knock at her door. She opened it to find Aminah standing there, eyes glowing with a strange excitement.

"Miss Callaway," she whispered, "I have something wonderful to tell you. I don't want anyone else to hear."

Hope smilingly drew the girl in and closed the door. With Christmas secrets flying around, she surmised that Aminah had come to consult her regarding a gift. As she turned from the door, however, the indulgent smile died on her lips. She stared in wonder at Aminah's radiant face. In the bright glow of the lamp, the girl's skin and eyes appeared to have a translucent quality, as if lit up by an inward radiance. Aminah

was too excited to sit down. Her words came pouring forth
eagerly.

"Miss Hope, I saw a vision of Jesus last night! I am sure of it.
I was asleep, and I was aroused by a soft glow in my room. The
door was shut, so it was not a reflection from the lamp in the
hall. Then I saw Him. He was very tall. He wore a shining robe
that glowed with light. The light was too soft for me to see His
face distinctly, but His eyes shone with such wonderful love that
I did not feel at all afraid. He stood at the foot of my bed, hold-
ing out a white robe like His own with both hands. He said,
'Aminah I offer you this robe. Will you wear it before your peo-
ple for My sake, and serve Me above all others?' I was so over-
whelmed by His presence and by the tenderness in His voice,
that I couldn't speak. I wanted so much to answer. He didn't ask
me again, just stood there patiently waiting. I felt His love pour-
ing right into my heart. Finally, I just held out my arms. He
smiled, and laid the robe across them. It was so soft and warm.
The next moment He was gone. The light disappeared with
Him. After a long while, I fell asleep, holding the robe in my
arms. I was so disappointed when I woke this morning and
found that I was hugging my pillow, that I cried."

At the recollection, tears came again to her eyes. She brushed
them away, and smiled at Hope. "I am sure that it was more than
a dream," she concluded earnestly. "What do you think, Miss
Hope?"

Hope hesitated. She had been deeply impressed by the sim-
plicity of the recital. She was also awed by the peculiar radiance
that still emanated from the girl's skin. She was reminded of
how Moses's face had shone after his encounter with God on
Mount Sinai. She did not discount the possibility that this might
have been a true vision. Such experiences were possible, she
believed, even in modern times.

Hope weighed her words carefully before replying.
Meanwhile, she opened the blinds. Then she extinguished the

lamp and drew Aminah over to the window. By daylight, the texture and coloring of the girl's skin appeared normal. But such joy and peace glowed in the depths of her expressive dark eyes, that Hope felt conviction deepening in her own heart that Aminah's experience of the previous night had indeed been something more than a dream.

"Aminah, I cannot tell you whether or not your experience was an actual reality or only a wonderful dream. The important thing to consider is your own reaction. Instead of constantly asking, 'Was it real?' You should ask yourself, 'Did it have a real meaning for me? Did I make an actual and total commitment of my life to Christ? Did I mean it? Will my decision be a lasting one? And, if so, how will it affect the purpose and direction of my life from now on?' These are the only questions of real significance for you to consider now."

Aminah answered readily, "I have been considering them, Miss Hope. I know I shall need much help in finding the answers. I did mean it when I accepted the robe, even if I didn't speak. He understood. My greatest happiness from now on will be to love and to serve Him."

Hope's eyes shone with joy.

"I am so glad for you, Aminah," she said. "But I believe this should be kept a secret between us for now. It could be mistaken for boasting, you know, and might lead to unpleasant misunderstanding by your friends."

"Why, Miss Hope," the girl exclaimed, with a hint of reproach in her tone, "I thought you knew that I could never share my vision with anyone but you. I know that most people would laugh. I could not bear to have them ridicule something that is so precious and wonderful to me."

Hope's heart suddenly began singing a Hallelujah chorus.

"Please forgive me, Aminah," she said humbly. "I fear that I have badly underestimated your grasp of the situation. You have already suffered so much among us, I should have known you would recognize the need for caution."

"You have said nothing to require forgiveness, Miss Hope," replied Aminah, with the gentle dignity that was an integral part of her nature. "But do you think it would be all right to tell the other girls that I have decided I want to become a Christian? I am afraid I will not be able to hide it from them for very long."

Hope hesitated, then replied, "Perhaps we should consult Dr. Dawson first. And don't you think that it would be wise to tell your father about your decision first of all?"

The light suddenly died in Aminah's eyes. Her face turned white. She stammered, "My father . . . I never thought . . . yes, I must tell him first. It will hurt him terribly . . ." Her voice faltered. Then she said very quietly, "Thank you for reminding me of my duty, Miss Hope."

The breakfast bell was sounding. Without another word, Hope swung the door open. They walked down the hall together in somber silence. Aminah's mountain top experience of the night before was over. Already, she was beginning to tread the dark valley. They both knew it. Only Hope realized that the close tie existing between father and daughter had been severed last night. Without one thought or backward glance for Mohammed, Aminah joyously stepped through an open door into a new life in which her father had no part.

That night Hope took Aminah to the Dawson home. There they held a long conference with the doctor and Margaret. With no prompting from Hope and with only a brief mention of her amazing experience of the night before, Aminah simply stated her conversion to the Christian faith and her desire to renounce her Moslem beliefs and confess Christ openly.

The Dawsons listened attentively to all she had to say. They were impressed by her sincerity, and by her mature grasp of the many difficulties involved in her decision. It was only when she approached the subject of breaking the news to her father, that her voice broke, and she wept. The three missionaries waited silently until she recovered her composure.

Then Dr. Dawson ventured to express his opinion.

"Aminah," he began, "we all know that this news will be a great shock to your father. You say that you dread to tell him because you love him too much to wish to hurt him. You believe that he loves you devotedly and that he desires your happiness above all else. You are blindly assuming that he will accept your decision with little or no objection. I assure you that this will not be the case. Mohammed is a staunch Moslem. Although he is gentle and kindly to his friends, there is another side to his nature. He can be ruthless and implacable toward all who oppose him. He does not hold his present position of power in the Moslem Brotherhood and in government circles by reason of the gentle side of his nature. It is because of a cruel strength that rides roughshod over all resistance. Do not fool yourself. You think now that you are strong enough to stand firm in your decision against any pressure your father may bring to bear against you. You are still only a 'babe in Christ.' You have never been up against the formidable strength of Islam. Your father will fight you with every weapon in his power. You will be unable to stand before him. He will either break you to his will, or break your heart."

Aminah listened to him in wide-eyed dismay. She spread her hands in gesture of helplessness.

"What am I to do, then?" she asked anxiously. "I have studied Jesus' teachings. If I don't tell my father, wouldn't that be denying Jesus?"

The chief smiled at her earnestness.

"Not necessarily, my dear," he replied. "If your father asks you if you are a Christian, and you say no, then you would be denying Christ. I certainly think that you should tell him eventually. I do not believe that Jesus requires you to make haste to volunteer the information. There were several occasions when

He instructed individuals to keep silent regarding their belief in Him, because 'the time was not yet ripe.' Many scriptures tell us to 'wait on the Lord.' I believe that advice applies in your case. You know a great deal about Christ's teachings, but you need to learn much more. His disciples walked with Him three full years before they were prepared to witness for Him.

"Nothing would be gained by too hasty a declaration. Meanwhile you will have a chance to become firmly grounded in your beliefs. Then, when the proper time comes for you to tell your father, I am sure God will prepare his heart and yours for the revelation."

He looked at Aminah inquiringly. Her face had been brightening as he spoke. Now she smiled, and said, "I will be happy to take your advice and wait, Doctor. But what shall I tell my classmates if they ask me?"

"There again," replied the chief, "I don't think you need to make an issue of it. If they ask you why you are studying the Bible so intently, the simple and truthful answer would be that you are seeking to learn more about Jesus."

It was nearing ten o'clock. Margaret lit the Coleman lamp. Just as the yellow glow began to brighten the dome of the wick, the electric generator shut off. The doctor stepped over and flipped off the electric wall switch. His guests rose to depart.

Seeing the wistful look in Aminah's eyes, he asked, "Would you like us to pray with you before you leave, Aminah?"

"Oh, yes, please," she answered quickly.

When the prayer was over, Hope again noticed the translucent quality about Aminah's face and eyes that she had seen by the light of her own Coleman lamp that morning. Evidently, the doctor saw it, too. He placed his hands gently upon the girl's shoulders, saying tenderly, "My dear, if your father ever sees that look on your face, you will have no need of words to tell him what has happened. We must all pray that God will mercifully divert the force of his wrath from you when that moment of revelation comes."

Something in the doctor's grave face as he spoke, suddenly awakened Aminah to a realization of the serious jeopardy in which she would be placing her dear Christian friends of the Mission by such a revelation. All the joy drained abruptly from her face.

"How could I be so thoughtless as to consider only myself when all my Christian friends stand in far greater danger of my father's wrath than I?" she exclaimed sorrowfully. "Indeed, I must pray instead that God will allow my father to vent the full force of his anger upon me alone, and not permit any harm to come to you or to the mission because of me."

She turned sadly toward the door.

Hope exchanged significant glances of understanding with the doctor and Margaret. Then she followed Aminah out into the darkness.

TWENTY-FIVE

About ten days before Christmas, Hope was passing through the lower hall one evening when she saw a light in the ironing room. The door was slightly ajar. She pushed it open, wondering who was there at that late hour. She ~~formed~~ Murshdeeyah preening herself before a small mirror on the wall. Hope's freshly laundered cap was perched on the girl's kinky braids, now worn around her head in imitation of her mistress's hairstyle. She was smiling and crooning to herself, totally unaware that she was being observed.

Hope slipped up quietly behind her and whispered, "Would you like to be a nurse, Murshdeeyah?"

Startled, the girl snatched the cap from her head and turned guiltily to face the questioner. Seeing Hope's laughing face, she carefully dusted the edge of the cap on her sleeve and offered it to her mistress, saying, "Hair clean. I wash today. Okay?"

"Of course, Murshdeeyah," said Hope. She accepted the cap gratefully. "But you shouldn't be working so late on my ironing."

"I not tired. I like," responded Murshdeeyah, unrolling a uniform and beginning to iron.

Hope knew there was no use to argue. She stood eyeing the girl speculatively as she worked. An idea was forming in her head. After a minute, she repeated the question, "Murshdeeyah, would you like to be a nurse?"

The girl favored her mistress with a brief glance.

"*Nam*," she answered simply.

She went on ironing with the cheerful air of one who entertains no false hopes of ever attaining an impossible goal.

Hope reached out and took the iron from the maid's grasp. She set it down firmly on the ironing board stand.

"Listen to me, Murshdeeyah," she ordered. "I mean this. If you really want to become a nurse, I think I can help to arrange it."

The girl folded her hands together, and waited resignedly for Hope to finish her statement. Hope continued, "You would need to go to school for at least two or three years. You would have to start in the younger grades. It would not be easy for you. I am sure you could learn quickly. They need a girl to help in the kitchen at the Ramallah Mission Home and School for Girls. Lydia Zaki is going there to board in January while she attends the Friends' School for her final year. Then she will come back here to enter nurse's training."

Murshdeeyah's black eyes were widening with incredulous hope. She gazed intently at Hope's face. Hope continued, "I am sure that the directors of the Mission School would be willing to give you board and free tuition in exchange for your help in the kitchen. With hard study, I believe you would be ready to enter nurse's training within three years. Do you want to do it?"

For answer, the tall black girl dropped to her knees before her mistress, seized her hand and bowed her forehead on it. Hope gazed down upon the grotesque creature. She realized that this half child, half woman was dearer to her than any of her students. But she was vaguely disturbed by the girl's position. It smacked uncomfortably of worship of herself. If so, it was high time that their relationship be severed for the best interests of them both.

Hastily she pulled Murshdeeyah to her feet. Then she stepped back a pace. The girl eyed her troubled face with quick concern.

"You not sorry you tell me I can be nurse, Missy Hope?" she asked uncertainly.

"No, no, it's not that at all," Hope replied. "It is just . . ." she paused helplessly, at a loss for words.

The girl studied her mistress's face gravely. Then her black eyes lit up with complete comprehension. She raised a huge hand and poked Hope's chest with a bony finger. "Missy Hope," she said, "you kind. You good. Very good." Then she swung the pointing finger upward and rolled her eyes toward the ceiling. "Allah great!" she concluded.

Hope was awed by Murshdeeyah's intuitive perception. She gazed at the girl in amazement. "Why, Murshdeeyah," she stammered admiringly. "You are positively uncanny! You are absolutely marvelous!"

Not understanding the words but sensing by the tone that her mistress was pleased, the girl's comical face split into a wide grin. With a nod of satisfaction she picked up the iron.

After several days of chill winds and threatening skies, the Sunday before Christmas dawned sunny and clear. The small hospital chapel was crowded for the morning service. A large flannelgraph board stood in the center of the platform. The five student nurses were seated beside it.

Hope was late. She joined Misprint, who was standing against the rear wall by the door. The congregation was singing an appropriate Christmas carol. This was followed by prayer and a brief message from Dr. Dawson. Then Aminah stepped forward and placed the background for the first scene on the board. It showed a simply furnished living room. She placed the figure of Mary seated on a low footstool in the foreground. Then she began in a clear, sweet voice to recount the story in the first chapter of Luke: "And in Elizabeth's sixth month, the angel Gabriel was sent from God into a city of Galilee, named Nazareth, to a virgin espoused to a man whose name was Joseph."

Aminah placed the figure of the angel Gabriel upon the board and continued her story. She was in the midst of repeating Gabriel's words, when Hope became vaguely aware that another latecomer had entered and was standing beside her.

Aminah concluded Mary's response. At the words, "and the angel departed from her," she removed the figure of Gabriel. Then she turned to face the audience and began Mary's Magnificat. Her face was radiant with love for her newfound Saviour as she repeated Mary's words, "My soul doth magnify the Lord, and my spirit hath rejoiced in God my Saviour. For He hath regarded the low estate of His . . ."

The man standing beside Hope uttered a violent exclamation at this point. He began pushing through the crowd standing in the aisle leading to the platform. It was Mohammed Abdullah. His face was contorted with rage.

Hope managed to reach him with great effort. She seized his arm and implored in a whisper, "Please Mohammed, don't make a scene before all these people."

His pride made him waver. He shook off the detaining hand and turned on her savagely. "I want to talk to my daughter," he announced loudly.

"I will have someone send Aminah to you at once. You can talk to her in private. Please come with me."

He yielded reluctantly to her tug on his arm and allowed himself to be led toward the entrance door. Misprint was edging her way toward them. As they went by, Hope whispered urgently, "Send Aminah right away to the classroom."

She led her unwilling companion to the classroom nearest the chapel. Thankful that they had created so little disturbance, she closed the door behind them. Limbs trembling, she sank into her own chair behind the desk. She invited Mohammed to accept a chair nearby. Instead, he marched to the opposite side of the desk. He leaned across it and transfixed her with such a wild glare of pure hatred that she was thankful the desk stood between them. She shuddered inwardly with cold apprehension.

Mohammed turned abruptly from the desk and began pacing the length of the room, loudly declaiming his hatred of all thing Christian. He cast baleful glances at Hope every time be passed by her desk in his furious pacing.

Soon the door opened. Aminah entered. She cast a frightened glance at Hope. Mohammed had reached the far corner of the room in his pacing. His back was toward her. Aminah advanced timidly to meet him. He turned. The Mohammed Abdullah who strode toward her was not the loving father she had known all her life. This man was a total stranger. She had never seen him like this before. She shrank back in terror. He seized her roughly by the shoulders and began shaking her violently.

"Aminah!" he shouted with pure rage, "I demand that you tell me the truth. Have you embraced this foul religion of Christ? If you have I would rather see you dead. I could kill you with my own hands!"

He kept shaking her with such violence that her teeth chattered. Aminah was speechless with terror. She broke into sobs and sank to her knees in her father's cruel grasp. Raising her eyes imploringly to his face, she clasped her hands in mute supplication.

Mohammed was utterly beside himself by now. His hands slipped from his daughter's shoulders to her throat. His lips drew back viciously from his teeth. Slowly his fingers tightened on the girl's tender flesh. She did not struggle. Her pupils became distended and she began choking for breath. All the time her eyes never left her father's face.

Hope struggled to rise and go to the girl's assistance. She was horrified at what was taking place. Some unseen force held her tight to her seat.

When it appeared that the last breath was leaving the girl's body, her father's fingers suddenly released their grip. It was as though they had been forcibly pulled apart. Aminah crumpled to the floor in a gasping heap. Mohammed stood there staring fixedly at his outstretched hands. He had a look of fear, horror, and utter bewilderment on his face. Then his hands dropped to his sides. He gazed wonderingly down upon his daughter. All hatred left his face. In its place was a look of deep contrition and sadness. He stooped over Aminah and raised her gently to a chair. As if fearing to trust his hands further, he quickly clasped them behind his back. He stood quietly regarding her with yearning tenderness. Her breath still came in laboring sobs.

At last he leaned toward her, and whispered hoarsely, "Aminah, never, never tell me that you are a Christian!"

She bowed her head in mute assent. He raised his right hand above her head in a curious gesture of benediction. Then he turned hastily and left the room.

Hope rose and came to put her arms around Aminah. The cruel bruises on the girl's throat were rapidly darkening. Her voice was faint from her recent trauma, but her eyes were glowing as she looked up at Hope.

"Did you see His hands, Miss Hope?" she whispered.

"His hands?" echoed Hope stupidly. "Your father's?"

"No, I mean Jesus' hands," whispered Aminah. "I saw them so plainly. They took my father's hands away from my throat. Didn't you see them?"

Hope shook her head. Then she remembered the force that had held her to her seat a few minutes before. She wondered.

"They were so strong and beautiful," Aminah continued. "I kept praying all the time. Then I felt His presence. I knew He would help me, and He did."

Her eyes clouded with sudden grief. She added sadly, "but I failed Him! I should have confessed and I didn't. Now my father has made me promise never to tell him. I shall have to live a lie. I have denied my Lord, and He will deny me."

"Don't be a goose, Aminah!" exclaimed Hope. "How could you confess when your father gave you no opportunity? And why didn't he? Because he already knew the answer. You should have seen your face when you were reciting Mary's Magnificat! He didn't need a confession. He wanted to terrorize you into a denial. When you didn't even attempt to struggle, he saw that he could not conquer you by fear, and his fury increased." She shuddered at the recollection, and added, "I believe he intended to kill you. How could you hold so still when he was choking you to death?"

"I had been asking God to let me bear the full brunt of my father's anger," Aminah answered simply. "I asked that He spare my friends and force his vengeance on me. He gave me the strength to hold still. I believe that the entire force of my father's anger has been spent on me, and that he will not attempt to harm the mission now in any way."

Aminah was right about her father. As days and weeks slipped by with no sign of developing hostility to the mission by either the government or the Moslem Brotherhood, it became apparent that Mohammed's wrath had indeed been spent on his daughter that day in the classroom.

After a month's absence he appeared one day with his usual gifts for Aminah. Thereafter, he again came regularly to visit her. It became increasingly clear that the strong tie between the father and daughter had been broken.

TWENTY-SIX

JANUARY WAS MARKED BY the addition of two new members to the Beth Hanani Mission staff. First to arrive was Matthew Mansfield, a gangling giant of a farm boy from the wheat fields of Kansas. He had two years of electrical engineering behind him from a Mennonite college. He was an earnest young Christian whose conscience forbade him to bear arms in violation of his religious beliefs. In place of military service, he was allowed to serve at his own expense for three years as a helper on some foreign mission field. Matt had come out to serve as general maintenance man. Just about everything of a mechanical or electrical nature at the mission station was badly in need of repair. In an underdeveloped country such as Jordan, all machinery, as well as all automobiles, had to be imported. A few native Arabs acquired a certain amount of skill at repairing automobiles by trial and error. They knew next to nothing about generators and the like. The X-ray machine required special knowledge, but there would be little use in importing new parts from America unless someone knew how to install them. It had been operating at less than full efficiency for sometime now.

Dr. and Mrs. Dawson brought Matt to the Beth Hanani compound straight from the Kalendia airport. They arrived in time for tea. All the missionaries, except the night crew, were present.

"Watch out for this boy's handgrip," the doctor warned the ladies. Young Matt grinned. His coltish frame betrayed the fact that he was not more than twenty. The motherly hearts of the older women promptly yearned over him. Esther Baxter resolved to share her home and dinner table with him as often as possible. She issued an invitation then and there, only to find that Margaret had already engaged him for the same night. The two women quickly agreed on separate dates. Matt accepted both with enthusiasm.

"I think I should warn you though," he said. "My mom says I eat enough for two people. She never could get me filled up."

Three days later Hope was passing the open door of the repair shop, when she heard roars of laughter coming from within. She entered to see Matt standing over one of the workmen with a puzzled look on his face. The man lay flat on his back. His hands were folded complacently across his chest. He was laughing as heartily as his two Arab companions, who stood nearby. The young American was scanning the pages of a little red notebook. He looked up at Hope with a grin.

"I must have said the wrong thing," he explained. "This fellow was turning a crank here for me. I thought I told him to stop. He just stretched out on the floor. Now I don't know what to say."

Hope joined in the laughter. "You must have said 'nammy,' " she said, "and he took advantage of it." She addressed the man on the floor reprovingly, "*Moosh kwyess, Suleiman! Oom!*"

The man rose with an unrepentant chuckle.

"What did you say?" asked Matt, producing a pencil.

"Roughly translated I said, 'Not nice. Get up,' " explained Hope. "My pronunciation is bad. I mix genders. But I manage to make myself understood. Our Arab friends find me amusing. I have learned to laugh with them."

"Oh boy!" exclaimed Matt. "I can see we are going to have a good time around here. These fellows don't know beans about machinery. Dr. Dawson gave me permission to teach them something about generators and other things. What I need to know right now is how to say stop before they get going too fast and wreck something. They sure don't lack enthusiasm."

Hope told Matt the words that would be of help to him. He busily scribbled them down in his small notebook.

"Thanks a lot. This ought to help me get by."

Hope departed with a warning shake of her finger at the three grinning Arabs and a smile of encouragement for Matt.

The day that Matthew Mansfield received his Jordanian license to drive, Dr. Dawson turned the wheel of his car over to the boy, much to Margaret's immense relief. She knew how sorely the doctor had missed Khaleed's strength. Now Matt slipped into the dual role of chauffeur and right-hand man.

The second new arrival was Dr. Morcus Kemalyian. He flew in to the Kalendia airport one week after completing his year of internship at the American University Hospital in Beirut. Hope was busy at the time of his arrival, so she met him a few nights later at the Dawson's dinner table.

She already knew something about him. The chief had met him in Beirut at the AUB Hospital the past fall. He had gone there in hopes of recruiting some temporary medical assistance. Dr. Kemalyian was introduced to the chief as a possible candidate. He desired to specialize in the field of tuberculosis. The chief liked him immediately. The young intern admitted that he lacked funds for further study. He had scraped together barely enough money to carry him through his present internship. The chief explained that the mission salary would be low, but that the young doctor would have the time and opportunity to open a private general practice in the town. Doctors were very scarce in that area. He might be able to save enough to finance further education in his chosen field.

Hope wondered at the young doctor's choice of the tuberculosis field of medicine. She ventured to ask him about it as they sat across from each other at the dinner table. Deep sadness appeared in his beautiful brown eyes.

"My mother died of tuberculosis," he replied, "after a long illness when I was sixteen. As you can tell by my name, I am Armenian. My mother saw my father and two older brothers dragged away by the Turks when they overran our country in 1915. She never knew what became of them. She and my sister escaped by hiding out in the fields. They nearly died of exposure and hunger before they made their way to Syria and then to Lebanon. I was born less than three months after my country ceased to exist. My sister died a year later. She was just four years old."

Dr. Morcus spoke quietly, with no hint of bitterness in his tone. But the lonely hunger of a man without a country and with no kin to love him, was in those expressive brown eyes.

"I saw my mother waste away after that," he continued. She sacrificed her own life in order that I might have strength and live. I vowed at my mother's death that I would become a doctor and devote the rest of my life toward eradicating the disease that killed her."

Hope was almost speechless with sympathy. She murmured, "I am so sorry." Then she turned to Matt, in hopes of cheering up the young doctor.

"How are you doing with the Arabic language, Matt?" she asked.

Matt consulted his little red notebook, then answered proudly, "*Kibeer kwyess, Sitt* Callaway. *Pumpkin becafee. Moosh awam. La! Bee swaysh, Kibeer swaysh. Nam Faheem?*"

Dr. Kemalyian choked and hastily covered his mouth with his napkin. The chief chuckled. Hope and Margaret giggled outright. Matt joined them with a roar of laughter at his own expense. Dr. Morcus finally gave up his valiant effort at seriousness and joined in the merriment.

When Hope was able to speak, she said, "Dr. Kemalyian, I fear I am a poor teacher. Perhaps Matt would appreciate your help."

"Would I?" cried Matt with enthusiasm. "That would be keen! Could you tell me what I said wrong?"

Dr. Morcus glanced at his hostess, who nodded approvingly.

"I am confused by your words 'pumpkin becafee,' " he explained to Matt. I am familiar with your American pumpkin pie, and 'becafee' means 'enough.' Surely you were not referring to this delicious dessert?"

Matt looked puzzled himself. Hope came to his rescue.

"I think Matt means '*mumpkin*' or '*impkin*,' " she explained. "I used to get both words confused with 'pumpkin' myself."

Dr. Kemalyian replied, with a smile of understanding.

"I can see now that Matt was not referring to the dessert. He was probably trying to tell us that he is 'getting by.' Right Matt?"

"Right, Sir!" Matt agreed. "*Shukran, Hakeem!*" he continued with spirit. "I know that means 'Thank you, Doctor!' Now will you answer me one more question?" He consulted his notebook, then asked, "What does '*mafeesh muk*' mean?"

Dr. Morcus laughed, then replied, "Not any brains."

"That's me!" Matt laughed. "*Anah mafeesh muk!*"

During the preceding winter, Hope had scoured the country for recruits to start a new nursing class. By January 24 she had only four girls signed up for the full two year nursing course, to start on February 15. All prospects were exhausted. Three young men and three young girls were due to begin the six months' aide course on February 5. Hope was keenly disappointed at the smallness of the full term group.

At eleven o'clock on the morning just mentioned, three crowded taxis pulled up outside the main gate. The first driver conferred with Saleem. Under the latter's guidance the entire cavalcade swept into the driveway and parked in the shade of some cypress trees near the front steps of the hospital.

Hope happened to be in her office. She watched in amazement as a dozen adults, and at least as many children of assorted sizes, spilled out of the taxis and headed for the entrance. Hope's eyes were drawn to a tall young girl who appeared to be leading the delegation. As they passed under her window, she recognized the girl as Annette Johannus. She had visited the family at Nablus in December. She had hoped to enlist the girl in the nursing class. An unexpected downpour at the dinner hour kept her there for an hour. Mr. Johannus was friendly, but adamant in refusing his consent to permit Annette to enter training. Both parents were with the girl now. Hope hastened to meet them in the hall. Annette stood beaming in the doorway, flanked by her parents and two other girls about her own age. Wondering why they had come, Hope shook hands cordially.

"Welcome to Beth Hanani, Mr. and Mrs. Johannus, and Annette," she said. "I trust that you have all been well?"

Annette could scarcely wait for her father's dignified replies to Hope's amenities before she drew the two girls forward, saying eagerly, "Miss Callaway, here are my friends, Samira Simone and Nejla Habeeb. They want to be nurses, too."

"Annette," said her father sternly, "you forget your manners. Remember, we have not yet given our consent." He stepped aside and introduced the other two couples. The children he introduced with a sweep of his hand.

Hope hastily shook hands with the parents and some of the older children. Then, before any of the youngsters could wander off down the hall into forbidden territory, she herded them into the staff tearoom. There were enough seats for the older people. The smaller ones played happily on the rug at their feet.

It soon developed that the visitors had come to inspect the hospital before deciding to permit their daughters to enter training. They evidently expected to be taken on a guided tour of the building. Hope was obliged to explain that the grownups would be restricted to visiting only certain areas of the hospital. The children would not be permitted to accompany them on the tour. A servant would stay with them during the parents' absence. She excused herself to fetch one of the maids.

As she opened the tearoom door, appetizing odors were drifting up the stairwell. Her guests sniffed appreciatively. Hastily closing the door she descended to the kitchen. She knew that Arab etiquette decreed that all guests present at mealtimes should be offered food. The Johannus family had shared their dinner with her in Nablus. With the prospect of not one, but three nursing recruits, she could do no less than issue the expected invitation.

Rose and Fatmy were just finishing portioning out the food on the patients' trays. Even Hope's inexpert eye could see that there was only enough food remaining in the pots to go around among the hospital staff and the outside employees. Her heart sank as she explained her predicament to Rose. But she had failed to reckon on the housekeeper's resourcefulness. Being a true Arab, Rose made a quick calculation. She came up with the only possible solution.

"The men employees and outside workmen will have to be served a regular meal in the men's dining room, of course," she said. "We can serve them smaller portions, a little earlier than usual. They won't starve for one day. The domestic staff and nurses can just do without the noon meal. We will serve it to your guests right here in the staff dining room as soon as you want it."

Hope stared at her in astonishment. "Will the staff be willing to do without their meal?" she asked doubtfully.

"Oh, yes," Rose declared confidently. "Not one of our people would want to disgrace the hospital by lack of hospitality. I will get the word around. We can give them an early tea and a little more substantial supper. Now, don't worry. Tamam will come up in a few minutes to get the children ready. She can stay with them while you take the parents around."

Two hours later, Hope stood on the hospital steps waving good-bye to the families from Nablus. The three precious signed agreements were safely clutched in her hand.

As the last taxi made the sharp turn onto the highway, a large basket toppled from the luggage rack on top, and came bouncing down the hospital driveway. Loaves of flat Arabic bread went rolling like cartwheels in all directions. Cheese, olives, and hard boiled eggs went tumbling after.

Saleem let out a great shout and the taxi driver heard. He brought his car to a stop several yards down the road. He got out and walked back. He surveyed the scattered food and shrugged his shoulders. All the while Saleem berated him soundly in Arabic. He retrieved the basket and restored it to the roof of the taxi and hurriedly drove off to catch up with his companions.

Saleem turned to Hope with an expression of such utter disgust that she sank down on the steps and laughed until the tears came.

"Don't feel so sorry for yourself, Saleem," she gasped, wiping her eyes. "The joke is certainly on us. After all, you and I were lucky enough to get part of a meal today. How could we possibly know that they brought their lunch and were not expecting to be fed?"

Twenty-seven

Hope awoke the next morning with a question in her mind: which of the five new students should she ask to share Christine's room? Since Hanni's departure, Christine had been steadily growing more difficult to live with. She was sharply critical of everything and of everybody with whom she worked. Her classmates shunned her whenever possible. She appeared to have retreated still further into the shell of reserve she had built up around herself years ago. Hope recalled with misgivings a conversation she'd had with Misprint shortly after the latter's arrival.

"There's something about that girl, Christine, that baffles me," Misprint had stated. "I agree with Eileen that she is a wonderfully efficient nurse. She spares no pains to make the patients comfortable. But she sets unrealistic standards of perfection for herself and everyone who works with her. There is a merciless quality about her that almost frightens me. She seems to derive a bitter satisfaction in making herself an unpleasant person to be around."

Hope told Misprint about Christine's experience in the cave, and that she was all that remained of her whole family. After a long moment of silence, Hope continued, "I thought I could help her when she came here. She has never confided in me. The wall she has built around herself seems impenetrable."

Misprint had placed a comforting hand upon Hope's shoulder, saying, "If the Lord could make the walls of Jericho fall flat, He can certainly break down Christine's barriers."

Thinking now of that conversation, Hope arrived at a decision. Upon finding Misprint alone in the tearoom that morning, she drew an envelope from her pocket and shook five small folded slips from it into a saucer. She asked Misprint to draw one. Obligingly she did so and read aloud, "Stephanie Stephanos." She handed it back to Hope with a look of inquiry.

"Thanks," Hope said with a smile of satisfaction. "Stephanie will be Christine's new roommate. I couldn't make the choice myself. Stephanie is of Greek ancestry, as you can tell by her name. Her grandparents came here from Cyprus years ago. Her folks attend the Greek Orthodox church in Jerusalem. As I remember, she is a big girl, about nineteen. She appears to be easygoing and ought to be a good choice."

The new class of aides and male attendants arrived on schedule. By the time they were settled in their class and working on assignments, the seven new full course students arrived. Stephanie Stephanos lived nearest and came before noon, ahead of the others. She was tall and well proportioned. Her dress was rather careless, but she had an attractive, outgoing smile. Her skin was fairer than that of most Arab people, and her eyes were a softer brown.

Before taking her up to her room, Hope conducted the girl to the office to have a little private talk. After a few words Hope plunged boldly into the subject of Christine. As briefly as possible, she sketched a few basic facts about the girl.

"Christine was badly burned several years ago in a fire that destroyed her home and her entire family," Hope explained. "She is much older and more reserved than the other students. You will find that she is very sensitive about anyone seeing her scars. She dresses and undresses behind a screen in her room."

Stephanie nodded understandingly.

"You can trust me to respect her privacy," she assured Hope.

"I must warn you that Christine can be quite difficult at times. Unfortunately, her tragedy has caused her to keep to herself a great deal. She can also be very unkind. You may find it an unhappy arrangement as her roommate. But I know she needs love and understanding. I am praying that you will try to love her and be her friend."

A warm smile curved Stephanie's lips. "I will try, Miss Callaway," she responded heartily.

"Thank you," said Hope. "I'll ask Saleem to take your luggage up to your room. You will have time to get your things unpacked before dinner."

Stephanie detained Hope at the door. She looked puzzled. "Did you say her name is Christine Gomry?" she asked.

"Why, yes," replied Hope. "Do you know her?"

"I think so," Stephanie replied slowly. "She must be the same girl who lived in a cave just above us in the valley below Ras el Ahmoud when I was about eight years old. That girl was badly burned when she fell over a charcoal brazier. The live embers were embedded in her flesh and her gown. They must have burst into flames when she ran out the door. It was early morning and still dark when my parents heard her screaming out on the hillside. She was blazing like a torch. My father was the first one to reach her where she had fallen. He smothered the flames and carried her into our cave. Her screams woke us all up.

"My father went out to see what had happened to the rest of her family, while my mother covered her with blankets. She kept on screaming and tearing at the blankets until mother lifted them. She found some live coals buried deep in her chest and shoulders. They made deep holes. The smell of charred flesh was terrible. I watched my mother dig out the hot embers with a spoon."

Stephanie shuddered at the recollection, then went on, "The girl was unconscious when my father came back and told us that the whole family was dead. But they didn't burn to death. They had been dead for hours, suffocated by the fumes from the charcoal brazier. There was no fire in the cave. The donkey was lying cold and stiff right beside the overturned brazier. She must have stumbled over him and upset the brazier on her way to the door. No one could understand how she alone ever survived the fumes. They were still so strong in the cave that the men hardly dared go in.

"They made a stretcher and carried her up the hill to the police station. The police took her to the hospital in an ambulance. We heard later that she was still living. Soon after that, we moved into a house in Ras el Ahmoud, and I forgot about her. But I am sure she must be the same girl."

"You are probably right," Hope agreed. "But please don't ever mention to Christine that you know anything about her past. It is too painful a subject for her to discuss with anyone."

With the advent of two classes of new students, both nursing directors had heavy teaching schedules. The senior nurses were given increasing responsibilities in the wards. Every night a check of the drug records for the day was made at each ward desk by one of the mission staff and the senior nurse on duty. By now the seniors were entrusted with all scheduled medications, and with much of the ward supervision of the junior students and aides. Thus they received far greater opportunities to develop initiative and the qualities of leadership than are ordinarily allowed senior students in similar American institutions. Of course, their working schedules were far longer and heavier each day than those of their

American counterparts. The graduate aides and male atten-
dants worked twelve hours on the day shift, with breaks during
the patients' afternoon rest periods. They took turns until nine
on the evening shift, assisting the senior nurses to settle the
patients for sleep before the night crew came on duty. All day
students shared the twelve hour day schedule, with one day off
each week.

The senior nurses were given time out for classes in the
forenoons, and the juniors and aides attended afternoon and
evening classes. Although the senior classes were fewer now,
they often had to catch up with their studying and personal
laundry on their one day off.

It was a rugged schedule for all concerned. But the
Palestinian Arabs are a hardy type, well accustomed to long
working hours. They would have considered an eight hour, five
day weekly routine as being conducive to laziness, if not an
actual invitation to indulgence in evil practices.

During the first few weeks of the new term, Hope and Eileen
were caught up in a whirlwind of activity. The midnight oil
often burned very late behind the closed door of the staff sitting
room upstairs. They struggled over class schedules, assignment
of ward duties, and preparation of lessons. But by mid-March
the two acquired a working schedule, and they began to catch
up on a little sleep.

Thus, for a while, the Beth Hanani Mission had rest from
trouble on all sides.

On a blustery day in late March, Matthew Mansfield drove
Dr. Dawson and Elizabeth to the Kalendia airport to meet
Yacoub Kakeesh. Yacoub had not once been home during the
more than eight months he had been studying in Beirut. A spe-
cial homecoming celebration was planned for him in Bethlehem
that night. Elizabeth was allowed the rare privilege of staying
overnight to participate in the festivities honoring her beloved
brother.

Breakfast was over the next morning when the bus bringing the day workers out from the city pulled up at the hospital gate. The bus was very late. The resident staff had taken up their duties for the day. The workers poured forth from both bus exits and hastened up the driveway. Eileen watched them idly from the window of Hope's office. Suddenly she exclaimed, "Here comes Elizabeth, but who is that fine looking young man with her? It can't be Yacoub!"

Hope had joined her at the window. They exclaimed in unison, "It is Yacoub!"

In another moment Elizabeth stood beaming in the doorway. She proudly presented her brother. Gone was the shy, stoop shouldered, gangling boy who had left them nearly nine months ago. In his place stood an erect, broad shouldered, distinguished looking young man. His keen dark eyes surveyed the world confidently through tortoise shell rimmed glasses. Hope and Eileen shook his hand warmly and began questioning him about his Beirut experiences. Elizabeth managed to whisper hurriedly to Hope, "I know I am late, Miss Callaway. I will go change into my uniform right away. But before I go on duty, may I take another few minutes to show Yacoub around? The new people here have never met him. I want them to know he is my brother."

Hope smiled at her eagerness and nodded assent.

The girl scurried off and Hope turned back to Yacoub. He was explaining to Eileen that he had just dashed out this morning for a brief visit. His family wanted him to spend a couple of days visiting at home with friends and relatives before resuming work at the hospital.

Warda appeared in the open doorway with a paper in her hand. She paused uncertainly. Yacoub's back was toward her and she didn't recognize him. He swung around as Hope called to the girl, "Come in Warda, and join us in welcoming Yacoub home."

Warda moved forward obediently. Her gaze was riveted in wide-eyed disbelief upon the face of the young man before her. He was staring at her with a look of startled admiration, as if he had never seen her before. Their glance held for a long moment. Then her eyelids drooped shyly and a lovely flush overspread her cheeks.

Yacoub extended his hand eagerly, forgetting that Arab women do not shake hands with men. "How are you, Warda?" he exclaimed. "You have changed so much, I hardly know you."

The girl confusedly shifted the paper she was holding to her left hand, and allowed her right to be imprisoned in both of his.

"Welcome home, Yacoub," she said. "It is you who has changed."

She freed her hand from his grasp. Her face was scarlet. Yacoub's eyes were glowing. He laughed delightedly as he surveyed her downcast face with the air of one who has just discovered a most unusual treasure. He seemed totally unaware of his amused audience.

Hope reached out and took the paper from the girl's hand, asking, "Did you want to ask me about this, Warda?"

Reminded of her errand, Warda answered, "I should be able to read Dr. Baxter's writing by now, Miss Callaway, but I can't make out these instructions."

"How familiar that sounds," laughed Yacoub. "Maybe I can be of help. I gained quite a reputation at AUH for deciphering doctors' orders."

Hope handed over the paper. He studied it intently for a minute. Then he picked up a pencil from the desk, printed a few clear letters above the obscure ones, and handed it back. Hope compared the two and nodded agreement. She returned the paper to Warda.

With a murmur of thanks, the girl turned to leave. She was almost knocked over by Elizabeth as the latter dashed in. Elizabeth put out her hand to steady her roommate, exclaiming,

"Sorry, Warda! I see you have already met Yacoub. I hope you don't mind my being late. I'll be along in a minute."

"Don't hurry," said Warda, with a shy smile at Yacoub. "Daoud and two of the new attendants are on duty this morning. We are managing fine."

Yacoub's eyes followed her admiringly down the hall. Then he turned to survey his sister. "Why, you are wearing glasses, too!" he exclaimed.

"Oh, yes," she replied with airy nonchalance. "I forgot them yesterday when I went to meet you. I missed them." Then she noticed the increasing amusement in the eyes of both her supervisors, and added hastily, "Shall we go?"

With a formal little bow to the two women, Yacoub excused himself to join his sister. They marched down the hall together.

Eileen subsided in her chair with a giggle.

"Except for the difference in sex, they look almost as much alike as two peas in a pod, and Elizabeth knows it," she remarked. "I doubt that she has ever worn those glasses outside this hospital. It is my guess that she will be wearing them everywhere now."

"Did you notice how they looked at each other?" asked Hope.

"Who? Elizabeth and Yacoub?" Eileen demanded.

"No, Yacoub and Warda," Hope replied. "They were positively starry eyed. I smell the beginning of our first romance."

"Don't tell me you believe all that bosh about 'love at first sight,'" Eileen scoffed.

Hope laughed at the disgust in her tone.

"I suppose we might call it 'love at second sight,' or rather 'four sight.' Yacoub's glasses have certainly sharpened his vision where Warda is concerned. She seems equally impressed with the change in him."

Eileen was preparing to depart. She picked up her books and papers and paused in the doorway to remark, "Dream on, little one, they will name their first daughter Hope, of course." Then in a very quiet undertone, "But maybe, just maybe, they could call their second one Eileen."

"Eileen, Cupid is usually not content to shoot his darts at only one couple. I wonder where he plans to aim next." Hope said.

Eileen laughed and strode out of the room.

TWENTY-EIGHT

THE VERY NEXT SUNDAY morning, Hope arrived late for chapel services. All the rear seats were taken. She saw one against the far wall in the third row. Murmuring apologies, she reached the seat in time to bow her head for the invocation.

The congregation remained seated during the first hymn. In the middle of the first verse, Hope became aware that Dr. Morcus Kemalyian was sitting directly in front of her. He was turned sideways, and she could see his profile. She noticed that he was not singing. Instead, his gaze was fixed on someone seated in the front row. So intent was his look, that Hope leaned forward to discover the object of his scrutiny. A group of student nurses was sitting there together. She soon reached the positive conclusion that he was watching Aminah Abdullah. Hope was startled by this knowledge, and settled back to assess her own reactions to the situation. She had been thrilled with joy by Yacoub's and Warda's interest in each other. Now she felt only pity and dismay over the plight of the obscure young doctor. With his double handicap of poverty and his Christian background, he would stand no chance against the wealth and violent prejudices of Mohammed Abdullah.

In vain she made an effort to keep her mind on the services. Her thoughts kept reverting to the man before her. Dr. Morcus turned squarely to face the platform as soon as Dr. Dawson began his message. From then on he became thoroughly engrossed in the service. By the time the service ended, Hope was wondering if she were only imagining that the young man entertained any romantic interest in Aminah.

To her surprise, she found Dr. Morcus at her elbow when she reached the door. He fell into step beside her.

"May I have a private word with you, Miss Callaway?" he asked respectfully.

"Of course," she responded.

At the foot of the steps she turned into the path leading to the clinic. It was always deserted on Sundays. They walked a few yards in silence until out of earshot of the others. Then she faced the doctor expectantly and waited for him to speak. His face was flushed with embarrassment. He appeared to be at a loss for words. Finally he began.

"I fear my question may seem very ungentlemanly, Miss Callaway, even when judged by your American standards." He paused to wipe the sweat from his brow, then struggled manfully on. "Ordinarily, it is against the custom of Eastern men to discuss young ladies among themselves. For this reason, I hesitate to question Dr. Dawson. I trust that I do not offend. I have an overwhelming curiosity regarding the religious beliefs of one of your nursing students. I refer to Miss Aminah Abdullah. Her name is Moslem. But I notice that she joins regularly in all our Christian worship services. I have seen and heard her praying with patients in the wards. Is she a Christian?"

"Oh, yes, indeed," Hope responded warmly. Then, warned by the leaping joy in his eyes, she added hastily, "But, as you probably know, her father is a powerful member of the Moslem

Brotherhood. He has absolutely forbidden her to discuss it with him. She is resigned to the fact that he would never consent to an open acknowledgment of her faith. Only we here at the hospital know that she committed her life wholeheartedly to Christ. I am telling you this in strictest confidence. Her father was furious when he first discovered it. Only his great love for Aminah and his long standing friendship with Dr. Dawson have prevented him from venting his wrath upon the mission. Without a doubt, he hopes that this is just a passing whim of his daughter's."

"Do you believe that it is?" Dr. Morcus persisted.

Hope spoke decisively. "No, I believe that she will remain unshaken in her convictions."

A warm smile lit up the doctor's features. Hope saw that he still did not fully grasp the situation. His next question showed her why he failed to do so.

"Have I ever met her father?" he asked uncertainly.

"Why, yes," she answered in surprise. "I am sure you have dined with him at Dr. Dawson's table. He is Mohammed Abdullah. I thought you knew all about him."

"I suppose I should have known," he replied in a rather subdued tone. "But the name is such a common one that the connection never occurred to me." The light of hope was dying hard in his eyes.

Hope continued deliberately, "Mohammed Abdullah is extremely wealthy. Aminah is his sole heir, as well as his dearest treasure. She is of marriageable age. He suspects that all men without comparable fortune are seeking to marry her for his wealth. He trusts Mrs. Dawson and me to guard her like dragons. He hopes to arrange a suitable marriage for her by the time she completes her training here."

She stopped abruptly, aware that she had said far more than was needed. Dr. Morcus's hands were clenched so tightly that the knuckle bones stood out whitely beneath the taut brown flesh. There was a long moment of painful silence. Slowly his clenched fists relaxed. With an effort he recovered his poise and continued without any expression in his face.

"I see," he said. "Thank you, Miss Callaway. You have been most kind."

As he turned and strode away, Hope muttered to herself, "Kind? Is it kindness to stab a friend?"

Her spirits lifted that afternoon when Aminah came to report that Hikmat had surrendered her heart and life to Jesus within the past hour. She wanted to talk to Hope about it. Hope had often seen the woman reading an Arabic Testament. She was quite well educated. The missionaries were forbidden by law to offer the books as gifts, but the patients could ask for them on lean, or buy them outright.

Hikmat looked up with a smile when Hope entered the ward.

"Miss Callaway," she said. "When I learned that Rehab was going to have a baby, my heart was filled with such hatred. She loves my children and is mothering them well. She comforts my husband. I had no reason to hate her. But I could not tear the hatred out of my heart. I kept reading about Jesus' love, and I asked Aminah and Regina to help me pray that I would come to know it. Now I have His love for Rehab in my heart, and there is peace and joy there too, just as He promised."

"That is wonderful, Hikmat," Hope assured her. "I hear that you are almost well now. How will you feel toward Rehab when you return home? How will she feel about you?"

"I do not know, Miss Callaway," Hikmat replied simply. "I trust Jesus now to tell me what to do. I know His peace will abide in my heart. I trust Him."

Hope regarded her with awe and amazement. As she left the woman's bedside, she pondered the outcome.

Dr. Kemalyian's license to practice medicine in Jordan arrived the following day. Within a week, he moved into a small rented office in Bethlehem, with sleeping quarters in the rear.

Regina Murad's mother was his landlady. She possessed a remarkable memory. She had learned that the doctor was in need of equipment and instruments, and recalled that a Bethlehem doctor had closed his office and left for South America five years before. He had stored his medical equipment with relatives. She located the stored equipment and dickered with the relatives for the doctor to purchase it on a long term agreement. He hoped to squeeze the monthly payments out of medical fees. He was very grateful for Mrs. Murad's help. The Murad family lived close by, and he took most of his meals with them. Mrs. Murad also did his laundry and cleaned his office weekly.

The office building was in a good location on the main street in a newer section of Bethlehem. It was one block above the Arab Hospital and overlooked the Bethlehem-Hebron-Beit Jala crossroads. In less than two weeks Dr. Morcus was offered a position on the staff of the Arab hospital. He had been highly recommended by Dr. Dawson. Since he lived only one block away, and was willing to stand by for emergency calls night and day, he was soon picking up the crumbs from the other doctors' practices. This was hardly fair, since he ended up with the poorest patients. But he struggled along cheerfully, managed to keep up with his financial obligations, and never refused care to anyone in need.

Hope rarely saw him. He still came to assist Dr. Dawson two mornings a week and on Friday afternoons. She often wondered if he were getting over his interest in Aminah.

One Friday afternoon in late April, Saleem found her sitting idly at her desk in the classroom, dreamily watching a wisp of cottony white cloud floating across the deep blue sky. A delightful spring fragrance drifted in through the open window. Classes were over for the day. There were none scheduled for that evening. Saleem handed her a note from Margaret Dawson. It was an urgent invitation to dinner at six o'clock. Margaret explained that she was faced with the prospect of having four men on her hands. She was depending on Hope for some feminine support. The note caught Hope in a perfect mood for an evening of social diversion, and she scrawled an acceptance, and gave it to Saleem for delivery.

As usual, the meal was excellent. It was served by Maryam, the Dawson's cook. The chief and Mohammed Abdullah were in an expansive mood. They began to engage in friendly banter. Dr. Morcus and Matt Mansfield were being highly entertained by the conversation of the two older men. The women began some quiet chatter of their own. Margaret broke off in the middle of a sentence, and Hope pricked up her ears.

As frequently happened at the Damson table, the Crusades of the Middle Ages were up for discussion. Had Dr. Baxter, or another Englishman been present, a heated argument might arise regarding the respective merits of the Arab champion, Saladin, and Richard the Lionhearted of England. Being an American, the chief remained content to parry each thrust of his opponent with goodnatured amusement.

Margaret was about to relax when Mohammed let slip an illadvised remark to the effect that Saladin's superior courage undoubtedly stemmed from the brave example of the great prophet, Mohammed; whereas, Richard's lesser degree of courage was easily accounted for by the lack of power of the leader whom he followed.

Dr. Dawson stared at his friend as if wondering if he had heard the man right. While he fumbled for a suitable reply, young Matt leaned forward and asked in a clear, low tone, "Sir, do I understand that, when you spoke just now of King Richard's leader as being less powerful, you were referring to our Lord Jesus Christ?"

The room became ominously quiet. For once, both women were tongue-tied. The two doctors exchanged apprehensive glances. Mohammed began to flush and to stir uneasily under

Matt's steady gaze. Finally, he cleared his throat and sttempted to speak in an offhand manner.

"Why, yes," he said, "as a matter of fact, I was referring to Jesus Christ. To us, he was merely a prophet, without much power."

Matt's voice, although still quietly respectful, now had the ring of steel in it.

"Sir," he said, "I am willing to concede that history appears to have shown that your Saladin had a few more generous and gentlemanly qualities than Richard. Possibly they were about evenly matched in physical courage, but we Christians are fairly well agreed that the Crusades were without a doubt the greatest mistake that was ever undertaken in the name of Christ.

"My Lord never advocated killing. He never once raised His hand against His enemies, although He possessed all the power of God to destroy them. He was, and is, the most courageous man who ever walked upon this earth. He has the power to inspire all those who truly follow Him."

"That is your opinion, young man," Mohammed countered with a sneer.

Matt's face was flushed with earnestness. Hope clasped her hands tightly together under the table to keep from applauding. Margaret cast an imploring look at her husband, but his eyes were upon Matt. The boy was studying the face of the man opposite with increasing interest. Now he leaned forward, fixed his guileless blue eyes upon Mohammed's scornful one, and inquired in a deceptively innocent tone, "Sir, have you ever studied the life and teachings of Jesus for yourself? I refer to accounts of his own contemporaries. Practically all the New Testament accounts were written by those who witnessed His miracles, His death, and His resurrection. Have you ever read the New Testament for yourself, Sir, or even one of the four gospels?"

"No," snapped Mohammed. "But I imagine we are even on that score. I doubt if you have ever read the Koran or any of our other books on Islam, yourself." He realized too late, that he had been fairly caught. Matt flicked a swift glance in Dr. Dawson's direction and answered readily,

"There you are wrong, Sir! Dr. Dawson has some excellent books on Islam. I have been reading all of them." Matt leaned forward and quietly drove his point home. "Does it not seem to a man of your intelligence that a man's opinion on any subject is of little value unless he has first made a thorough study of the subject himself?"

The company could not have been more startled if a bombshell had exploded in the room. With a roar of rage, Mohammed was on his feet. His face was purple with anger.

"Boy!" he hissed, "do you presume to offer advice to me? If so, By Allah, you need to learn some manners!"

Matt replied with humble and sincere contrition.

"I am sorry to have offended you, Sir. I had no right to say what I did. I apologize to you and . . ." he glanced around the table ". . . to everyone present, especially to the ladies."

Mohammed allowed himself to be mollified. He nodded curtly, saying, "I accept your apology, in view of the fact that there are ladies present."

Hope breathed a sigh of relief. The men relaxed back in their chairs, and Matt rose to face Mohammed. His huge farmer's hands gripped the edge of the table as if summoning strength. The chief laid a warning hand on the one nearest him. Then Matt spoke. His voice was low and tender.

"Sir," he said earnestly, "I feel impelled to beg you, no, to challenge you, to search the Scriptures for yourself. Then draw your own conclusions regarding the merits and claims of Christ."

Mohammed was staring at Matt as one mesmerized. Once before Hope had seen that look on his face as he stared at his own hands while his daughter lay gasping at his feet. Now she saw his fierce eyes soften. Suddenly, a warm smile lit up his haughty features. He extended his hand to Matt.

"Young man," he said heartily, "I must admit that you certainly have the courage of your own convictions. I will accept your challenge! Here is my hand on it!"

Matt's huge hand reached eagerly across the table to engulf Mohammed's in a grip that made the older man wince.

Before anyone else could move or speak, Margaret rose and said hurriedly, "I move that we all adjourn to the other room for coffee."

The chief linked arms with his volatile Arab friend. They fell into step behind the women, leaving the two younger men to follow. Hope glanced back from the doorway in time to see Dr. Morcus grasp Matt's hand and pump it vigorously.

A few days later Hope was alone in the tearoom when Dr. Baxter came bursting in with news.

"Guess what?" he exclaimed as soon as he saw her. "Mohammed Abdullah dropped into the clinic a few minutes ago on the pretext of having a little indigestion. There was nothing wrong with his stomach, of course. I prescribed some bismuth. He continued to stay, and seemed to be looking for something. I guessed what he was up to and asked him right out what it was he wanted. He admitted that he wanted a New Testament. I had a small one in my desk that sells for five piasters. He laughed when I told him the price, and handed me fifty. Then he slipped the book into his inside coat pocket and buttoned his coat tight so that no one could see it. I wonder if he will read it by flashlight under his blankets by night, as I did with forbidden books when I was a youngster."

They both laughed. Hope asked, "Did you hear about Margaret's dinner party the other night?"

"Oh, yes," he replied. "The chief gave me a thorough briefing. He was mighty proud of Matt. I take off my own hat to the lad. He showed more courage than all the rest of us put together."

" 'Out of the mouths of babes . . .,' " Hope quoted happily.

TWENTY-NINE

IN MID-MAY MUSTAPHA Hussein brought to Hikmat the eagerly awaited news that Rehab had given birth to a daughter. Since the four other children were boys, the arrival of a baby girl was particularly gratifying to the whole family. Along with his news of the baby's arrival, Mustapha brought a written invitation to both nursing directors from Rehab to visit her and the new baby as soon as possible. They could not both be spared from the hospital on the same day, but each promised to visit Rehab soon.

The new staff home was now being prepared for occupancy. In the bustle of getting staff and equipment moved, and the vacated hospital rooms ready for waiting patients, neither nurse found time to make the promised call until several weeks later.

For some time the metalsmiths, carpenters, and other craftsmen in Bethlehem and Jerusalem had been busily constructing new beds and furniture for both buildings. As rapidly as each former staff room in the hospital was equipped with suitable furniture, it was promptly filled.

Ever since Hikmat had become a Christian, she had been making remarkable progress toward recovery. By mid-June her X-rays were normal, and Dr. Dawson gave his permission for her to be discharged. Hikmat departed happily on the anniversary date of her own arrival. Hope accompanied her to the taxi. She made Hope promise to come to tea at her Ramallah home two weeks later.

On the appointed day Matt drove Hope to the Hussein home in Ramallah. He left her there and went on to visit an American pal at the Friends' School nearby. Rehab met her former superintendent at the door and greeted her warmly. She ushered her into a large, tastefully furnished living room. The guest was instantly impressed by its unobtrusive beauty. Hikmat sat in a luxurious armchair holding the baby in her arms. A handsome little boy between three and four years of age stood at her knee. A neat young maid came to take Hope's coat. After warm expressions of admiration for the children, Hope began inquiring politely after the health of her two hostesses and all the rest of the family. They assured her that everyone was well. Then, with equal politeness, the two Arab women inquired after the health of everyone in the hospital.

Having exhausted this topic of conversation, Rehab passed Hope the customary dish of foil-wrapped chocolates. Then she placed the dish on a table at Hikmat's elbow. Hope noted how solicitously Rehab hovered over the older woman. She adjusted a pillow more comfortably at her back and placed a footstool beneath her feet. In a few minutes she sent the boy off to be cared for by the maid, lest he tire his mother. Then she took the baby from Hikmat and settled down in a chair to nurse her.

Since no one seemed disposed to volunteer the information that Hope was secretly dying to know, she came right out and asked the baby's name.

A rosy flush overspread Rehab's face.

"I know that I promised to name her for you, Miss Hope," she answered with obvious embarrassment. "But we all liked 'Eileen' better for a first name. Her second name is 'Hope.' I actually spent more time in the wards with Miss Eileen than I did with you in the classroom, so I got to know her better. I do hope you don't mind?"

"Of course, I don't mind, Rehab," Hope assured her hastily. Actually, the news came as quite a shock. She was amazed to find that she really did mind. However, she forced herself to add heartily, "I am sure that Miss Anderson will be very pleased."

Rehab looked greatly relieved.

"Please tell her we want her to come next week to see her namesake, Miss Hope," she begged. "I really do plan to keep my second promise and send little Eileen to the Beth Hanani Hospital to become a nurse when she is old enough."

The baby had finished nursing and was now fast asleep. Rehab carried her off to lay her in her crib. Hope moved to a seat closer to Hikmat and asked in a low tone, "Are you happy, Hikmat?"

There was a flicker of quiet amusement in Hikmat's eyes.

"You are wondering how Rehab and I are getting along in the matter of sharing a husband," she stated with a smile. "There has been no difficulty. I just told Abu Ameer that I should not give birth to anymore children. He believed me. I think he was actually relieved. My position here is now that of a loved sister. There will be no jealousy between Rehab and me."

"But," said the astonished listener, "surely you were told at the hospital that if you accepted the full cure and were once healed, you would have no difficulty in pregnancy if you maintained the health and diet rules and took plenty of rest? I am sure Rehab knows these rules."

Hikmat's eyes twinkled. "Of course she does. She knows that I know it, too. But Abu Ameer doesn't know it. There is no reason why he should. He is satisfied with the arrangement. So are we."

Their conversation was interrupted by the return of Rehab. She was followed by the maid, wheeling a heavily laden tea cart. The maid placed the cups and teapot before Hikmat, who poured the tea. Rehab piled their guest with an amazing variety of sweetmeats, explaining proudly that she had made most of them herself. In spite of Hope's protests that she could not possibly dispose of so many, her plate was soon heaped with a delicious assortment.

Before long the ring of the doorbell announced the arrival of Matthew Mansfield. It was only when the maid switched on the hall and living room lights on her way to the door, that Hope realized the day was nearly over. Matt accepted a sweetmeat from Rehab, then waited while she escorted Hope to the bedroom to get her coat. They both paused to admire the sleeping baby in her crib beside the large double bed of her parents. Hope noted the lovely imported furniture and the exquisite quality of the drapes. They expressed the wealth and good taste of the owner. Rehab proudly showed her the bathroom, and the two bedrooms in which the boys were paired off. Then she opened a door at the far end of the hall saying, "This one is Hikmat's."

The room was large. It was beautifully furnished. A leather bound Bible lay on the bedside table. Above the bed was an unusually striking painting of a lifelike Jesus standing before the empty tomb. Hope had never seen a painting like it. She asked where it had come from.

"It is an original," she explained. "It was done by a local artist who has a shop here in Ramallah. I bought it for Hikmat."

"You?" exclaimed Hope in surprise.

"Yes," Rehab answered. "We were out for a stroll with Fareed and the baby in her carriage a few days ago. Hikmat saw it in the shop window. She like it so much that I asked Abu Ameer for the money to buy it. We hung it here yesterday."

Seeing that Hope still looked amazed, Rehab burst out, "Miss Callaway, I was so afraid and jealous when Hikmat first came home. But she has brought so much love into this house that I am ashamed. She has given up her husband to me. I feel that I can never do enough for her. She tells me it is Jesus' love that He has put within her heart which enables her to be so loving. I can't understand it, but I can feel it. So can Abu Ameer. We both realize that it is a powerful influence for good in our home. We are willing for her to teach the children about Jesus. It brings her so much happiness."

Rehab closed the door. They returned to the living room, where Hope and Matt made hasty farewells to Hikmat. The latter rose from her chair and accompanied Rehab to the door to see them off. As Matt drove rapidly away in the dusk, Hope looked back to see Mustapha's two wives standing in the doorway. Rehab's arm rested protectingly about the shoulders of the older woman. Hikmat's arm encircled the waist of her slim younger companion.

It was dark when the car reached the outskirts of Bethlehem. Supper was long finished by the time Matt drove into the hospital grounds. They stopped at the Dawsons to report their arrival. Matt was ready for the sandwiches and coffee that Margaret offered. Hope was still too stuffed with Rehab's cakes to want any more food that night. They listened with interest to the chief's report that the law had finally caught up with Jaleel Yusef. He was caught using duplicate keys in a robbery. He was now behind bars for a term of ten years. On the day of his arrest, the neighbors called in Dr. Kemalyian to treat Jaleel's wife. She had received an unmerciful beating at the hands of her husband for revealing the hiding place of his loot when the officers came to search the home.

For many years the neighbors had suspected that the poor woman was losing her mind. Now Dr. Kemalyian discovered an old injury of many years standing. Undoubtedly, the beating had intensified the existing brain damage. All that Dr. Kemalyian could do was to bind up her wounds and administer a sedative. No sympathy was expressed for Jaleel. The neighbors were caring for his demented wife as best they could.

The American missionaries wondered what had become of Aida. No one in Bethlehem had laid eyes on her since her departure for Nablus with her husband nearly a year ago. If her mother knew anything of her whereabouts, the secret was now locked in her befuddled brain.

On the way to her own room Hope stopped at Eileen's door to inform her that Rehab's baby was named after her. She also delivered Rehab's verbal invitation to come to tea the following week. Eileen was overwhelmed with delight at the news.

Hope closed her own door with a sigh of relief that she had been able to conceal her own disappointment at Rehab's choice of a name.

Hope sat reading her Bible for a long time that night. She was tired, but her guilty conscience would not let her rest.

Now she recalled the day in the fourth grade, when, for the first time, her name stood second on the list of those who passed the class examinations, instead of first. She vowed then that it would never happen again. She saw to it that it never did. It had taken a long time for her to get over her resentment of the boy who stood first on the list.

She thought of how fond she was of mentioning the fact that she was valedictorian of her high school graduating class. That meant four years of the highest grades in every subject. She never failed to add that she was among the ten highest, out of over fifteen hundred graduate nurses, who took the State Board examinations. She never admitted to anyone but herself the acute disappointment of not ever knowing if her name headed the list of those ten. She was practically certain that it did.

At last she faced the awful truth. It was pride and self-love that had taken her off to the mission field. Even there, she had never been content to play second fiddle to anyone. How blind she had been to her own love of her miserable self.

Self-revelation is never pleasant. She rose and faced herself accusingly in the mirror, and began hurling scornful epithets at the image she saw reflected there: "Hope Callaway, you liar! You hypocrite!" she stormed. "You are so jealous of Eileen that you can't even stand yourself! Pretending that you love the girls so much you can't bear to discipline them. You are really afraid if you do they will love someone else better than they do you. You can't stand the thought that Rehab liked Eileen just a little better than yourself. You are just wallowing in self-pity.

"These girls have enough sense to appreciate Eileen. You haven't any sense at all. You are just as childish as those Nigerian natives you were training. You knew they needed discipline. But because you knew they were like little children, who always resent restraint, and that their affections often turned to bitter hatred of anyone who tried to discipline them, you left that part of their training to the other missionaries. You always made sure that you stood highest in the affection of the natives. Your fellow workers must have sighed with relief when you decided to leave the work there.

"Eileen has more genuine love for these girls in one of her little fingers than you have in your whole body," she continued hotly. "You fraud! These girls are not children. Her discipline is winning their love as well as their respect. You make me sick. You don't like to admit even now that you were never capable of loving anyone as much as you love yourself."

Overcome with remorse, she dropped into her chair and wept bitter tears of repentance. It was a long time before she became quiet enough to hear God's gentle voice asking, "Child, lovest thou Me?"

She considered the question for several minutes, then answered humbly, "Lord, You know that I do."

Then He asked, "Hast no man condemned thee?"

Hope carefully searched her heart and memory and found that she could reply in all honesty, "No man, Lord."

"Neither do I condemn thee. Go, and sin no more."

These words were blessed assurance and loving encouragement to her contrite heart. Hope gratefully sought her bed. Her spiritual vision was yet too imperfect to perceive that a far more grievous sin still stood in the way of a perfect relationship between them.

THIRTY

TOWARD THE END OF June an airmail letter from America arrived postmarked from the town where Hanni was staying. Hope tore it open eagerly. A small snapshot of a baby fell from it into her lap. The letter was from a cousin of the Mennonite sisters in Hebron. She wrote guardedly to say that her niece had taken a baby girl to care for while the mother worked to support herself and the child. The baby was born June 5 in the Mennonite Maternity Home. The child weighed barely five pounds at birth, but was sturdy and healthy. She showed promise of becoming a beautiful little girl. The mother had a very easy delivery. Her husband was dead. Near the end of the letter the writer casually mentioned that Hanni was well and working nearby. She would enter the fall class of nursing students in the large Mennonite hospital a few miles distant.

Hope read the letter through twice. Then she picked up the snapshot. It was evidently taken in the hospital within a few hours of the child's birth. She studied the picture with a curious concern. The tiny features seemed to resemble Hanni, but the chin was somewhat similar to Khaleed's. This could become a good asset to her character. On the back, in Hanni's handwriting, was, "Her name is Hope." This brought a thrill of joy to Hope's heart, mingled with a feeling of unworthiness and a stab of regret over her selfish reaction to the naming of Rehab's child. She shared the news and the picture with her fellow missionaries, but did not let them see the writing on the back.

Knowing that Christine was anxiously awaiting news, Hope waylaid the girl after dinner. She drew her into the isolation room, and closed the door. Then she produced the letter and picture. Christine's eyes filled with tears of joy and relief as she read that the baby weighed only five pounds at birth, and that Hanni had an easy delivery.

"I was so afraid for her, she was so little and frail," said Christine, wiping her eyes. "I am glad it is a girl."

"So am I," said Hope. "Now Hanni will have a second chance to become a nurse. Indeed, God has been merciful to us all." She slipped her arm about the girl as they moved toward the door. "Remember, not a word of this to anyone, Christine," she warned. "Our hospital could still be endangered."

A shiver passed through the girl.

"I cannot forget, Miss Hope," she answered quickly, "I know this is my second chance, too, and my last. I want so much to be a nurse that I lie awake sometimes worrying for fear I will do something wrong and lose this chance."

Hope was genuinely distressed.

"Oh, Christine, you shouldn't do that," she exclaimed. "You will just tie yourself up in knots. You must have faith."

"Oh, I do," the girl replied. "But I can't trust myself."

"Why not, Christine?" Hope probed gently.

For an instant she thought that the "wall" was about to crumble. Then the girl pulled away from her arm.

"I can't tell you, Miss Hope," she cried despairingly. "It is just too terrible." She pulled open the door and fled down the hall to the men's ward as if pursued by a demon.

Hope was conducting a junior class the next morning when Marika, the new bookkeeper, appeared to tell her that Mrs. Milad was waiting to see her. Hope's heart contracted. Since the morning tea hour was over, she asked Marika to have the woman wait in the tearoom. Then she hastily assigned some written work to the students. She directed them to leave the completed papers on her desk, and went to face Hanni's mother.

Mrs. Milad was staring out the window when Hope entered. She turned quickly. The eager look in her eyes confirmed Hope's suspicions that the woman knew something. Not being certain as to how much, Hope decided to be casual.

"Please sit down, Mrs. Milad," she began cordially, indicating a chair. The woman perched obediently on the edge and clasped her hands tightly in her lap. Hope sat down facing her, and chattered on brightly, "It is good to see you again, Mrs. Milad. I hope that your husband and all the children are well?"

Her guest managed a nod.

What do you hear from Hanni?" Hope asked. "She promised to write you regularly."

Hanni's mother flung out her trembling hands in a gesture of despair. "She writes, yes, but what does she say? Nothing! To her own mother. She tells me nothing!" She hitched her chair closer to Hope's. "Please, Miss Callaway, you must know something by now. Did the baby come yet? Is my Hanni all right?" She clasped her hands in an imploring gesture.

"Mrs. Milad," Hope said kindly, "I will tell you. But first you must promise me that you will never tell anyone else."

"Before God, I will never tell," she promised breathlessly.

Hope leaned down and whispered in her ear, "Hanni is fine. She has a baby daughter."

"Thank God!" the poor mother exclaimed. She covered her face with her hands and rocked back and forth. Tears of relief trickled through her fingers. Hope sat down and waited quietly.

In a few minutes, Mrs. Milad recovered herself. She wiped her eyes and smiled mistily at Hope.

"Did Hanni tell you anything before she left?" asked Hope with curiosity. "How did you know?"

Mrs. Milad shook her head sadly. "She told me nothing. But what sort of a mother do you take me for, Miss Callaway? I knew my Hanni was in trouble. I saw it in her eyes the week before Mrs. Dawson came with that paper. She fooled my husband with her fine tales about America, but she didn't fool me. Why else could I ever have signed that paper and let her go? I knew we could do nothing to shield her from shame and disgrace. But my daughter did not trust her own mother. She has never told me anything." Her voice broke on the last words.

"Mrs. Milad," Hope assured her. "Hanni did love and trust you. It wasn't that at all. We couldn't take any chances on the news leaking out. It would have ruined our hospital. Dr. Dawson made Hanni take a solemn oath on the Bible that she would tell no one, not even you. I am glad that she kept that oath. I am trusting you to keep the one you made just now, also," she added.

"I will never tell, Miss Callaway," Mrs. Milad assured her. "Not even my husband. He doesn't need to know. It would only hurt him. You people have saved Hanni. I can never repay you, but I can pray God's blessing upon you and your mission here." She hesitated, then asked, "The man was Khaleed Khalil, wasn't he?"

"Yes," Hope admitted. "But it wasn't Hanni's fault."

"You needn't tell me," said Hanni's mother grimly. "I knew that man was a scoundrel. We suspected that he seduced a Moslem girl in Bethlehem before the Dawsons came. You know what happens to them. She just disappeared. I always felt that Dr. Dawson made a wrong choice in trusting that man with his business. If I had ever thought then that he would ever dare approach my Hanni, I would have come straight to Dr. Dawson. But I had no actual proof about the Moslem girl."

Hope was thankful that Hanni's mother would never know about her daughter's suicide attempt. She thought it best to change the direction of their conversation. "Hanni expects to enter nurse's training this fall. She will probably write to tell you about it."

Mrs. Milad's eyes brightened. Then she asked uncertainly, "But what about the baby, Miss Callaway? You said she was all right, didn't you? Who will take care of her?"

"She is just fine," Hope assured her. "A cousin of the Mennonite sisters will take care of her. Wait a minute. I have something to show you."

Hope hurried to her room and took the baby picture out of her locked desk drawer. She returned to the tearoom with it concealed in her pocket. There she handed it to Mr. Milad. The woman studied it carefully for several minutes. Then she turned it over and saw Hanni's handwriting.

"Her name is Hope," she read aloud. "Hanni has named her for a good and lovely woman." Then she held out the picture to Hope.

Hope hesitated, then asked, "Would you like to keep it?"

Mrs. Milad eyed it wistfully, then shook her head. "No, someone might find it," she decided. "I shall just keep it here." She indicated her heart, then rose, saying, "I must get back to the children. I hope I haven't just missed a bus."

Hope accompanied her to the door and glanced up the road toward Hebron. A service taxi was just rounding the bend by the refugee camp. "Saleem!" she called to the gateman. "Please hail that taxi and ask if they have a vacant seat."

Mrs. Milad started to protest, "No, please, I . . . " she stopped, crimsoning with embarrassment, then ended lamely, ". . . I will just wait for the bus."

Hope guessed instantly that the poor woman's shabby purse contained only the three piasters needed for the bus fare. The taxi seat would cost five. The driver had stopped. Saleem motioned for them to hurry. Hope left her reluctant companion to follow, and ran down the driveway, fumbling in her pocket for the shilling she always kept there for such emergencies. Her fingers encountered nothing but her keys, the baby picture, and a handkerchief. Saleem was holding the rear door open. She stepped close to him and whispered, "Saleem, please loan me a shilling to pay her fare."

Saleem dug down in his pocket and produced a handful of piasters. He counted out five into the hand of the driver. Mrs. Milad arrived with downcast eyes in the midst of the transaction. She offered no protest, merely thanked Saleem as he helped her into the taxi and closed the door.

As the taxi drove off, Hope's searching hand found the shilling tucked deep down in the corner of her pocket. She drew it forth with triumph. "Thanks, Saleem, she said. "Now I can pay you back right away. It was in my pocket all the time."

She held out the coin to him as she spoke. He made no move to take it. She stepped closer and tried to thrust it into his hand. He put both hands behind his back and retreated with a smile.

"This is ridiculous!" Hope stormed. "I just borrowed it from you. I never would have asked you to loan it to me if I didn't think you would let me pay you back. An American man would have more sense . . ." Too late, she clapped her hand over her mouth.

The smile vanished from Saleem's face. With flashing eyes, he drew himself to his full height. "You forget, Madame," he reminded her proudly, "I am an Arab!"

Hope recovered herself quickly. "Of course you are, Saleem," she said contritely. "You have every right to be proud of it. I am sure my own countrymen could learn many lessons in courtesy from the men of Jordan. I thank you for coming so nobly to

Mrs. Milad's rescue, and to mine. My offer to pay you back was an insult. I beg your pardon. Will you forgive me?"

She looked up meekly and saw with relief that the familiar friendly warmth was back in his eyes. He bowed gravely.

"For nothing, Miss Callaway," he said. "It is forgotten."

There still remained one person who was entitled to know about Hanni. That person was Murshdeeyah. When the Ramallah Home and School closed for vacation in early June, some of the orphans had no place to go. They stayed on at the home throughout the summer. Murshdeeyah was given one week off to visit her mother, then she returned to cook for the remaining children and the mission staff while the regular cook took a rest. Hope had a standing invitation from the English directors of the Ramallah Home to visit whenever she was free to come. She sent them word that she would be there for lunch on her day off the following week.

When she rang the doorbell, Murshdeeyah appeared. The girl had such an expectant look on her face that Hope pulled her head down and whispered in her ear, "Hanni has a little girl. They are both fine."

With a wide grin of delight, Murshdeeyah whispered back, "Baby little?"

"Oh, yes," Hope replied. "Very little. Only five pounds."

Murshdeeyah looked quite puzzled.

Kate Jones, one of the missionary staff, caught Hope's last remark as she hurried forward to great their guest. She shook her finger reprovingly at her.

"Don't let Miss Callaway fool you, Mary Martha," she said. "Five pounds is a lot of money."

"I was speaking of American weights," said Hope with a smile. To Murshdeeyah she explained kindly, "Five pounds is about equal to two and one-half kilos. Your Arabic kilo is about two American pounds in weight. Five pounds is not very big."

The girl nodded.

"*Nam*, I see," she said, moving toward the kitchen door. "Very little. Allah is good!"

"Come, take off your things. Let us sit in the living room for a while," invited Kate. She led the way into the other room. "Dinner will be ready soon. You will find that Mary Martha is a good cook."

"Is that what I heard you call Murshdeeyah?" asked Hope.

"Didn't she tell you we had a new name for her?" Kate asked. "She is always reading the Bible. When she read about Mary and Martha, she was very impressed. She is such a good combination of both sisters, that we decided to call her Mary Martha. She is very pleased."

"The name certainly fits her," Hope agreed. "I would like to have a little visit with her some time today when she is free."

"She will like that," Kate said. "We will tell her when she serves the dinner."

Later, Hope sat talking with Murshdeeyah in her small bedroom upstairs. It adjoined the dormitory where the smallest children slept. The girl was assigned to mother them at bedtime and throughout the night.

"How have you been doing with your special lessons this summer, Murshdeeyah?" Hope asked with interest.

"Fine, Miss Hope," the girl answered with care. "Mrs. Holmes says she can stand under me most of the time now."

Hope giggled.

"You mean understand, don't you?" she asked.

"Nam, yes," agreed Murshdeeyah. "Under-stand, stand-under, are they not the same?"

Hope tried to explain. "You stand under an umbrella when it rains. You understand when you come to know what a word, or a person really means. If Miss Holmes 'stood under' you, you would be standing on top of her."

Murshdeeyah chuckled heartily, then said, "I tell you something very funny, Miss Hope. One day Miss Holmes say, 'make sentence with words 'off-ten' and 'seldom.' I say, 'I off-ten go to Beth Hanani, I seldom come back.' Mrs. Holmes laugh and laugh. She say, 'How you do it, Mary Martha?' I see what she mean. I understand mistake."

Hope joined in the girl's hearty laughter at her own expense.

Near the end of Hope's visit she became serious.

"Miss Jones is sure you will be ready to enter training school two years from next spring, Murshdeeyah."

The girl clapped her hands in delight.

"Suppose I am not at Beth Hanani then?" Hope probed. "Would you still want to come there to train?"

Murshdeeyah looked astonished. "You go away, maybe, Miss Hope?" she asked. "Why?"

"Well, perhaps the Lord will want me somewhere else," Hope said. "If this is so, would you still want to come?"

The girl considered the question. Then she answered simply, "Miss Hope. I would miss you. But I have many sisters now. You are my dearest one."

Hope was completely satisfied. This best loved one of all her children, now became her dearest sister.

THIRTY-ONE

IT WAS THE LAST day of June. Dr. Dawson entered the tea-room that morning bringing a large stack of mail from Bethlehem. It was rather late. Hope was the only staff member still present. She poured the chief a cup of tea. He gave her her letters and they settled down companionably to read. Presently the doctor handed her an open letter.

"I wrote this fellow a couple of weeks ago," he explained, "and asked him to do me a favor. This is his reply. We roomed together in college and went through medical school together. I was able to do him a couple of favors in those days."

The address on the letterhead was that of the chief of staff at a large New York hospital. Hope glanced down the first page with mounting interest. The American doctor wrote that he was glad to inform his old friend, that two sizeable scholarships for the coming class of graduate doctors, were still open. As chairman of the scholarship board, he could practically guarantee to secure one of them for Dr. Morcus Kemalyian on the strength of his old friend's recommendation. The young man would be required to present satisfactory credentials to the board. This should be no problem, although Dr. Kemalyian lacked experience. American scholarship boards were very sympathetic these days to the urgent medical needs in the Middle East. His board was especially inclined toward leniency in the case of ambitious young doctors from that area.

The letter went on to state that both scholarships provided two full years' tuition. This included use of laboratory equipment and materials, textbooks, special instuments, etc. Hospital uniforms, laundry, and board were also provided. During the first year, resident living quarters were unavailable. Outside living costs were very high, and the scholarships covered far less than half the amount usually needed.

Hope finished the first page. "Oh, this is wonderful," she exclaimed. "Does Dr. Morcus know you were going to ask?"

"No," replied the chief dryly. "Before you get completely carried away, I suggest that you read the rest of the letter."

She picked up the second sheet. The New York doctor explained that lodging expense during the second year would be eliminated. Graduate students could live in a special section at the hospital. Here they were required to help out with emergencies and to assist some of the older doctors. These men were quick to detect a bright upcoming doctor, and quite often made attractive offers of junior partnerships to young men completing the course. In such cases, the future financial success of the younger doctor was assured. A small salary was provided during the second year for services rendered. However, it was a mere pittance. The doctor strongly advised Dr. Morcus not to consider accepting the scholarship unless he had a minimum of at least three thousand dollars. With no relatives in the States to help him, he could not possibly get by on less.

The letter went on to state that all scholarships would be awarded by the end of July. Application blanks were being forwarded under separate cover. The doctor wished his old friend and the young doctor the best of everything and said he would keep in touch.

Hope folded the letter with a sigh.

"I am sure Dr. Morcus could qualify, but where would he get the money?"

The chief echoed her sigh.

"I doubt if he has saved anything to date for further study. However," he continued, "I will urge him to send in the application forms."

His tone was so disconsolate that Hope felt impelled to cheer him up.

"Now, doctor, let's not be pessimistic. You believe in miracles more than any of the rest of us."

With a twinkle in his eye he quickly challenged her with a question, "Are you willing to join me in a prayer pact for the money?"

Seeing his grin, she went a step further.

"I will, doctor," she asserted. "But your friend said that three thousand was a bare minimum. Why not ask for another five hundred? This is the last day of June. The scholarship will be awarded by the end of July. Dr. Morcus will have three months after that to consider the offer. Let us pray for that miracle!"

The chief solemnly extended his hand. Hope grasped it eagerly.

"Thirty-five hundred," she stipulated.

"Thirty-five hundred," he agreed.

They shook on it.

After supper that evening, Hope was rereading her mail in her room when she heard the sound of running footsteps. There was a quick rap on her door. She sprang to open it. Aminah stood there. Her face was white.

"Dr. Dawson sent for us," she gasped. "My father just had a heart attack at the doctor's dinner table."

Before Hope could put on her shoes, Aminah was gone. She was nowhere in sight when Hope emerged from the side door of the hospital. Dr. Baxter and Matt were racing up the drive to the Dawson home ahead of her. She followed them into the Dawson's hallway. The three doctors were conferring in low tones. In the sitting room beyond, she could see Mohammed Abdullah resting on a couch. Aminah was beside him.

Dr. Baxter examined Mohammed and returned to consult with Dr. Morcus and the chief.

"I concur with your opinion," he said in a low tone. "It seems to be an acute heart attack."

Dr. Morcus flushed, hesitated, then said respectfully, "I am afraid I must disagree, Sirs. It appears to me to more nearly resemble the symptoms of an acute gall bladder attack, rather than a true heart condition."

The two older doctors exchanged indulgent glances. Then Dr. Dawson said genially, "You may be right, Dr. Morcus. But I believe we all agree that we should get Mohammed to a hospital. The Arab Hospital in Bethlehem is nearest. I will telephone to ask if they have a private room available, and if they can get a local doctor there for consultation when you arrive. I don't think I will need to go. Let us move into the sitting room while I put in the call."

While the call was being made, Dr. Morcus stepped over to the couch to place his fingers on Mohammed's pulse. The man's glazed eyes opened drowsily at the touch. Hope realized that he must have been given a strong injection of morphine before her arrival.

Dr. Morcus bent over to ask, "Are you feeling better now, Sir?"

Mohammed spoke weakly, "Yes, Doctor, thanks to your powerful shot. Remind me to recommend you to the King." His eyes closed.

Dr. Morcus smiled reassuringly down into the troubled eyes of Aminah.

"Your father is going to be all right," he assured her.

"Of course I am," Mohammed growled, without opening his eyes.

Plans were made quickly as soon as the chief hung up the phone. Matt was to drive Mohammed in his own car, with Dr. Morcus and Aminah riding in the back seat to care for him. Dr. Baxter would take the Dawson car and follow them.

Hope told Aminah to run and get her things, so that she could go with her father and stay the night, if needed.

The next afternoon Matt took Dr. Dawson into the hospital to visit Mohammed. They were back in time for supper. Aminah was with them. She reported briefly to Hope that her father had spent a restful night. Several X-rays were taken this morning. Her father's own personal physician had come from Jerusalem for consultation. He was transferring Mohammed even now by ambulance to the new French Hospital in the Jerusalem suburbs. Special nurses were already engaged. Aminah's help was not needed. Hope hastened over to the Dawson home to get the chief's report. Margaret asked her to join them at the table. "We need you to help us eat last night's leftovers," she urged.

When the chief had returned thanks, he turned to Hope. "Dr. Morcus was right," he said. "The electrocardiogram was normal. Gall bladder X-rays showed definite shadows of stones. Mohammed's personal physician has persuaded my friend to let him schedule surgery in the new French Hospital on Monday morning. Mohammed held out against surgery until the doctor consented to have Dr. Morcus assist him, and to retain Morcus as consultant afterward." He chuckled. "Abdullah has developed a great confidence in that boy. Dr. Baxter and I both muffed the diagnosis last night. Our Arab friend is nobody's fool."

After a moment he continued. "Dr. Morcus could become an outstanding surgeon and diagnostician. TB is far too limited for a man of his talents. I believe Dr. Morcus should acquire a well-rounded education in all types of major surgery."

"Do you think he will want to?" asked Hope.

"You didn't realize that my letter yesterday was from one of the greatest surgeons living in the world today," the chief replied. "I learned this summer that he would be teaching that post-graduate course in surgery personally next January. Like me, he isn't getting any younger. That's why I am anxious for Dr. Morcus to try for that scholarship this year. I think he will be interested when he reads the application forms."

Mohammed Abdullah made a rapid and uneventful recovery. He was out of the hospital in two weeks. He began encouraging his friends to patronize Dr. Kemalyian. His own car was often seen parked before the young doctor's office in Bethlehem.

At the end of July, Dr. Morcus received notification from the scholarship board, offering him a two-year scholarship in surgery. The offer would be held open until the first of November. School would start on the fifth of January.

Hope was present when Dr. Morcus brought the notice to show the chief.

"I haven't the money to accept just now, of course," the young doctor said. "But at least I know that I have the necessary qualifications to try again later. I thank you very much, Sir, for your efforts on my behalf."

There was no bitterness in his tone, but his eyes betrayed a deep disappointment and hunger.

"How soon do you expect to have enough money?" the chief asked.

Dr. Morcus shrugged his shoulders.

"I don't know," he answered frankly. "I still owe a few instalments on my office equipment. I expect it will take at least another two or three years. I must leave the time in God's hands."

"And how old are you now?" the chief pursued.

"Forty years last month," replied Dr. Morcus.

Dr. Morcus bowed his head and was silent. Hope's heart ached with pity for him.

The chief's eyes began to twinkle, and he leaned across the desk and touched Dr. Morcus's arm. "I want you to promise me something," he said.

The young man raised his head and gave the older doctor his respectful attention.

"I want you to give yourself the full time allotted before you write to turn down that scholarship," the chief said briskly. "We never know what might develop in three months."

Dr. Morcus looked astonished. "I can't see that it will make any difference," he said. "But I will take your advice and wait."

After Dr. Morcus left, Hope eyed the chief reproachfully. "Don't you think you are being a little cruel to ask him to wait?" she asked. "It will only prolong his agony."

"Why, Miss Hope, I'm surprised at you," he replied. "Where is your faith? You asked me for a miracle. Is anything too hard for the Lord?"

A week later Dr. Dawson brought a newspaper from Jerusalem containing news of a terrible bus accident at the top of a steep grade between Jerusalem and Nablus. The bus missed a sharp curve and plunged down a steep ravine. The driver and two passengers were killed. No one at the hospital knew any of the people.

A few days later, Regina returned from a day in Bethlehem. She bubbled over with excitement. She timed herself to arrive in the midst of the supper hour. Then she made a dramatic entrance.

"Listen, everybody!" she exclaimed. "I have the most exciting news! One of the men killed in that bus accident was Aida's husband. When two neighbor women went with the policeman to tell Aida the news, they found the door locked from the outside. The big iron key was sticking right in the lock. Aida's husband had locked her in the night before and gone off to Jerusalem to gamble with friends. He often stayed away all night and never allowed anyone to visit her."

Regina stopped to make sure she had everyone's undivided attention, then she continued, "When they unlocked the door they saw Aida crouched on the bed. She was staring at them like a wild woman. She had a big knife in her hand. A newborn baby was lying beside her. She hid the knife when she saw the women and policeman. When they told her that her husband was dead, she didn't move or cry. Just stared. But when they told her that his body would be brought there for her to prepare for burial, she jumped up and grabbed the baby. She said she would run away before they came, and that she never wanted to see him again, ever.

The policeman stepped outside while the women got her to bed. When he returned he told her that a cousin would take charge of the funeral. She would not be expected to do it, because she had just given birth. He told her she should go to her mother in Bethlehem. She refused until she found out that her father was in jail and her mother needed her."

Regina took a quick breath, then went on with her story.

"All Aida had was an old suitcase with a few baby clothes and diapers in it. The women brought her a faded cotton house dress and some ragged underwear from the cupboard. She wouldn't let them help her dress or get near the baby. She wouldn't even let them look at the baby.

"The policeman had ordered a taxi, and when it came they helped her in. One of the women decided to go with her. The other woman locked the door and offered the key to Aida. She told her to keep it and everything that went with it.

"When they arrived at Aida's mother's, my mother had just brought some food for Mrs. Yusef, so she saw it all. The baby was crying, but Aida refused to let Mother carry it. Mother helped Aida into the house. The Nablus woman followed with the suitcase. Aida's mother didn't even know her daughter. Aida started crying along with the baby. Then Mrs. Yusef put her arms around both of them. 'Don't cry, little one,' she said. Mother thinks she was just talking to the baby. Aida laid the baby on the bed in the other room and shut the door so that no one could see in. Then she drove everybody out of the house. They all heard the key turn in the lock.

"Mother invited the woman from Nablus to our home for a cup of tea. That's how Mother learned about all that happened there."

The missionary staff exchanged significant glances.

"That first day," Regina continued, "everybody thought the shock of her husband's death and having given birth to the baby, had made Aida a little lightheaded. They brought food to the house to help. She would let no one inside. Now it has been three full days since she has come to the door at all. At first the food would disappear when no one was around. Now the dishes just sit there on the step until the dogs come and eat it.

"The neighbors hear the baby crying a lot. They think there must be something wrong with it, and with Aida, too. I knocked and called today, again and again. I could hear her moving about inside, but she wouldn't open the door."

Having told all her news, Regina sat down. She began placidly devouring her supper amid a buzz of excited conversation.

Hope pushed her scarcely tasted plate of food away from her. She glanced restlessly at her watch. She had wondered, all these months, what had really become of Aida. Now she feared the worst.

"Eileen," she said, "it's too late to go tonight. Aida might not let me in. If you will take over here tomorrow, I am going to catch the first bus into Bethlehem in the morning. I won't come back until I have seen Aida—even if I have to call the police to break down that door!"

THIRTY-TWO

Hope reached Dr. Kemalyian's office at eight o'clock the following morning. He was already caring for a patient. She waited until he was finished. She meant to enlist his aid in case medical help was needed for Aida or the baby.

He had been kept well posted by Mrs. Murad, and was greatly concerned. He had another patient waiting, and would not be free for about an hour. They agreed that Hope would attempt to gain entrance to the Yusef home immediately. She would prepare Aida to accept medical help, and the doctor would arrive as soon as possible.

Hope walked up the hill. She passed the Murad home and turned into a narrow, poorly paved street leading into an older section of the town. She came to a short blind alley. A group of dingy stone houses with windowless fronts were crowded together. Each presented a single, heavily constructed iron door toward the garbage littered alley. Hope stopped at a door midway of the alley. She rapped sharply upon it.

Receiving no reply, she pounded on it with both fists. She sensed that someone was standing listening on the other side. A feeble wailing cry sounded from somewhere within. She pounded harder, calling, "Aida! It's Miss Callaway! You might as well let me in. I am going to stay here until you do."

She waited a few minutes and then began to pound again.

Finally an iron key turned in the rusty lock. The door creaked open a few inches. The pale, haggard face of a woman peered out at her. Hope stared at the face in shocked disbelief. It was the face of the girl she had come to see.

She had enough wits about her to push against the door that Aida still gripped firmly. To her relief the girl relaxed her grasp. She stood aside without a word, allowing Hope to enter. The heavy iron door clanged shut behind them. Hope heard the swift turn of the key in the lock.

Hope made a rapid survey of the dreary room before her. On her left was a sink supported by rusty iron pipes. A single water tap protruded from a roughly chiseled break in the stone wall behind it. A shallow open cupboard contained a few cracked dishes. There was half a loaf of stale-looking aish, a glass container with some rice, and a jar with a drop or two of oil in the bottom. In the corner was a tea cannister. Along the side wall stood a large unpainted wooden table with a single primus oil burner standing on it nearest the sink. A blackened teakettle simmered on it. Two backless stools of woven rushes stood beneath the table.

A frail Arab woman sat rocking in the only piece of furniture in the room. It was an ancient English walnut rocker. Hope realized that she must be Aida's mother.

The one note of cheer was the fact that Mrs. Yusef's face was clean; also her hair was freshly combed and neatly braided. No doubt, this was Aida's doing.

A feeble wail was coming from an open door on the right. Hope moved swiftly toward that inner room. Before Aida could bar her way she was gazing down at the tiny mite of humanity who appeared too frail to emit any audible sound. The dark eyes were wide open. There was something in that blank stare that struck a chill to Hope's heart. In spite of Aida's half-hearted protests, Hope gathered the baby up in her arms and sat down on the edge of the double bed to cuddle her. She rocked and patted the child gently. After a minute the wails ceased. The baby's lips moved expectantly in a sucking motion.

Hope looked up questioningly at Aida. "She seems hungry, Aida," she said.

The girl flung out her hands in a despairing gesture. "I know she is starving," she said dully. "I've been trying to nurse her. She can't seem to swallow right, nor to suck the way she should. The milk doesn't come in. There is nothing there for her."

She took the baby from Hope and pressed it tenderly to her breast. The eyes were open in that strange stare, and the lips sucked expectantly. Aida dropped to her knees and held out the child to Hope. "I am afraid there is something wrong with her brain, Miss Hope," she whispered desperately. "Maybe she would be better off dead, the way she is. But I love her. I can't just let her die. I have done so many wicked things. Surely God wouldn't let me commit murder. I prayed last night that you would come. Then I could not believe that it was really you at the door. I don't deserve your kindness, but please help my baby."

Tears were running down Hope's face as she took the child. "You are still one of my girls. You always will be," she said.

Aida laid her head down on Hope's knee. All the pent-up grief and bitterness of the past year flowed out in the healing therapy of tears. Finally she raised her head and began to speak in a subdued tone, "Miss Hope, I wanted to tell you so many times how sorry—"

She got no further. Hope rose, holding the baby over one shoulder. With her free hand she reached down to pull Aida to her feet.

"Not now, Aida," she said. "We can talk later. Dr. Kemalyian will be here any minute to examine you and the baby. You must get some rest. He can prescribe a formula for the baby to satisfy her hunger. You look as if you need some medicine yourself. I see some clean clothes here for the baby. Go splash your face at the sink. Then get your hair combed while I bathe her. I want you to lie down and rest until he comes."

Hope gathered the baby clothes together. She carried them and the baby to the sink. Using the warm water in the kettle, she bathed the scrawny little body. When Hope went to lay her in her makeshift crib, Aida was sound asleep. The girl's hair was neatly brushed and braided. She was so painfully thin that Hope wondered when she had eaten her last meal.

Hope was busily washing the dishes when Dr. Morcus arrived. His knock woke Aida and she started to get up. But the kindly doctor ordered her to lie still while he talked to her. Although the girl had never met him, his gentle manner quickly reassured her. She frankly answered his questions regarding the unattended delivery of the baby just six nights before.

"I remembered Miss Callaway's instructions," she said. "I used a hot iron to sterilize old pieces of sheets and a piece of strong material to tie the cord. I prepared them several days beforehand. When labor started I boiled strong coffee to drink when everything was over. I was able to tie the cord and take care of the baby and myself within a few minutes. I examined the afterbirth carefully to be sure it was all there and massaged my abdomen several times during the night. There was no hemorrhage."

Dr. Kemalyian smiled his approval at Hope. "You had an excellent teacher, Aida," he said. "Very few women would have the strength and courage to do what you did alone." He gently probed the girl's abdomen, asking, "Have you had any pain or fever since?"

"No, doctor," she replied.

"Well, then," he said cheerfully, "just move over a little and I'll have a look at the baby."

Hope laid the baby on the big bed. The doctor sat down on the stool she brought. He checked the child thoroughly with his stethoscope. Noting the staring eyes, he produced a flashlight from his bag. He flashed it several times across the baby's face. Each time her eyelids blinked. Aida watched anxiously.

"She can see, can't she, doctor?" she asked.

"Yes, her pupils react to light," he replied.

"Is there something wrong with her tongue?" Aida asked. "She can't seem to suck or to swallow. I try to squeeze a few drops of milk into her mouth, but most of it comes back through her nose."

Hope had set a basin of water with soap and towel on a stool beside the doctor. After washing his hands, he probed far back in the baby's mouth with his finger. She retched a little. While he washed his hands again, Dr. Kemalyian explained, "Your baby has a partially cleft palate, Aida, which keeps her from sucking or swallowing properly. She will need to be fed through a stomach tube for a while. When we get her started on a good baby formula she should pick up strength and weight right away. Later, some grafting can be done to close that palate gap between her nose and mouth."

"What about her mind, Doctor?" she queried. "She stares so. Is there something wrong with her mind?"

Dr. Morcus hesitated, then replied frankly, "That I can't say, Aida. I am not a pediatrician. She is still very young, perhaps too young yet to really tell much. I want to take a blood sample from both of you."

Aida lay quietly while Hope applied the tourniquet to her upper arm and swabbed the needle site. The doctor unwrapped syringes and sterile test tubes.

When both the blood samples had been drawn Aida sat up and Hope propped a pillow behind her back.

"I know why you took the blood, doctor," she said. "I want to know the results. I am almost positive that my husband had syphilis. I believe he gave it to me and to the baby."

Hope capped the test tubes and carried the syringes to the sink to rinse them. She heard Aida saying to the doctor, "My husband must have known that he had it. When I became pregnant he beat me because I refused to get rid of the baby. He said it wouldn't be normal and besides he needed me to help him work in the fields. He had cancelled my father's debts to use me as a workhorse and meant to get his money's worth."

Hope returned and went to stand beside Aida. The girl seemed completely unaware of her presence. She was staring at the doctor with a strange intensity. As one hypnotized, she went on speaking as if moved by a strong compulsion:

"He said his first wife believed him when he told her that she could never have a normal baby. He helped her to get rid of two. The third time she did the job herself and died of hemorrhage."

Hope shuddered. She glanced appealingly at the doctor. He was eyeing the girl with a keen, professional look.

Aida continued in that strangely monotonous tone: "He said his second wife wasn't so smart. She didn't believe him when he said she couldn't have a normal baby. She wouldn't let him get rid of it. She carried the baby seven months, when she started labor. It had been dead for several weeks. She died of a bloodstream infection. I asked him if the baby looked abnormal, He laughed and said it was so decayed that he couldn't tell."

Hope shuddered again. She looked appealingly at Dr. Morcus. His hands gripped the handles of his bag. He ignored Hope's silent plea.

"Even with all that," Aida continued, "I wouldn't kill my baby and run the risk of killing myself, too. He was furious. He tried for weeks to do something about it. Many times I had to fight him off. I hardly dared sleep for fear he would tie me up and do something to me."

Hope put her arm protectively about the girl's shoulders. "Doctor," she implored, "please tell her she must stop!"

"No!" shouted Aida. "I must tell this to somebody!" She indicated her chest. "It is poisoning me in here."

The doctor glanced at Hope for a second then back at the girl. "Go on!" he ordered harshly.

Aida's voice dropped again to its former monotone, "Finally he gave up and left me alone. He took to staying away two or three nights a week—always locking me in. He never took me anywhere. Years before he had forbidden the neighbors to set foot on his property. Our home was isolated. He always locked me in when he went to buy groceries in town. I had no contact with anyone.

"At first I was glad to be left alone. Then I remembered that he had shown me a small tumor or boil in his groin a few days after we were married. He said it didn't hurt, but it was ulcerating. I tried to treat it with what ointments we had, but it wouldn't heal. He must have had it for years. I realized he was going crazy. He was going to wait and kill the baby when it was born. I tried to plan some way to escape. The windows were heavily barred. The door was made of iron. I had no tools to break through the stone walls. When he left me outside to work with him he stayed close by. The neighbors were too far away and I was too heavy by then to outrun him.

"The morning the labor pains started," the girl continued, "I managed somehow to keep going. He must have suspected and lost his nerve. Late that afternoon he dressed in his best robe and said he was going into Jerusalem. I knew he would spend the night gambling with friends. I barely had time to get things ready before the baby came. I took care of everything as soon as I could. Then I sharpened a big knife. I laid it on the bed beside me. I was going to kill him when he came home. But it wasn't necessary. God saw to that."

Up to this point Aida had spoken unemotionally, but now her features contorted with violent passion. She screamed out, "I hated him, hated him! Do you hear? I am glad he is dead!"

Her voice dropped as suddenly as it had risen. She added in a more normal tone, "I have said it at last. It had to be said. You understood, didn't you, Doctor?"

Suddenly, she stretched out both hands imploringly to him. The words came in a pitiful whisper, "My mother has lost her mind. My poor baby has none. Have I gone crazy, too?"

Dr. Morcus's bag dropped with a thud. He sprang to grasp those two shaking hands in his own strong brown ones.

"No, Aida, you are not crazy," he stated firmly. "God has kept you sane under circumstances that would have driven most women mad. Your mother's mental condition is not hereditary. She is not in pain. If you did acquire syphilis from your husband this past year, it can be completely cured with antibiotics in short order. There will be not future ill effects to your mind or body. If your child has it, the damage already may be irreparable. But even her condition is not completely hopeless."

Hope was dawning in Aida's eyes as the doctor spoke. Still holding her hands he sat down beside her and continued, "Yes, Aida, you and I both knew that this had to be said, so I listened. Now I want you to listen very carefully to me. You already know that hatred is a very poisonous thing."

She nodded mutely. He had her full attention.

"We must not judge your husband," he went on. "Only God has that power and that right. You must put all the unhappiness of this past year completely out of your mind. You have your child and your mother to think of now. They both need your care. We will stand by to help you all we can, but you yourself must make a deliberate effort to regain your health and strength as quickly as possible."

For the first time in almost a year, a smile appeared on Aida's face.

"My little Angele is the one thing that kept me from losing my mind. God gave her to me to love and to care for. Although she is weak and imperfect, He has used her to redeem my soul from my wicked ways. I know that He will use her to remove the sin of hatred from my heart. I named her Angele because God sent her to be my guardian angel. For her sake I will get well and strong again."

"Amen!" said the doctor heartily. He rose, adding, "You don't need any more advice from me, young lady. But right now little Angele needs nourishment and you need some vitamins and food. If Miss Callaway will come with me to my office, I will send some samples of canned baby formula and some vitamins. She will see to getting some food for you. I will let you know the results of the blood tests as soon as I get the reports."

"Thank you, Doctor," Aida murmured. Her eyes were shining.

While Hope collected her things, Dr. Kemalyian walked over to the occupant of the rocking chair. "*Keef halik* (how are you), Sitt Maryam?" he asked quietly.

Mrs. Yusef drew her black scarf more closely about her head. She regarded him blankly, with no sign of recognition. She just resumed her incessant rocking.

The doctor looked at Hope. They both shook their heads sadly.

She followed him outside and pulled the door shut behind them. As they walked, he tried to accommodate his strides to her short steps.

"Dr. Morcus," she began hurriedly, "I am sure you don't have any more money to spend than I do." She didn't wait for his reply, but continued on, "So I have been thinking. What we do today won't even last a week. We do not know if Aida's husband left anything. Even if he did, it will take months to settle his estate. Aida can't leave the baby with her mother to go out to work. She will not want the neighbors to see the baby. So they cannot help her. Besides, Aida needs to become occupied with something outside that dreary place right away."

"So . . .?" he asked, as he unlocked the door to his office.

"So . . ." Hope continued eagerly, "What about Madame Wadea Malik's Shelter for Unfortunate Women and Children. You are on the staff there, aren't you?"

He gave a start and looked at his watch.

"Good heavens!" he exclaimed. "Thanks for reminding me. I have an appointment to meet Madame there in less than an hour. She invited me to lunch. She wants me to examine a crippled boy and give her my opinion as to whether surgery might cure his defect."

They stared at each other in delighted amazement. The same thought was in both their minds.

"What perfect timing!" Hope exclaimed joyfully.

"Yes, it is," Dr. Morcus agreed. "I will ask Madame to take them in this very day. I have thought for some time that Mrs. Yusef should be there. But I didn't have authority from her family to move her. Now Aida can give it. I am sure Madame will make room for her and the baby, too, when I explain the circumstances. The two will have to be isolated, of course, until we get the blood tests. If they are positive, I can start treatment at once. I believe you have found the perfect solution."

Half an hour later Hope again stood before the heavy iron door of the Yusef home. She carried a well-filled shopping bag. She raised her hand to knock, then changed her mind. Instead she pushed gently against it. To her great satisfaction, it swung inward on its creaking hinges.

At four o'clock that afternoon a taxi drew up before a large three storied stone building set well back from the Beit Jala Road near the Hebron crossroads. An old fashioned English rocking chair was tied atop the luggage rack with three suitcases. Hope emerged from the front seat beside the driver. Requesting that he wait a minute, she hurried up the short path and began climbing the steep steps leading to the main entrance on the second floor level. Before she reached the broad stone porch, a large, stately woman, with beautiful silvery gray hair, came out to meet her.

"I have been expecting you since three o'clock, Miss Callaway," she said cordially. "Does your driver need help with the luggage?"

"I think he can manage," said Hope. "But I am afraid I must ask you to loan me the money to pay him. I have only three piasters left in my purse for bus fare back to the hospital."

Her hostess threw back her head with a hearty laugh. She started striding down the steps so briskly that Hope had to trot to keep up with her. The driver had already taken the three suitcases down from the luggage rack, and was untying the rocker.

Thrusting her hand into a capacious skirt pocket, the Madame drew forth a fat money pouch. She addressed the taxi driver sternly as he began bowing delightedly to her. "These are my guests that you have brought, Ahmed. How much did you expect to extort from Miss Callaway for this insignificant little trip in your miserable taxi?"

"Fifteen piasters only, Madame," he declared, "including the luggage, too, of course."

Madame Malik surveyed the three suitcases and the rocker. "Did you carry these out to the taxi yourself?" she demanded.

"Yes, indeed, Madame," he replied with another bow.

"I suppose you are expecting my servants to carry them up the steps from here?" she pursued. Her eyes were twinkling, as were those of the taxi driver.

"Oh, no, Madame," Ahmed protested. "I will carry them myself."

"Well, what are you waiting for?" she demanded imperiously.

"For your permission, Madame," he replied with another bow.

"Open the door of your miserable taxi first," she ordered. "I want to greet my guests. Then you have my permission to proceed."

With a broad grin, he obediently swung the rear door of the taxi open. Then he picked up the two largest suitcases.

Madame Malik bent down to peer at the passengers on the rear seat. Her large, well-molded mouth curved in a heart warming, motherly smile. She held out her arms. "Give me that baby!"

Without a protest, Aida meekly surrendered her child.

"What do you call her?" queried the Madame.

"Angele," murmured Aida.

She pulled back a corner of the blanket to see the child's face. Then she smiled and said, "I like girls, especially an angel." Tucking her hand under Aida's elbow to help her out, she continued, "Come along, my daughter. We have a small private room for you and Angele right next to the nursery. You can catch up on your sleep while nurse Adeeba cares for baby during the night. Your mother will sleep in the ward for elderly women."

Ahmed had returned from his first trip. He was transferring pillows and odds and ends from the back seat into the rocker. Madame spoke a few rapid words to him in Arabic. He nodded and smiled. She dropped several coins into his hand. A nurse came hurrying down the steps to help escort Aida. Madame followed, carrying the baby. Ahmed brought up the rear, carrying the rocker. He set the rocker on the porch. Hope picked up Aida's suitcase and tried to escort the tottering old woman. Ahmed hastened to relieve her of the suitcase. Then with his strong right arm, he gently encircled the frail little figure of Mrs. Yusef and practically carried the bewildered little woman to the top of the steps. There he surrendered her to the care of an attendant, with a bow as courteous to her as if she were a queen. There was a tender light in his eyes as he returned to his taxi. Hope's heart glowed with gratitude. She knew that Ahmed had been well paid for his services. But this was not the first time that she had witnessed the compassion of Arab men for the elderly and feeble in their midst. She knew the man's tenderness was genuine. Ahmed sat at the wheel of his taxi and did not start the engine.

She turned and entered the wide entrance hall. Madame Malik was talking to the head nurse at the far end. The Madame was now wearing her voluminous circular woolen cape and a headscarf.

"Miss Callaway, I must ask you to excuse me now," Madame Malik said as Hope approached her. "I am in a great hurry to get back to Jerusalem. Please tell Sitt Azizy about the baby's formula and anything else she may need to know. I sent Aida and the child off with Sitt Hilweh to rest. She asked me to say goodbye and to thank you for all you have done. Leila is bringing you some tea. Ahmed is well paid, so don't give him anything more. He doesn't expect it."

Before Hope could begin to thank her, Madame Malik smiled graciously and hastened out through a side door to the driveway where her chauffeur awaited in her private limousine.

A few minutes later, Hope was being borne swiftly along the highway toward Hebron. Dusk was falling. She leaned back with a sigh of contentment. Mentally she began to review all that she knew about Madame Malik. Already the Madame was a legend in her own time. Many tales were related of her numerous kindnesses.

She was the only child of an Arab father and an Armenian mother. Both had been devout Christians. It was said that theirs was a storybook romance. Her father had been tall and handsome and fabulously wealthy, her mother the poor, beautiful Cinderella. Their devotion to each other was so great, that one followed the other in death within a few short days. They had given their only child a college education in an exclusive school in France. They had brought her home to marry a Christian Arab who was even wealthier than her own father. She, too, bore an only daughter, who was sent abroad to be educated.

When her husband, Milad Malik, died a few years later, his widow sold his extensive properties in the fertile lowlands of Palestine at a handsome profit. These funds were invested in giltedged securities abroad, together with her inheritance from her father.

With her well-assured income, Madame Malik was able to extend the philanthropic enterprises that she and her husband had started. In time, her daughter, Eloise, brought a French husband to share a summer home in the suburbs of Ramallah. She gave birth to six grandchildren. Now, except for summer vacations in Ramallah, the family spent the school years of the children on the continent, much to grandmother Malik's regret.

No one ever thought to call her by any other title than that of Madame. She spoke several languages fluently. Madame's favorite charity was the shelter, where Aida and her family were given refuge. Madame was the sole owner and director. She had bought and developed it from a decrepit poorhouse into a well built and well staffed home and hospital. It not only sheltered destitute widows and feeble, elderly women, but also housed crippled children and outcast infants.

Madame was kind and generous, but intolerant of deceit, cruelty, or neglect of patients. The love in her own heart for her unfortunate "children" spilled over into the hearts of her employees. They all loved her devotedly.

Hope recalled with a smile, how easily and trustfully Aida had surrendered her baby to the Madame's arms. She mused on the totally different characters of the three girls who had left the Beth Hanani training school under such dissimilar circumstances. Each had recently given birth to a daughter. Each had done so under strikingly different circumstances. She knew that neither Rehab nor Hanni would have survived an experience similar to Aida's. Aida had inherited the steely stamina of a proud and hardy race. This quality refused to be beaten down or broken by oppression.

THIRTY-THREE

Dr. Kemalyian came as usual to assist Dr. Dawson on Friday afternoon. He did not stay for dinner at the Dawson's home. Encountering him in the hall on his way out, Hope ventured the innocent remark that Matt reported seeing Mohammed's car twice that week parked in front of Dr. Morcus's office. She expressed the hope that Mohammed was bringing him some business. Resentment flared in the young doctor's eyes. He glared angrily at Hope.

"I don't need, or want, Abdullah's business," he muttered fiercely.

Without another word, he strode out the front door, leaving Hope openmouthed with astonishment. She had never seen Dr. Morcus roused to anger before. She wondered what she could possibly have said to cause such an outburst.

Monday she went to seek the chief's advice on a trivial matter. In response to her knock, he called out, "Come in, please." She entered to find Mohammed Abdullah already there. He was leaning across the doctor's desk. Hope was about to withdraw, but Dr. Dawson said, "Don't go Miss Hope. We need a woman's viewpoint on a grave matter just now. Come in and sit down, please."

Hope obeyed.

"You'd better sit down, too, Mohammed," he advised.

Mohammed subsided with a sullen growl.

The chief's eyes were twinkling with mischief. He addressed his next remarks to Hope.

"I just happened to mention to Mohammed the other day that Dr. Morcus had received an outstanding offer of a graduate scholarship from a New York hospital. I said he was planning to turn it down for lack of personal funds. Then what do you suppose? Abdullah went straight to Dr. Morcus and offered to finance his education."

Hope opened her mouth. The chief held up a warning hand, saying, "Wait until you hear the rest. There is a string attached to Mohammed's offer, namely, Aminah."

Hope stared at him blankly.

"Mohammed's 'string' is the hand of his daughter in marriage."

Mohammed leaped to his feet. He pounded the desk in rage.

"He refused!" he shouted, glaring at Hope. "The fool! Does the fellow think he is too good for my daughter?"

Hope managed to keep a straight face.

"I am sure it is not that at all, Sir," she began soothingly. "I believe Dr. Kemalyian loves your daughter and would like to marry her. But he has no fortune to offer. He is too proud to accept your help."

"Proud?" snorted Mohammed. "Of course we Arabs are proud. But it is quite customary in our country for a man to expect his wife's parents to provide a suitable dowry for her. He has no reason to refuse my offer unless . . ." he paused as a new thought suddenly occurred to him. He glanced suspiciously from one to the other of his companions, then asked craftily, ". . . unless the fellow is holding me off, expecting me to offer more."

"I am sure Dr. Kemalyian has no such thought, Sir," Hope said hastily. "Perhaps you have forgotten that he is not an Arab, but an Armenian. There is no doubt that he leans much more toward our Western views regarding marriage. Parents allow their children to select their own mates. Also, it is considered unmanly and dishonorable for a man to accept support for himself from his bride's parents."

Mohammed subsided in his chair while he pondered this new angle to the problem.

"That possibility never occurred to me," he said. "You are probably right. I expect I have misjudged the young man. I have been impressed for some time by his medical ability. I have found him to be upright and honorable. He may have taken my offer as an insult. It is possible that I owe him an apology. I see that I have made a most unfortunate approach."

He spread out his hands to his friend in a pleading gesture. A pathetic note crept into his voice, as he continued, "What is a man to do for his only child? I am getting old. Everything I have will go to Aminah. She will need a strong, wise husband to care for her and help her manage her fortune. So far, Aminah has refused to consider any man that I thought acceptable. I noticed how she looked at Dr. Kemalyian when he attended me during my illness. She has not seemed averse to my hints in that direction. I want to see my grandchildren before I die. Is there any way, my friend, that you could help to persuade him to accept my offer?"

Dr. Dawson and Hope exchanged glances. He voiced the thought that was uppermost in both their minds.

"Have you considered the fact that Dr. Morcus is a Christian, and that he would want a Christian marriage?"

A warm smile lit up Mohammed's grave features.

"Indeed, I have considered it," he answered readily. "I guessed Aminah's secret long ago. I knew why she refused to consider a Moslem husband. Besides, I kept my promise to Matt. I have read the New Testament not once, but many times. I have come to believe in Him. I understand the three-fold nature of God, and have asked the Holy Spirit to guide my life."

He held up his hand as Dr. Dawson was about to speak.

"No, my friend," he continued, "do not ask me to declare my belief openly. I love my country. I would lose my influence here if I were to publicly renounce the Islamic faith and desert the Moslem Brotherhood and my King now. I feel that Aminah should respect my wishes, and make no public declaration for herself here in Jordan at this time. I planned to take her to America after Dr. Kemalyian takes up residence there. She could profess her faith openly in that country and receive Christian baptism. They could be married in a Christian church of their own choosing.

"If the news leaked out over here, my friends would not hold it against me. By the time she returned for visits, or for permanent residence, her faith would be accepted. There would be no embarrassment. As long as my country needs me, that is as far as I am prepared to go."

Dr. Dawson regarded his friend earnestly for a long moment. Then he rose, moved around the desk, and placed an affectionate arm about Mohammed's shoulders. Their hands met in a warm clasp.

"So be it, my friend," the chief said kindly. "I will not attempt to press you further. I promise I will do all I can to change Dr. Kemalyian's decision."

After Mohammed Abdullah left, Hope looked at the chief.

"So you expected your scheme to work?" she asked.

"Not for one minute," the chief replied smoothly. "I merely told Mohammed out of curiosity. I wondered what his reaction would be. I wanted to know what opinion he had formed regarding Jesus. I am completely satisfied with his declaration. Aren't you?"

"Well . . ." began Hope doubtfully, "It is wonderful that he believes in Jesus, and that he approves of Dr. Morcus as a son-in-law, But do you think you can persuade Dr. Morcus to accept his offer?"

The chief shook his head. "Not if I know that young man! I did promise to try, and I will. But frankly, I will be quite disappointed in Morcus if he does give in to Mohammed."

Hope's face fell. "Why do you raise false hopes, Doctor?" she mourned. "Dr. Morcus has only three weeks left now before he must send his answer to the scholarship board. How can he possibly raise three thousand five hundred dollars in that time?"

"Oh, ye of little faith, Miss Hope," he said. "One tiny mustard seed of faith, is all it takes."

Several days later Dr. Dawson reported to Hope the result of his conversation with Dr. Kemalyian. The young man admitted that he did love Aminah. He stated that, if he were in a position to accept the scholarship now, and to support himself during the next two years of training, he would be happy to marry Aminah. He expected it would take him another three or four years to acquire enough funds for his support. He did not expect either Mohammed or Aminah to wait that long for him.

"I must say that I admire him for his stand," the chief concluded.

Hope sighed. "The one I feel sorriest for is Mohammed," she said wistfully. "I am sure he will not be able to persuade Aminah to marry anyone else. If he has to wait four years for them to get married, and then another year or two until they have children, he may never live to see even one grandchild."

"Who said they would have to wait four years to be married?" Dr. Dawson said. "Weren't you the one who stipulated three months for that miracle? Where is your faith, woman? We still have nearly two weeks."

His tone was severely reproving. But Hope caught the merry twinkle in his eye. "What are you up to now, Doctor?" she demanded.

He laughed outright. But all he would say was, "Mind your own business, young woman. Your business is to keep right on praying and using that grain of mustard seed."

"Oh, by the way," he continued casually, "Madame Malik's car was stalled at the crossroads when Matt and I drove down from Dr. Morcus's office. Matt helped the chauffeur get it started. We followed behind them to the 'shelter.' Matt worked on the car while Madame and I had a chat over a cup of tea. She and Aida send you their love."

On the morning of October 26, the mission staff were relaxing for tea in the staff tearoom. The next day was the deadline for airmail letters to be mailed in time to arrive in New York by the first of November. Hope was thinking of this when she glanced out the window. A large private car was entering the driveway. She rose and peered at it. Then, recognizing the limousine, she exclaimed, "Why it is Madame Malik's car. But she isn't in it. There is only a man sitting beside the driver."

All the other missionaries were craning their necks at the windows, too. Dr. Dawson spoke quietly from behind them, saying, "It is Dr. Morcus. I am expecting him." The chief gave Hope a deliberate wink. "Everyone please return to your seats," he ordered. "Miss Hope and I will talk with him in my office."

He gallantly offered his arm to Hope. He marched her into the hall in time to intercept Dr. Morcus on the way to his office. The young man looked slightly disconcerted when he saw that Hope was accompanying the chief. Dr. Dawson opened the door of the office and ushered them both in.

"I am sure you will not mind if Miss Hope listens in on our conversation, Dr. Morcus. Madame Malik telephoned me a short while ago to say that you were coming."

He closed the door, and seated Hope. Dr. Morcus stood look-
ing uncertainly from one to the other. The chief moved to his
own chair behind the desk. Dr. Kemalyian remained standing.

"Well, Morcus, what can I do for you?" inquired the chief.

Dr. Morcus looked bewildered.

"Didn't Madame Malik tell you why I was coming, Sir?" he
asked.

"Was she supposed to?" countered Dr. Dawson.

"Well, I thought . . ." began the young man, ". . . that is, well,
sir, Madame Malik walked into my office this morning and
offered me an outright gift of two thousand pounds to clear off
all my debts and finance my education in America. Did you tell
her about the scholarship?"

Caught off guard by the direct question, Dr. Dawson
squirmed a little. Hope held her breath. She knew the doctor
was incapable of lying, and feared his answer would arouse sus-
picion. The chief recovered quickly and leaned back in his chair.

"It is quite possible that I did," he admitted. "I was rather
proud that you got the award, you know. I didn't think that it
was necessary to keep it a secret."

To Hope's relief, Dr. Kemalyian accepted the plausible
explanation without resentment.

"It doesn't really matter," he said. "In any case, I could not
accept her generous offer. She insisted, however, that I come
out here and consult you."

"Why can't you accept this offer?" asked the chief.

"Why Sir!" he gulped. "Surely you don't think I would take
money from a woman."

"Do you have any grounds for suspecting that Madame
Malik has any matrimonial designs regarding you and herself?"
demanded the chief.

Dr. Morcus gazed at him in openmouthed astonishment.

"No, I can see that you haven't," the chief went on imper-
turbably. "She is old enough to be your mother. Well, then, has

she attached any strings to her offer? No? Any talk of repayment with interest? No? Then what is your objection?"

"She—she is a woman, Sir," Dr. Morcus protested weakly.

"Fiddlesticks," scoffed Dr. Dawson. "Do you think all my gifts for mission work have come from men? I assure you the largest number have come from women. Without women, where would Christian world service be today? It is certainly no disgrace to accept money from a woman for a worthy cause. Madame Malik can well afford to finance your education."

He leaned back in his chair to allow the younger man time to digest what he had been saying. Confusion and bewilderment were written all over Dr. Kemalyian's face. He seemed unable to accept the truth that the older man had just pointed out to him.

Dr. Dawson leaned forward.

"Dr. Morcus, you once told me that your greatest desire was to be fully used in the ministry of healing," he stated. "I ask you now; is that still your chief ambition?"

Dr. Kemalyian lifted his head.

"Yes, Sir, it is," he replied.

"You are aware that you need much more medical training before you are qualified to do more than dispense a few pills to a few people in a small office," the chief continued. "Only mediocre ability is needed for a job like that. "I believe God has endowed you with far greater talents and abilities. Do you imagine that He will be pleased to wait four or five more years while you satisfy your stubborn pride, by rejecting this gift?"

Dr. Dawson paused again, then added, "I happen to know that Madame Malik is always seeking new opportunities to serve the Lord with her money. Have you any right to deny her that pleasure because of your silly scruples?"

Dr. Morcus's eyes were now glowing with dawning hope. Finally, he stated, "Madame Malik has offered far too much, Sir. She specified two thousand pounds. One thousand should be enough. I could manage on that. I would not feel justified in accepting more."

"You still have a few debts to settle, and your transportation to pay," warned Dr. Dawson. "Also, my friend only mentioned that amount as a rough estimate. I doubt if one thousand would cover your barest necessities. You would have absolutely nothing for emergencies. Just what did Madame Malik say about the amount that she offered?"

"She said that God told her to give me two thousand pounds," replied Dr. Morcus wonderingly.

"Well then," said the chief derisively. "That settles it! Accept the full amount as a gift from God, which it really is, then thank both Him and Madame Malik for it."

For one more incredulous moment Dr. Kemalyian hesitated. Then he sprang to his feet with a radiant smile, exclaiming joyfully, "I will, Sir! Thank you, Sir! God bless you."

Dr. Dawson rose and shook the outstretched hand warmly.

"Good," he said. "Now that you have things settled in your mind, come have a cup of tea with us."

"No, thank you, I had better not stop," replied Dr. Morcus, shaking hands with Hope, who had risen to offer her congratulations. "Madame's car is waiting, and so are my patients. And I must get that letter of acceptance off to New York today."

He was already at the door when Dr. Dawson raised his voice, "Better send a cablegram, too," he advised, "In case the letter is delayed. You can afford it now, you know."

Dr. Morcus laughed. "So I can!" he exclaimed in boyish delight. "I'll do that, Sir. Thank you!"

He fairly ran from the room and down the hall.

Hope faced the chief accusingly. But her own eyes were sparkling with joy.

"You old schemer, you," she chided affectionately.

The doctor waggled his head mournfully.

"I didn't expect you to use such unkind words, Miss Hope," he said, with an air of complete innocence. "Why are you so suspicious? Didn't our miracle happen?"

"You made a pact with me for a miracle three months ago," said Hope slowly. "Then you started planning all this without ever letting me know. Am I supposed to consider the working out of your own scheme as a miracle?"

They were standing face to face. The doctor sobered as he saw the confusion in her eyes.

"My dear, I trust you have learned today that God often uses human, as well as natural means, to bring about His miracles. Does that make them any less miraculous? I did not cause Madame Malik's car to break down at the crossroads just as Matt and I passed by the other day. I never mentioned the amount that Dr. Morcus needed."

With a fatherly smile he gallantly offered her his arm.

"Now, let us go finish our tea," he said.

They found Misprint alone in the tearoom with an open letter in her hand. There were tears in her eyes.

"My son's wife is having a nervous breakdown," she said sadly. "They need me right away. They have six little children. I have that money waiting right here in your Jerusalem bank. How soon can you get a plane reservation for me, Doctor?"

THIRTY-FOUR

"I AM GOING TO miss you," Hope said. "I feel that we are 'kindred spirits.' "

"I feel the same way about you," Misprint said.

They were waiting in the Kalendia airport for the afternoon plane to Beirut. It would take the older woman on the first leg of her flight to America.

Margaret Dawson was over in a corner chatting with friends. Matt stood at the large observation window, watching the planes taking off and landing. Dr. Dawson had remained behind at the hospital, standing by for emergency calls in place of Dr. Baxter. Esther Baxter had started labor at noon. On the way to the airport Matt had taken her and her husband to the Arab hospital in Bethlehem. So only three of Misprint's colleagues were there to see her off on her long journey.

"This has been a wonderful experience for me," Misprint went on. "I thank God for it and for you dear people. When I came out last year I thought I had outlived my usefulness as a mother. My children were all raised and married. Now I realize that situations arise in which a mother can be of some help to her children as long as she lives. It is a rather pleasant feeling."

"By the way," she continued, "has there been any change in Christine yet?"

Hope's eyes clouded. "I am afraid she is getting worse," she confessed. "The new class recognizes and respects Christine's efficiency. They accept her authority without resentment. But her strict discipline and sharp tongue keep her from winning their friendship. Stephanie is such a warmhearted girl that I thought surely she would be able to make friends with Christine. But she is careless and untidy. A week ago I discovered Christine's screen has been stretched clear across her side of the room. She threatens to confiscate anything of Stephanie's that she finds on her side of the screen. She and Christine rarely speak to each other. I don't see how things can go on this way much longer."

"Please keep me informed about her," Misprint said. "I shall continue to keep her in my prayers. They are calling my plane now. God bless you! We shall meet again somewhere, somehow, I know."

Matt and his two passengers arrived back at the hospital in time for supper. Afterward, Hope taught two subjects to her junior students. It was eight-thirty when she dismissed them. She sat at her desk a few minutes, wondering if Esther had delivered her baby by now. There was no reason to feel concerned. Esther had had no difficulty with previous deliveries.

She recalled that Dr. Baxter had carried Tim, their oldest son, over to the isolation room just before he and Esther left for the hospital. Tim was subject to asthmatic attacks. He was in the midst of one now. She decided to look in on Tim before retiring. The door of the sick bay was wide open. The usual dim lamp was burning on the floor in a corner. She approached the bed. She saw that Tim was sound asleep. His quiet breathing told her that the asthma attack was over. She went on down the hall to the chart room. Christine was putting the last chart in the rack.

"How are you getting along tonight, Christine?" Hope asked.

"Everything is finished," replied Christine. "The medications are all given. The men are settled for the night. I sent Zacchia off duty a few minutes ago. Nasri will be here soon. My charting is finished. I will be ready to go off duty as soon as Sister Marta comes and we count the drugs together."

"Tim was sleeping when I looked in on him just now," Hope observed.

"Yes, I checked him a few minutes ago," said Christine. "He was wheezing badly at six o'clock. I gave him the half ampule of ephedrine intramuscularly that Dr. Baxter ordered if needed. He quieted down and has been sleeping ever since."

Hope noted the drawn face of the girl, and the tired, unhappy set of her lips.

"You look tired, Christine," she said kindly. "I am afraid you push yourself too hard. Suppose I count drugs with you now. Then you can go as soon as Sister Marta gets your report."

Christine unlocked the medicine cabinet and brought out the box of drugs that were to be counted. She handed Hope the list. The daily oral drugs, which were administered in large quantities, were checked only when supplies ran low. But the seldom used drugs and the injectibles, must be signed out by the nurse administering them.

"Demerol 100," Hope began. Christine counted. "Fourteen," she replied. "Demerol 50." "Seven," was the reply. "Ephedrine 50," continued Hope. "Three," answered Christine. Hope shook her head.

"No, there should be only two," she said. "You signed one out for Tim at six and noted that half the amount was discarded."

Christine looked puzzled. She examined each label carefully.

"What about Epinephrine 50?" asked Hope.

Christine examined them carefully. "There are six," she announced. "There should be seven," replied Hope.

The two nurses stared at each other. Sudden terror leaped into Christine's eyes. Her face turned white. "Oh, my God!" she gasped.

The next second she was running wildly down the hall to Tim's room. Hope stopped to replace the box of drugs in the cupboard. She locked the door and dropped the key into her pocket. Then she hurried after Christine.

The girl was on her knees beside Tim. Her fingers were on his pulse. She was watching his every breath. Hope moved to the other side of the bed. She placed her fingers on the boy's other wrist. The pulse was strong and steady. Christine looked up.

"Oh, Miss Hope, have I killed him?" she whispered.

"He is all right, Christine," Hope assured her.

Christine was unconvinced. The terror remained in her eyes. "Maybe this is only temporary," she quavered. "Maybe the drug hasn't taken full effect yet."

"No, dear, you must believe me that he is in no danger," Hope repeated firmly. She picked up the lamp from the floor and set it on the table. "See that natural color in his cheeks," she said. "The asthma attack is over and he will sleep until morning now."

The girl was partly convinced.

"But I gave him the wrong medicine," she whispered. "I could have killed him."

"Yes, you could have," Hope agreed, "but you didn't. Of course, we will have to tell Dr. Baxter as soon as he returns."

"Tell me what?" asked a deep voice from the doorway.

Dr. Baxter strode into the room. Christine shrank back into the corner and cowered there. The doctor took the place she had vacated and lifted his son's hand. As he felt the boy's steady pulse, he looked inquiringly at Hope.

"Christine gave him the wrong medicine," Hope explained. "She won't believe me when I tell her he is all right."

Hope explained exactly what had happened while the doctor pulled his stethoscope from his pocket and checked his son's chest very carefully.

When he finished and straightened up, he said, "No harm done. Ephedrine is milder. There is less danger of side effects. Some doctors prefer the Epinephrine for older patients. Tim gets along with the other. I prefer it for a child of his age."

He started to step back from the bed and almost toppled over. Christine had both arms wrapped about his knees. She looked up imploringly through a mist of tears, begging, "Doctor, forgive me, please! I can never forgive myself."

He stooped over and gently tried to loosen Christine's clinging grip.

"Pull yourself together, Christine," he said. "There's no harm done. Get up before you awaken Tim."

The mention of awakening Tim produced the desired effect. She let Dr. Baxter help her up, and he led her to the chartroom. Hope replaced the lamp on the floor and followed.

The doctor was talking when Hope arrived. He faced Christine across the desk. Both were seated. Her face was still white.

"Christine," the doctor began, "you are not the first one to make this very same mistake. I am certain you will not be the last. I doubt if you will ever make another, however."

"I know I won't, Doctor," she replied tonelessly. "You have helped me, but I can never forgive myself. I will never give another medication. My nursing days re over."

Dr. Baxter and Hope exchanged understanding glances. Hope put her arm about the shoulders of the drooping girl. The doctor reached across the desk to take one of the trembling hands.

"Christine, listen," he said earnestly. "I have been through this thing myself. I'll venture to say that Miss Hope . . ." (he paused to glance inquiringly at Hope, who nodded) ". . . has been through it, too. If all the truth were known, there are very few in the medical profession who have never made at least one mistake in medication. Every one of us felt just as you do now. But if we all lost our nerve and quit, what would the world do for medical healing? This mistake will make you doubly careful. Don't give up because of it."

He continued as Christine started to protest. "Understand that I am not excusing you, Christine," he said. "There is no excuse for carelessness. We all know the rules: 'check order and medicine three times before giving it.' One slip is usually enough to make us doubly careful thereafter. We can thank God that the mistake wasn't fatal."

There was the click of a key in the latch of the side door down the hall. Hope held up a warning finger. Nasri appeared in his white jacket. He looked surprised when he saw the three in the chartroom.

"Sorry I overslept," he apologized. "Where is Sister Marta?"

"She must have overslept, too," replied Dr. Baxter. Then with a broad smile, he held out his hand to Nasri. "Man to man, Nasri, how would you like to be the first to congratulate me on the birth of a fine new son?"

Nasri beamed with delight. He shook the proffered hand with vigor. "*Mabrouk*," (congratulations) he said. "You are fortunate to have sons. May God grant you many more!"

Hope was crestfallen. "How could I have forgotten to ask?" she moaned. "Congratulations from me, too. How is Esther?"

"Fit as a fiddle," he answered proudly. "Young Matthew Mark is a fine big boy, with long legs and my looks—at least that is what the nurses say."

Christine had risen. She offered her best wishes also, then returned to Tim's room until Sister Marta arrived.

The doctor addressed Nasri, "Young man, Miss Callaway and I have some private business to discuss. Have you something you can do elsewhere for a little while?"

Nasri donned his isolation gown and took a flashlight. Then he went into the men's ward to take a bed check.

"Let me have Tim's chart," said Dr. Baxter.

Hope found it in the rack. He crossed out some orders and wrote in new ones. Then he signed the paper. He found the page of nurses' notes and studied Christine's entry. Handing the chart and pen to Hope, he said, "I can't imitate her handwriting. I'll leave this to you."

Hope made the alteration, wrote "error," and initialed it. "She will have to sign it herself tomorrow," she said. "But this will do for now. Thank you, Doctor."

"Glad to do it," he replied. "Christine is too good a nurse to lose. Now, I'd better relieve Maryam of her baby sitting."

He paused briefly at his son's door, then went off down the hall.

Sister Marta arrived a few minutes later, and Hope briefed her on the events of the evening.

She accompanied Hope down the hall. They stopped at Tim's door. Christine was kneeling beside the boy's bed. Her head was bowed upon her hands.

"Tell Christine I will be waiting when she is ready to come," whispered Hope.

The kindly deaconess nodded.

A half hour passed. The hospital generator shut off. Hope lite her coleman lamp. At length, some inner sense warned her that Christine was present. She looked up to see the girl standing in the doorway, holding her cap in both hands.

"Come in, Christine, I have been expecting you."

Christine advanced slowly. Her face was pale and set. When she reached Hope, she dropped to her knees and laid the cap in Hope's lap.

"Take it, Miss Hope," she said flatly. "I have forfeited the right to ever wear it again. I could have killed Timmy tonight. I am not fit to live. When God spared my life eleven years ago, I wanted to be a nurse and help others. Now I know that I never can. I am just too wicked to ever be good for anything."

She buried her face in her hands.

Hope picked up Christine's cap and turned to place it on the table. She pulled Christine's hands away from her face, and held them firmly. The girl raised her head and stared dully at Hope.

"Christine, there is something in your past for which you have never forgiven yourself," Hope stated.

The girl's eyes darkened with bitter memories. She bowed her head. Satisfied that she was on the right track, Hope resolved to force the issue, no matter how dire the consequences.

"Why do you hate yourself so, Christine?" Hope demanded sharply. "I will not be put off any longer."

"You already know why, Miss Hope!" Christine cried despairingly. "I am a murderer! I set the cave on fire and ran away. I killed my whole family. I can hear my sister's screams even now. I never even tried to rescue her. I just ran and left them all to burn to death. I was wicked! I can never forgive myself. Never!"

She snatched her hands away and buried her face in them again. Hope stared at her in amazement. Then she again seized the girl's hands and dragged them away from her face.

"Christine, you are wrong, absolutely wrong," she declared. "Listen to me! Your family all died of asphyxiation long before you got out of the cave. You couldn't have done anything to save them. Your robe was the only thing that caught fire when you stumbled and fell over the brazier."

Christine shook her head. "I know better, Miss Hope," she said dully. "You don't know. You weren't there."

"No, Christine, I am telling you the truth," Hope insisted. Then a sudden inspiration came to her. "You say you don't believe me because I wasn't there," she continued. "Perhaps you will believe the word of someone who was there that night. Come with me."

She pulled Christine to her feet and led her down the hall. She picked up the oil lamp from the stair landing and ushered the girl to the door of her own room. They entered. Stephanie was sound asleep in her bed nearest the door.

"Please remove the screen and sit down on your bed, Christine," ordered Hope. Then she gently shook Stephanie's shoulder.

"Wake up, Stephanie," Hope prodded. "We must talk to you."

Stephanie was wide awake in a moment, and swung her feet to the floor and sat up. She looked puzzled.

"I want you to tell Christine what happened that night in the cave eleven years ago," Hope asked. "She thinks she set fire to the place and burned her whole family to death."

"Why, Christine, you are mistaken! There was no fire in your cave. You were the only one that burned. Your whole family bad all been dead for hours from the charcoal fumes when the men found them. Everyone wondered how you ever got out alive."

"That's what you say," said Christine stubbornly. "You weren't there!"

"But I was there," Stephanie insisted. "Not in your cave, but in the one just below it on the mountain. Don't you remember me? I was only eight then. But you must remember my father, Stephen Stephanos?"

A flicker of recognition appeared in Christine's eyes. "I do remember the name," she acknowledged.

"Well, then," continued Stephanie triumphantly, "perhaps now you will believe me when I tell you I was there. I remember everything distinctly. It was barely light, maybe about four o'clock in the morning, when you began screaming. People all over the mountain were wakened by your screams.

"My father was the first to reach you. He said you were blazing like a torch. I woke up when he carried you into our cave. He had smothered the blaze and wrapped you in his robe. Mother covered you with a blanket. You kept screaming and plucking at the blanket. Mother lifted it and saw some big coals turning holes in your chest. I watched her dig them out with a spoon."

Stephanie shuddered at the recollection, then went on. "You were unconscious when my father came back and reported that everyone else in the cave was dead. They had been dead for hours. You must have fallen across the brazier when you were trying to get out. It was overturned. Ashes and coals were scattered all over the floor, but most of them were burned out. There must have been a few live embers left in the bottom that got buried in your gown. Nothing caught fire but your gown when you opened the door. The fumes were still strong in the cave when the men got there. They hardly dared enter. No one could ever understand how you managed to survive those fumes."

Christine was listening as if she were hypnotized. Now she spoke as one in a dream, "There was a big crack in the wall of the cave right beside the head of my bed," she whispered. "The cold wind blew in. I always slept with my head under the covers. I think I was beginning to feel dizzy when I wakened and tried to get out."

Stephanie nodded. "That explains it," she said.

"But the fire?" Christine persisted. "I know there was a fire! I was so dizzy when I got up that I fell over the brazier. I believe I lay there until the pain from the hot coals roused me enough to crawl to the door. I couldn't breathe. I know I managed to get to my feet and raise the bar. Then I fell against it and it swung open. I felt the cold air, and suddenly, everything burst into flames. I heard my sister screaming. The pain in my chest was terrible. I got up and ran away. I let them all die."

Stephanie stared at her roommate helplessly.

"How can I convince you, Christine?" she asked. "I tell you there was no fire in the cave. Your folks were already dead. The rooster and hens were lying dead below their perch. Think Christine! Can't you remember anything else? You must have tripped over the donkey when you fell across the brazier. He was lying right beside it, stiff and cold. Do you suppose the donkey would just lie there without moving if he were still alive when you tripped over him and scattered the coals?"

A light was dawning in Christine's eyes.

"The donkey!" she exclaimed. "Yes, now I remember. I felt his stiff hairs against my ankle when I tripped. I wondered why he did not move. Then I didn't remember anything more except the terrible pain and the screaming. You are right. He must have been dead!"

Stephanie moved over to sit beside her. Christine looked up pitifully into her face, saying, "Stephanie there must be some mistake. My sister wasn't dead! I could hear her screaming. Her screams followed me all the way down the hill."

Stephanie's strong young arms went about her roommate. The tears were streaming down her own face.

"Christine, those were your own screams you heard," she said tenderly.

For a long moment Christine searched the earnest, honest eyes of the younger girl. Then she cried, "It is true! Oh, God, it is true! I have been believing the devil all these years and refusing to forgive myself for something I didn't do."

She rested her head against Stephanie's comforting shoulder. The tortured grief of those eleven years poured forth in a torrent of tears. Stephanie held her close and rocked back and forth with her, like a mother soothing a hurt child.

After a few minutes, Hope wiped her own eyes, and rose, "Thank you, Stephanie," she whispered. "I will be in my room."

Stephanie nodded and continued her rocking. Hope slipped quietly out and closed the door.

This time she did not have long to wait. Christine came in with a rush and flung herself down again before Hope. Her face was radiant with a newfound joy and peace.

"Oh, Miss Hope," she cried, "I don't feel mean or hateful anymore."

"Not even toward yourself, Christine?" asked Hope.

"Not even toward myself," the girl replied emphatically.

The eyes of both nurses turned instinctively to the small white cap that still lay beside Hope's Bible on the table.

"Please, may I wear it again?" Christine asked wistfully.

Hope picked up the cap and held it out to her. "It is still yours, Christine," she said with a smile.

Hope dispatched an airmail letter to Misprint a few days later. She gave her friend a brief account of what had taken place. The letter stated: "Christine radiates love to everyone now. This morning she made a public apology to all the students and employees. They were glad to meet her more than halfway. The junior class has always looked up to her. Now her own classmates recognize and accept her leadership. They seek her advice on all their problems."

In her next letter to Misprint, Hope was delighted to report: "For the first time since her dismissal, Christine visited the Mount of Olives Hospital on her day off last week. She went with the intention of apologizing to Leila, the nurse whose face she had slashed. The nursing superintendent, Sitt Maryam, was glad to tell Christine that Leila had resigned from nurses' training just a short while later. Before leaving, the girl confessed that she blamed herself for the death of the patient that night. She said that when she and Christine removed the dressings and she saw the horribly disfigured face, she had thoughtlessly exclaimed, 'I can't bear to look at her. No one else ever will, either. She would be much better off dead.' Both girls saw, from the stricken look in the woman's eyes, that she had heard. When the woman died that night, the cause was diagnosed as extreme shock. Leila knew that she, not Christine, had caused the death. She was too ~~scared~~ to confess at the time. By the time she found the courage, it was too late to help Christine."

Hope's letter went on to say, "Eileen has been keeping up her Arabic studies, and is becoming very proficient. Neither Dr. Dawson nor I ever made more than a feeble attempt to learn. She is finished teaching all her classes now, so I have sent her out to do the recruiting for a new spring class. She is meeting with much more success than I did. Maybe it means a beginning breakdown of prejudices against nursing in this part of the world. We are having a large new influx of patients, so will need a large new class of recruits.

"Three of our five graduates will be staying on with us next year. Warda and Yacoub plan to be married in early May. Aminah will help out for a while. She and her father will follow Dr. Kemalyian to America by the end of the year. The mission board is sending out an assistant doctor in early spring to help in the hospital work here.

"We are all most grateful for the lovely flannelgraphs you left with us. Aminah is already rehearsing the juniors to present the Christmas story again in the wards and chapel this year. We shall miss you very much at Christmas, and always. I, for one, will never forget you. I hope to see you out here again some day."

THIRTY-FIVE

SHORTLY AFTER AIDA AND her family became residents at the shelter, Aminah paid them a visit. She had purchased a beautiful layette imported from abroad. The garments were exquisitely made of the finest material. There was a tiny white dress and slip to match. When Aminah presented them to Aida, the girl cried. Then she carefully replaced the gown and slip in their tissue paper wrappings and laid them away in a drawer. "These will be my little Angele's shroud," she said quietly.

A week before Christmas, Saleem brought a note that little Angele had slipped away quietly in the night, and would be buried that afternoon. Neither Hope nor Eileen were free to go. They sent Regina and Aminah as their representatives.

The two students returned to report that Aida was quite calm and composed. They said Angele looked like a little wax doll in her tiny coffin. She was dressed in the beautiful garments Aminah had provided. Aida told them that her child's face always reminded her of Zoohrah's. Both nurses could see the resemblance. Regina told Aida that Zoohrah's mother had come to take her and her dolly home the week before. Both were in blooming health. Aida had smiled and said, "I am so glad I gave her the doll. I didn't realize then that the only real joy in life is in giving, especially of yourself. My little Angele taught that to me. There are so many opportunities here for sharing a part of myself with these little ones, that I have no time for sorrow. My child is well and happy now. I shall meet her again some day."

At five o'clock on the afternoon on Christmas Eve, Hope repeated the gist of Aida's remarks to her hostess. She was seated in Madame Malik's private office at the shelter.

Jimmy and Ruth Dyson's youth group were still enjoying a bountiful tea with several of the nursing students. They were gathered in the large sitting room. Madame Malik had invited them to sing Christmas carols in the wards that afternoon. The bus they had chartered for the evening was waiting out front to take them on to the Shepherd's Fields for an early gathering around a bonfire. There they would be joined by the blind children and their attendants as well as by various missionaries from other points in the area, for the yearly singing of Christmas carols. Eileen was on duty that night, but would have her holiday the next day. Special services were traditionally held in Christ Church and in St. George's Cathedral on Christmas day.

When Hope quoted Aida's words about sharing a part of herself, Madame Malik smiled appreciatively.

"That is exactly what I brought you in here to talk about," she said. "As you know, Aida did have a faint trace of syphilis in her bloodstream, which responded rapidly to Dr. Kemalyian's treatments. Angele had such a severe case that we had no hopes of saving her. As soon as Aida was cured and felt strong enough, she undertook to help in the nursery. She has been a real blessing to my little ones."

Madame paused to consult a handsome watch, which she wore on a chain about her neck, saying apologetically, "I must not absent myself too long from my other guests, but I want to tell you something of my plans before I discuss them with Aida. I am sure you have a special interest in her welfare.

"Miss Callaway, I am not getting any younger. I have been praying for a long time that God would send me exactly the right person to take over the management of this Home when I am no longer able to do so. My daughter is in sympathy with the work, but her loyalties are divided between her husband's country and her own. She also has her six children to keep her busy. I could not expect her to handle the problems of personnel, patients, tradesmen, and everything else.

"I have wonderfully capable and compassionate nurses on my staff here now," Madame continued. "But they lack the executive ability for managing the Home. I know others with executive ability who do not have the compassionate understanding that I demand of my successor. Do you follow me, Miss Callaway?"

Hope nodded excitedly. "I think I do," she replied.

Madame Malik went on, "I believe God has sent me His choice. A fully trained nurse is not needed. Aida has enough knowledge in that field to understand the type of nursing service that is required. She is young, strong, and highly intelligent. She is able to handle her own problems and those of other people without friction. The entire staff accepts her wholeheartedly. She shows leadership and brings out the best in others.

"Suffering has developed a courage and spiritual strength in the girl that is rarely found in one so young. I believe she fits my purposes, and is the one for which I have been seeking."

She paused. Her eyes held Hope's in a long, steady gaze. "Miss Callaway," she stated quietly, "it is my intention if Aida is willing, to send her abroad for training in accounting, hospital management, and study of similar work in several institutions like this. Perhaps in three years or so, unless I should need her sooner, I expect to bring her back here to take over most of my duties. I will want to keep my hand in the work to some extent as long as I am physically able. But in case my health should require her presence here sooner than I anticipate, I will have a trust fund set up with my daughter and her husband as executors. She could draw on the account at a moment's notice and continue the work as planned. Do you think she will accept it?"

"The challenge is almost overwhelming," Hope replied slowly. "But I do agree with you. I believe that Aida can be trained to fully qualify for the position. I feel certain that she will accept."

Madame Malik rose with a satisfied smile. "I must get back to my other guests now," she said. "Aida has asked to have a word with you alone before you leave. If you wish to stay here, I will send someone to fetch her. I will tell her of my wishes sometime before the holidays are over."

Aida appeared almost immediately. She invited Hope to her room. It was a tiny, neat cubicle adjoining the nursery. She offered Hope the only chair and seated herself on the bed.

"Did you know that my father died in prison about three weeks ago, Miss Hope?" she began.

"Why, no," replied Hope, greatly surprised that the news has escaped Mrs. Murad's sharp ears, as well as Regina's.

"They sent word from the prison hospital that he was dying," Aida continued. "Mother would not have understood. So I went alone to see him. I could scarcely believe that the man lying on that hospital bed was my father. Instead of the big, strong bully I remembered, I saw a frail, shrunken, terrified little man who was afraid to die. He clung to me like a child and begged me to forgive him. I found that I could. He could not seem to grasp that. He died the very next day."

"Miss Hope," Aida continued earnestly, "I inherited the strength and determination of my father. If he hadn't beaten some of his stubbornness out of me when I was little, I might have been a bully like him. After a while I didn't mind the beatings for myself, but I couldn't bear to see him beat my mother. She never stood up to him. His greatest delight was in terrorizing my brother. My brother and I both learned to lie and to steal from his example. He was always gambling and demanding that we give him every cent we stole. I began holding out on him, until one day he found that it hurt me far worse to see him beat my mother. So then he threatened to beat her whenever I didn't obey him.

"I had to turn over my hospital allowance to him each month. The only spending money I had I stole from the clinic cash box. When I bought the doll for Zoohrah with my allowance, he was furious. He threatened to beat my mother unmercifully if I didn't get him a wax impression of the keys to the office safe. He promised he would leave mother alone if I did. He gave me the wax in a box.

"The day that I stole Faiza's money I saw your keys on the bureau in your room. I knew I couldn't get hold of the safe keys, so I took the impression of your dulab key instead. I promised I would steal as much as I could. Then, when you offered to keep the staff money, he made up the scheme for me to 'bank' what I had, and as much more as he could give me, so I could steal all the deposits and never be suspected. If I didn't do it, he swore he would beat mother half to death. It would be my fault. You know what happened when I tried it.

"When Dr. Dawson and Dr. Baxter took me home that night, they warned my father that they would have him imprisoned if he beat me. He started in on my mother as soon as they were gone. I pitched into him. We had a terrible battle. I was a lot stronger than he thought and was slowly getting the best of him. But Mother leaped on my back and held my arms. She helped tie me up. Then he beat me as hard as he dared where it wouldn't show much. I swore then never to steal again. I only hurt myself. Mother didn't want help. She was always weak and admired my father's strength.

"I knew that I couldn't stay at home any longer. But I had no other place to go. When my father brought a man home a few days later who was willing to marry me, I agreed to go with him. The marriage contract was signed that night. My husband cancelled the gambling debts my father owed him and paid my father twenty pounds beside."

"Twenty pieces of silver," Hope murmured.

"Yes, I know," said Aida. "I found much time to read my Bible this past year. It was a comfort while I was locked in, waiting for Angele to arrive. I knew I had been spared my father's fate, and I found that I no longer felt hatred for my husband, only pity for his weakness."

Hope moved over to put her arm around the girl, saying, "I am glad that you told me all this, dear. You have learned more lessons in one year than most people learn in a lifetime. I can safely predict that this next year will be a far happier one for you."

"Now I want to give you something I have been treasuring," said Aida, rising and going to the cupboard. "I didn't really steal it, but it does belong to the mission. You may want to use it for someone else. I have no need for it any longer."

She brought forth her battered old suitcase and took from it an oddly shaped bundle. Carefully she started to unwrap it.

"I know you must have wondered what became of my cap," Aida said. "I am so ashamed of the way I trampled on it. When you reminded me that night that I was wearing it, I suddenly realized how much I was giving up. My heart was already breaking. I just couldn't stand anymore. When you cried out and ran from the room, I picked it up and hid it among my things. It has been my most treasured possession ever since."

Aida produced the cap and turned it lovingly around in her hands. Hope noted that it was immaculately laundered.

"I kept it hidden," Aida continued, "even from my husband. When I knew I was going to have a child, I got it out and looked at it whenever he wasn't around. It gave me courage."

She held out the cap to Hope, saying, "Now I don't need it any more. It should belong to some student who has the right to wear it."

Hope made no motion to take the cap. Instead, she smiled.

"Keep it, dear," she said, "as a reminder of God's goodness. My heart came near breaking, too, that night. But Murshdeeyah told me about the cap the next morning. I knew you had it all along. I believe that you will have a far wider opportunity of service here than you would ever have had at Beth Hanani."

"Thank you, Miss Hope," said Aida humbly. "I pray that it may be so." She replaced the cap in its wrappings and put it away.

As the two walked out into the hall, Aida's sharply attuned ears caught the sound of a faint whimper in the nursery. She stepped into the room and picked up a frail little boy about two years old, with clubfeet. His dark eyes were wide and frightened.

"He has only been here a few days," Aida explained, wrapping a blanket about him. "Madame Malik is making arrangements for an operation on his feet. He is afraid when he wakes up in the dark and finds himself in a strange place. I will hold him for a while until he goes to sleep again."

The child snuggled his head contentedly under Aida's chin and the three continued on down the hall. They met Madame Malik coming in search of them. Her long woolen cape swirled about her as she hurried toward them.

"Everybody is on the bus. They are waiting for you, Miss Hope," she exclaimed, tucking her large hand under Hope's elbow to help her along. "The driver wants to follow the signs out to the spot reserved for your group in the Shepherd's Fields while there is still a little light remaining. He wants to get a good parking space before they are all taken."

Sitt Azizy was waiting at the door with Hope's thick coat and warm woolen scarf over her arm. She helped Hope into them, while the later thanked Madame Malik, and wished everyone a Merry Christmas. They followed her out onto the porch to wave good-bye. The wind was quite chilly. Hope wrapped her warm coat more closely about her. She glanced anxiously at Aida, who was the only one out there without a wrap.

Madame Malik had also noted the lack, and she moved close to Aida and the child, saying, "Come under my wing quickly, child, before you catch your death of cold." Aida obeyed. The warm woolen cloak closed about her and the child in a loving gesture. It made a pretty picture—the large silver haired woman, the tall dark-haired younger one, and the child, wrapped together in the sheltering cloak.

As Hope ran down the steps, she saw several brilliant stars already gleaming in the clear evening sky. She thought of that one great star that had once shone over Bethlehem almost two thousand years ago, and of the birth it had foretold. What a glorious night it must have been, and what a glorious message it had brought to lighten the hearts of all mankind, for all eternity.

THIRTY-SIX

HOPE SAT AT HER window on a crisp morning in mid January gazing with unseeing eyes at the rocky mountains in the distance. Her mind was visualizing a far different kind of countryside. She could see lush green hillsides with rice paddies and tea fields. There were sparkling rivers and huge stone buildings, yellow skinned natives.

She picked up a letter lying on her lap and read it slowly. It had arrived more than two weeks before. It was nearly committed to memory. The other missionaries were having morning tea. She had slipped away to her room to read the letter once more before discussing its contents with Dr. Dawson. Her decision was already made. Now she must tell the chief. It would be difficult.

At last, she folded the letter resolutely, put it in her pocket, and knelt for a moment beside her bed. Then she rose and went in search of the chief.

He was alone in his office. She slowly spread the letter before him on his desk, explaining, "This arrived several days ago from the Mennonite Board in America. They want me to start a training school for native nurses in their mission hospital in Taiwan. I have spent much time in prayer about it ever since. I feel that God is calling me to go."

The chief gave her a long, searching look as he picked up the letter.

"Please sit down," he invited. She did so. He skimmed quickly through the pages, then read it slowly again. Finally, he folded it carefully and handed it back.

"So you believe that God wants you to go, Miss Hope?" he asked quietly.

"I believe He has told me that I should accept," she replied.

The chief nodded. There was a look of sadness in his eyes, he spoke cheerfully as always.

"If God has already told you to go, I will not try to dissuade you. I myself have always been blessed whenever I have obeyed His commands. He has led me into many strange and wonderful adventures during my lifetime. I hardly need tell you how much you have done for us here, and how greatly we shall all miss you. Have you made any decision as to how soon you must leave us?"

"The letter states that the board would like me to start the training program in June. I will need to have at least a month in America to outfit myself for a different climate and to select the necessary textbooks. I must also attend to some financial matters. If at all possible, I would like to leave by the first of May. I am sure that Eileen Anderson is fully qualified to take over here as superintendent. If you approve, and she is willing, I believe the mission board would appoint her. I have said nothing to her about this. The decision is entirely in your hands."

"I agree that Miss Anderson is thoroughly capable," said the chief thoughtfully. "I will be honored if she is willing to accept. The board would be happy to appoint her on the strength of my approval. I suggest that we ask her right now."

He rose and opened the door to the adjoining office. "Marika," he said to the secretary, "please find Miss Anderson and ask her to come to my office right away."

"If Eileen does accept," Hope continued, "she will need an assistant director from America, of course. I believe that Christine Gomry could help in the teaching program. Christine plans to stay on here indefinitely after graduation. She will be a great help in many ways. I could stay on until an American assistant comes. But I believe it would be best for Miss Anderson to assume the superintendency immediately after the senior class graduates next month. The new class will be starting a few days later. She has recruited them. She should be given a free hand to carry out her own methods with them from the start. I will be glad to help as her assistant until you can get a permanent replacement."

The chief was eyeing her with keen regret.

"Your ability to consider and plan all the little details far in advance has always amazed me, Miss Hope," he said. "Truly our loss will be Taiwan's gain."

Hope's eyes suddenly misted.

"I shall miss your encouraging compliments, Sir," she said with a little choke in her voice.

There was a knock on the door and Eileen entered. The doctor rose and offered her a seat. Then he broke the news to her of Hope's plans to leave, and formally asked her to assume the position of Nursing Superintendent. Her eyes widened in amazement and disbelief. She turned to Hope.

"I—I thought, that is, I hoped, that some day this position might be offered me," she stammered. "Do you really think that I can handle it now?"

"Yes, Eileen," Hope answered unhesitatingly. "You are ready. I have known it for some time."

"I will be honored if you will accept the appointment," the chief added.

Eileen looked from one to the other, then answered gravely, "I am happy to accept. I will do my best to fill the position creditably."

"Good," said the chief, rising to shake her hand, while Hope smiled at her delightedly.

"There will be no mention of this until after the senior class has graduated," the chief warned. "Miss Hope wishes you to assume the position immediately afterward. She will stay on as your assistant until we get another one from America. It may take some time to find one, I fear."

"Why, Dr. Dawson," Eileen exclaimed excitedly, "I don't think you need to apply to America for an assistant. We could easily use a short-term teacher, of course, to help with the larger class. But I believe that Christine Gomry could be trained to make an excellent assistant. She has executive ability. She is an efficient teacher and supervisor in the wards, and the students accept her authority. With added responsibility she could learn to take over the position of superintendent here, if and when I should have to leave."

Eileen had their undivided attention now.

"I have heard you say, Doctor, that missionary work should be turned over to the nationals themselves as soon as possible," she said.

"We never know how much longer we foreigners will be allowed to carry on here. Christine and I work well together. I would be quite satisfied to train her as my assistant."

"Your logic is sound," said the doctor. "She would certainly not need to spend time in learning the language and the customs. Her own people would like the idea. I will be glad to give the girl a trial, provided she understands that it is just that—a trial. I believe the young lady has the ability to make good. We will put her on probation for, say, a year. If she shows enough promise by then, I will ask the mission board to appoint her to the position. We could also assure her of a chance at your position at some future date. I believe she should have a complete under-standing of the situation as soon as possible."

He rose to his feet. The two nurses rose with him.

"I suggest that you ladies have an interview with Miss Gomry immediately," he said. "Then let me know her reaction. If we need just a short-term teacher from America, I will send a letter off this very afternoon. It may be possible that we can let Miss Hope depart a little ahead of her schedule."

A short time later, Eileen and Hope were seated in the tea-room with a very mystified Christine.

"Christine," Hope began, "I know you can keep a secret, for you have kept Hanni's well. We now want you to keep another one."

Christine's eyes widened with apprehension.

"This is nothing like the other one," Hope hastily assured her. "We think you will be pleased."

Hope began telling of her plans to go to Taiwan, Christine grew apprehensive again. The girl turned quickly to Eileen, and queried, "Are you going to leave us, too, Miss Eileen?"

"No," Eileen assured her. Hope continued, "The reason we are telling you now, Christine, is that Miss Anderson has agreed to take over as superintendent here. We want to make sure that you are willing to stay on and help her."

Christine looked surprised. "But I told you some time ago that I would, Miss Hope," she said.

Eileen took over smoothly. "That was before you knew that Miss Hope would be leaving and that I would be in charge. I do hope that you will stay, Christine," she went on. "But I don't want you just as a nursing instructor and a supervisor. I want to train you as my assistant, with the understanding that you will be on probation here for one year. If you handle the responsibil-ity well, Dr. Dawson will recommend you to the mission board for a permanent assignment to the position, with the under-standing you will be in line to succeed me here at some future time. It is important to the plans of the mission that we know if you are interested enough to consider devoting your whole life to this ministry."

Christine had been listening intently, with clasped hands resting quietly in her lap. Now she bowed her head. There was a long silence. The two older women began to exchange questioning glances. Finally, Christine raised her head and looked pleadingly at Hope.

"Miss Hope," she said earnestly. "I love you very dearly. You have been more than a mother to me. Please don't be offended when I say that Miss Eileen and I think much more alike. The girls all love you, as I do, but they need firm discipline. When you are too kind to them, they take advantage of you. Everyone of us has done so."

Hope stared at her in astonishment. She opened her mouth to speak, then thought better of it.

Christine went on, "I know that I can work better with Miss Eileen. She understands the Arab temperament, and knows how to deal with it. I am glad and willing to try to work under her supervision. I know that I have very much to learn and that I must depend on her to teach me." Her eyes filled with tears, as she concluded, "I shall miss you very much." She turned to Eileen.

"Miss Eileen," she said wistfully, "I have no family left. My sister and I were very close. I still miss her very much. Will you teach me and be a second sister to me?"

Eileen Anderson, the unemotional, hardboiled, Eileen Anderson was already on her feet. She held out her arms. Her voice held a note of tenderness as she answered, "Oh, Christine, my dear, I never had a sister, and I always wanted one!"

Christine flew into her arms. Over the Arab girl's shoulder, Eileen cast an anxious glance at Hope. Rightly interpreting that look, Hope smiled, and silently clapped her hands in approval. A look of unutterable relief swept across Eileen's face.

Hope cleared her throat ostentatiously. "If you two will permit me to leave this touching scene, I will go so that you can make your plans in private."

The two stepped apart and giggled. Hope stalked stiffly past them with her nose in the air. At the door she turned, dropped them an elaborate curtsy, then closed the door firmly behind her.

All the way down the hall, her heart was singing with a paean of thankfulness. It was not so much for the added assurance of God's definite call to Taiwan, as for the fact that not one single pang of jealousy marred the delight she felt in Eileen's new-found joy.

THIRTY-SEVEN

GRADUATION DAY DAWNED CLEAR, crisp, and cold.

Early in the morning Rolf and Matt, with Daoud and Saleem assisting, started preparing the chapel. Everything but the small lectern was removed from the platform to make room for the large number of chairs needed to seat the many distinguished guests who had accepted special invitations to attend. These included three emissaries of King Hussein, one of whom was to present the diplomas.

The mayor of Bethlehem, various officials, church dignitaries and representatives from all over Jordan, would be present. Innumerable friends and relatives of the graduating class, as well as friends of the mission, were expected also; for this day marked a very important milestone in the annals of the Beth Hanani Mission Hospital.

The little pump organ and bench were relegated to a position on the main floor below the platform. Every possible inch of space on the platform was utilized in the placing of the folding chairs. But when the final count was made, it was discovered that there was only room to seat two of the mission staff on the platform beside the five graduates and all the dignitaries who had received special invitations. It would be considered unforgivable discourtesy to seat any of the guests on the main floor.

It was decided that the chief and the Reverend James Dyson should be the staff members to occupy the two platform seats. Two seats were reserved in the front row for Dr. Baxter and Hope. Daoud hid two extra folding chairs in the storage space beneath the platform. Being astute, and well-versed in the unpredictable ways of his countrymen to show up unexpectedly and uninvited, he was not about to be caught napping. As it happened, one extra official did put in an appearance. The Reverend Dyson had to occupy one of the extra chairs placed hastily up on the main floor.

The guests began arriving long before the stated time of two o'clock. The junior nurses arrived at half past one and settled themselves in a center section that Rolf was holding for them. They were in full uniform. The chapel filled rapidly after that. The guests waiting outside were assured that they would be allowed to fill the aisles and the back and sides, just as soon as the graduates and officials entered.

Eileen arrived in crisp uniform and cap. She seated herself at the organ. With a noisy clatter of footpedals and alarming squeaks from the ancient bellows, she filled the bags with air. Then she began playing a beautiful prelude from one of the famous oratorios. The audience quieted down to enjoy the music.

The officials arrived with the mission doctors and staff. Eileen waited until they were all seated, then she struck up the opening bars of the entrance march that she and Hope had chosen. Dr. Baxter rose to his feet and turned to face the audience.

"Let us all stand and sing two verses of hymn 205. Two verses only, please! Then we will remain standing for the invocation."

Dr. Baxter's powerful tenor voice led off with enthusiasm on the first words:

"Lead on, O King Eternal, the day of march has come . . ."

For the second and last time Hope Callaway marched proudly down the aisle leading her senior students. This time there were only five, but she was well satisfied. She knew that no finer young women could be found anywhere in the world. She felt only a passing twinge of regret for the loss of the four others who had started the course two years ago. Each, in her own way, was wearing the earthly crown that God had designed especially for her.

Before the second verse ended, the five students reached their assigned places on the platform, and turned to face the audience. The Reverend Dyson mounted the platform to offer the invocation, while Hope slipped into the place reserved for her beside Dr. Baxter. A short burst of applause for the graduates followed. Jimmy invited everyone to be seated. Then he introduced the Mayor of Bethlehem, who was to speak a few words of welcome. That portly individual unctuously proceeded to express his extreme delight in the very great honor that was being conferred upon him and upon all his constituency, by the presence of the King's emissaries. He went on to say, in flowery language, what a great day it was for these five very charming young ladies before them. Scarcely pausing to take a breath throughout his speech, he proceeded to elaborate upon this theme, with variations, for a full thirty minutes. Then, beaming and perspiring profusely, he reluctantly yielded the floor to Dr. Dawson.

Dr. Dawson immediately introduced the highest ranking guest, the king's personal ambassador. That tall, handsome individual, rose in his place with dignified military bearing and expressed in a few simple words his monarch's regret at being unable to attend today's ceremony in person. He stated that King Hussein wished him to convey to Dr. Dawson and his staff, and to the graduating class, his congratulations and assurance of a warm personal interest in their welfare. He also expressed the king's deep gratitude for the humane services that the Beth Hanani Mission was rendering to his needy subjects. He concluded by saying that he and his companions wished to add their own personal thanks and congratulations to those of their king. He then introduced his two companions.

To Hope's great relief, they merely rose and bowed, while the audience applauded enthusiastically.

Several other officials were called upon. Each, responded in turn with a congratulatory speech, some lengthy, others mercifully short. Meanwhile, the hours of daylight were rapidly slipping away.

At last, Dr. Dawson rose to deliver the baccalaureate address. It was simple, and of necessity, considerably shorter than what he had planned to say. He closed with a fervent prayer for God's blessing upon the future ministry of these five young nurses and upon all those associated with them. Then he called upon Hope.

In anticipation of a protracted meeting, Hope had prepared the shortest possible speech. She managed to find a place for her two feet on the platform between the lectern and the chairs of the graduates. After a word of greeting to the assembled guests, she addressed a few brief complimentary remarks to her graduating students. Then she turned to the king's ambassador and requested him to come forward.

At last the high moment had arrived for the presentation of the diplomas. Dr. Dawson produced the box containing the five precious rolls from beneath the lectern. They were tied with ribbons of blue and gold, the class colors. All eyes were upon them, as the ambassador struggled through the closely spaced seats on the platform. Hope glanced anxiously down at her own two small feet, which occupied the only available space on the edge of the platform. She stepped hastily down to the floor below. She wondered if the space she had vacated was big enough to accommodate the tall ambassador's feet. She turned to see him towering absurdly above her on one foot. Her head was barely upon a level with his waistband. Eyes twinkling, he stepped down beside her.

"Madame," he said with a gracious smile, "I believe we need to change places. Allah has blessed me with sufficient height that I can be seen without having to stand on an elevation. Please allow me."

He put a hand under Hope's elbow and assisted her back up to the platform. Hope tingled with gratitude. Truly, this noble man was a worthy representative of his king. Now their eyes were nearly on a level. She addressed the audience.

"Will you please hold all applause until the last diploma has been given?" she requested.

Dr. Dawson began handing her the diplomas. As she called out each name, she passed the rolls one by one to the ambassador. Each student rose to her feet as her name was called, and accepted the precious document from his hand, then remained standing. He accompanied each presentation with a warm handshake and a special word of congratulation. Hardly had the final diploma left his hand when the thundering ovation began. Hope let it continue for nearly five minutes, then laughingly held up her hand for silence. Eileen was already standing beside the graduates at the other end of the row.

"We will now recite the Nightingale pledge together," Hope announced. "I invite all nurses in the audience to stand and join us in the pledge."

The junior students in the center section rose in a body. From scattered seats all over the chapel, women, and a few men, of various ages and nationalities, also rose to stand at attention.

At a signal from Hope the seven nurses on the platform led in reciting the solemn pledge that Florence Nightingale had required of all nurses serving under her leadership. It was now in universal use throughout the world. A variety of languages could be heard all over the chapel, repeating the solemn words:

"I pledge myself before God and in the presence of this assembly to pass my life in purity and to practice my profession faithfully . . ."

Hope could hear Christine, who was standing next to her, repeating firmly, "I will not take, or knowingly administer, any harmful drug . . ."

Her glance traveled past Christine to Elizabeth and Regina, who stood side by side with rapt faces, saying earnestly, "I will do all in my power to maintain and elevate the standard of my profession . . ."

Warda stood next to them, beautiful as a rose, the queen of flowers, for which she was so appropriately named. Warda was merely parroting the words. Her eyes and thoughts were evidently upon Yacoub and their approaching wedding. Hope could see him in an aisle seat, gazing adoringly at his bride to be through the spectacles that enabled him to see her clearly even at a distance.

Aminah was next to Eileen at the end of the line, loveliest of them all, with the patrician grace of a princess. She, too, was gazing directly into the eyes of one man. There was a tender smile upon her lips as she repeated, "With loyalty will I endeavor to aid the physician in his work . . ."

Hope followed her gaze to Dr. Morcus Kemalyian, who was returning her tender look from where he sat in the front row. His scholarship course had been postponed until March, while he recovered from a heart attack. He was leaving by plane for America within a few days. Mohammed Abdullah had extracted a promise from him that he would make preparations to marry Aminah within the year.

Mohammed was sitting beside him now. But Aminah's father was not looking at his daughter. He was regarding the young man beside him with the peculiarly proud and tender expression that a father reserves for a well-loved son. As Hope watched, Mohammed lifted his hand from his own knee and placed it affectionately upon the knee of his companion. Without shifting his eyes from Aminah's face, Dr. Morcus covered the older man's hand with his own.

The pledge was now ended. Hope requested the nurses in the audience to be seated. Eileen began pumping the squeaky bellows.

"Our graduates will now sing their class song," Hope announced. "It is sung traditionally by my own Alma Mater and is especially dear to me. I am happy that the Beth Hanani nurses have chosen to sing it today." She stepped from the platform and resumed her seat.

As the five voices started to sing, a host of poignant memories crowded in upon Hope. Some were happy, some sad. Her own graduation day passed before her, now more than twenty-eight years ago. How fast the years had flown! She recalled the many years of service in Nigeria. The black faces of those she had trained there rose and passed before her, one by one. She had loved them all, too, but never as dearly as she loved these five young Arab girls before her. How could she bear to leave them?

For the first time since she had made her decision to go, Hope felt like weeping. Could she have been mistaken in her call to Taiwan? She had been in charge here for only a little more than two years. Was she deserting her post because of a vain assumption that she was indispensible elsewhere? Perhaps she was still needed here? Maybe Eileen couldn't . . .? Hope sternly checked the unworthy thought. She admitted honestly to herself that Eileen was fully able to cope, and only vanity was leading her to imagine otherwise. With a resolute effort she brought her mind back to the present.

The girls had finished their song and had resumed their seats. The Reverend Dyson stepped up to the lecturn to deliver a few concluding remarks, and to pronounce the benediction.

Hope bowed her head and closed her eyes.

She was roused from her reveries by the sound of her own name. The Reverend Jimmy was saying, "Miss Callaway has likened your nursing caps to 'cotton crowns,' which represent an earthly crown of love and service. You have earned the right to wear them proudly. From now on . . ."

Hope's thoughts drifted off again. "From now on, what?" she mused. What did the future hold for these five girls before her? Were they strong enough to wear their "crowns" worthily and well?

A voice spoke from within.

"They are ready, my child. Your work is finished here. From now on, you must trust them to me." She closed her eyes to think.

In the beginning Hope had wondered about her ability to not take sides. Now she knew that these sides existed only in her imagination. She was completely on the Lord's side now, and that was what really counted for the rest of her life.

She suddenly became aware that people were beginning to stir around her. With a start, she opened her eyes and raised her head. Five white clad, white capped figures, diplomas in hand, were standing stiffly at attention on the platform. Five loving pairs of warm brown eyes were fixed on her with eager anticipation. Everyone was standing except her.

Hope got to her feet. The ceremony was evidently over. But still the five graduates stood eyeing her expectantly. What were they waiting for? Were they expecting her to say something? Do something?

Suddenly Hope Callaway knew exactly what she was to do. She squared her shoulders and lifted her chin. She smiled radiantly back into those five pairs of eager young eyes. Then she took a deep breath and issued her last command.

"Class dismissed!"

There was a roar of laughter as the five graduates broke ranks.

The crowd surged forward.

Eileen's waiting fingers struck the keys of the faithful organ and the long suffering bellows pealed forth a noble chord of triumph.